WHY I AM A HINDU

Shashi Tharoor served for twenty-nine years at
the UN, culminating as Under-Secretary-General.
He is a Congress MP in India, the author of fourteen
previous books, and has won numerous literary
awards, including a Commonwealth Writers' Prize.
Tharoor has a PhD from the Fletcher School, and
was named by the World Economic Forum in
Davos in 1998 as a Global Leader of Tomorrow.

SHASHI THAROOR

WHY
I AM A
HINDU

SCRIBE
Melbourne • London

Scribe Publications
18–20 Edward St, Brunswick, Victoria 3056, Australia
2 John St, Clerkenwell, London, WC1N 2ES, United Kingdom
3754 Pleasant Ave, Suite 100, Minneapolis, Minnesota 55409 USA

Published by Scribe 2018
Reprinted 2021, 2023

Printed and bound in the UK by CPI Group (UK) Ltd, Croydon CR0 4YY

Scribe is committed to the sustainable use of natural resources
and the use of paper products made responsibly from those resources.

9781947534551 (US paperback edition)
9781947534568 (US hardback edition)
9781925713534 (ANZ edition)
9781925693355 (ebook)

Catalogue records for this book are available from the
National Library of Australia.

scribepublications.com
scribepublications.co.uk
scribepublications.com.au

for my mother

*Lily
Tharoor*

*whose devotion
is untainted
by her scepticism*

What thing I am I do not know.
I wander secluded, burdened by my mind.
When the first-born of Truth has come to me
I receive a share in that self-same Word.

— *Rig Veda*, I.164.37

May we not anger you, O God, in our worship
By praise that is unworthy or by scanty tribute.

— *Rig Veda*, II.33.4

May He delight in these my words.

— *Rig Veda*, I.25.18

CONTENTS

PREFACE AND ACKNOWLEDGEMENTS

I wrote this book for two main reasons. The first was to try and understand for myself, and for whoever else was interested, the extraordinary wisdom and virtues of the faith I have lived for over six decades, a faith that I have tried to absorb through beliefs and practices handed down to me by my father and others, my own observations, as well as an extensive reading of the scriptures in translation and numerous scholarly treatises. The second reason I wrote this book was to show that the intolerant and often violent forms of Hindutva that began to impose themselves on the public consciousness of Indians in the 1980s went against the spirit of Hinduism, that most plural, inclusive, eclectic and expansive of faiths.

I am neither a Sanskritist nor a scholar of Hinduism and did not set out to write a scholarly exposition of the religion. Mine is a layman's view of Hinduism, and my exposition seeks to give the reader an overview of the faith as I understand it, as well as accessible summaries of its main features. As will be apparent, I have relied on some of its greatest teachers and adepts to explain its essence. My narrative weaves between personal witness and an attentive reading of the relevant scriptures and academic texts. I seek to bring together ideas of Hinduism from ancient texts, their development by many thinkers, and the practices and the challenges of Hindutva ideology. My approach is to present both the ancient texts of Hinduism and the modern beliefs of Hindutva descriptively and on their own terms, rather than through the theoretical approaches of historians, theologians and social scientists. In this way I seek to arrive at what I hope the reader will find is a lucid and reflective account of one of the world's oldest and greatest faiths and its contemporary existence.

But I do not pretend to offer a comprehensive view of Hinduism: that would go well beyond the space and scope of this book. Instead, I describe aspects of Hindu thought that matter to me, question practices I am less enthusiastic about, outline Hinduism's capacity to grow and reform and be revitalised for subsequent generations, summarise the history of Hinduism in India and provide a feeling for what being Hindu means in a multi-religious country. In the process I devote as much space to the ideological contestations and political challenges swirling around the faith today as I do to its timeless metaphysics.

The book is divided into three sections. The first section, 'My Hinduism', looks at every aspect of the religion—its principal schools, tenets, teachers, and teachings, as well as some of its more questionable social practices. The second section, 'Political Hinduism', explains the ways in which political leaders, strategists, thinkers and their religious allies have attempted to hijack the faith for their own ends. The third section, 'Taking Back Hinduism', talks about how we might free Hinduism from the excesses and perversions it has been subjected to, and restore it to its truest essence, which in many ways is that of an almost ideal faith for the twenty-first-century world.

To some readers, my title—'Why I am a Hindu'—begs the question of who really is this 'I' that I refer to. Is it the thoughtful Hindu layman, the product of a modern English-language education in contemporary India, who is interrogating himself about the faith to which he claims adherence? Or is it the politician steeped in the issues of the day, who is writing with a sense of urgency and despair conditioned by the experience of being called 'anti-Hindu' by those who understand far less of the faith but are inflamed by their own ideological certitudes? My claims about being Hindu are undoubtedly mediated by political contestations around the public expressions of Hinduism by those who see it as a badge of identity more than a system of transcendental beliefs. But where I disagree with them, I do so not as a secularist—or as they would allege, a 'pseudo-secularist'—standing outside the faith, but as a believing Hindu who seeks to challenge them from within the bounds of the religion to which we both claim allegiance.

In some ways I am guilty of the old Indian failing of trying to depict the elephant by describing its tail, tusk, girth and so on. As a result I can at best approximate a number of truths in my effort to describe the unknowable whole truth. Hinduism is uniquely difficult to encapsulate for reasons I describe in my opening chapter: no single founder or prophet, no organised church, no single holy book, and so on; the faith is almost Wikipedia-like in the authorial diversity of its scriptures and tenets. The metaphors used by scholars to describe Hinduism have ranged from the banyan tree and the jungle to a kaleidoscope and even a pan of lasagne. One scholar has pointed out that 'Hinduism' can stand for a civilisation as 'Hellenism' does, and also for a faith as 'Judaism' does; political ideologues in the mid twentieth century insisted it also stood for a 'race' of people embraced by its beliefs. But isn't it also true that our Indian understanding of what 'religion' means has been so drastically affected by colonisation, secularisation, modernity and interaction with global currents, that our own way of conceptualising our native conglomeration of tradition, belief and faith is irretrievably lost?

I cannot be sure, and yet I would argue it does not matter. Some might suggest that this book is an exercise in attempting to fit something unwieldy and unclassifiable into terms an English-speaking twenty-first century reader can understand.[1] Would what we call today 'Hinduism' be recognised by Yajnavalkya (mentioned in the Upanishads, as distinct from the putative author of the *Yajnavalkya-smriti*, mentioned later) or even Adi Shankara who reinterpreted the same faith nearly 2,000 years later? In essence, can today's Hinduism be divorced from the journeys that this aggregate of faiths took over three millennia of enquiry and exploration, resistance to assault and creative reform? Is it even possible, a thoughtful friend asks me, to think of Hinduism as 'pristine' and thus implicitly to say 'I am Hindu' without acknowledging that what one means is not some eternal category of belief but a set of self-descriptors that is contingent on history?

Some may well suggest that my portrayal of Hinduism means that I too have joined those who seek to 'tame' this most unruly of belief systems. Critics allege that the Indian secular liberals want to do just that to Hinduism because they cannot understand religious belief, while the Hindutvavadis want to do so because they cannot control too diverse a set of beliefs. Both sets of attempts result in an effort to 'homogenise' Hinduism for various ends. But the quotidian practices of Hindus involve intense prayer and meditation as well as fierce and bloody rituals, slavish devotion to gurus as well as philosophically abstruse speculations—a range of conduct that has little respect for a writer's need to describe religious phenomena in coherent terms.

As a Hindu, I write of my own faith, and confess that I am incapable of the detachment that one might find in conventional scholarly studies of Hinduism. Rather, mine is an engaged view of the religion, from within its confines—if something so capacious can be seen as confining at all. Though I have read a great deal of Western academic work on Hinduism, I do not partake of the hypercritical views of some twentieth-century Indologists, whose Orientalist gaze upon Hinduism, based perhaps understandably on modern notions of egalitarianism, rationalism and social justice, has sparked hysterical accusations of Hinduphobia. While I do not go as far myself in rejecting their right to express such views, I fear that some Western writing on Hinduism has paradoxically provoked a backlash that has driven many Hindus into the arms of radicals. Despite the flaws in some of its practices, my admiration for and pride in Hinduism outweighs my critical concerns, and I make no apology for this.

This book could not have been written without the help of numerous people who have been kind enough to comment on various drafts of the text. My former aide and associate Manu S. Pillai, a gifted historian himself, offered me useful guidance, as did my 'sister from another womb', Dr Nanditha Krishna of the Indian Council of Historical Research, who has authored several books herself on various aspects of Hinduism. (She has asked me to point out that she agrees with my depiction of Hinduism but not with my rejection of Hindutva.) My thanks to Nanditha for allowing me to use her translation of the Nasadiya Sukta (the Creation Hymn). Keerthik Sasidharan, an intellectual moonlighting as a banker, raised a number of the questions I have summarised in this Author's Note and offered other insights into the faith. Devdutt Pattanaik, undoubtedly India's most popular interpreter of Hinduism, came up with a number of pertinent suggestions on an earlier draft, which have helped influence my final text. Professor Sheeba Thattil's research was invaluable in assembling vast amounts of material on Hinduism, including several works now out of print. I would like to thank Dr Karan Singh for allowing me to use his translation of Mirabai's poem. As always, family played a vital part. My son Kanishk Tharoor and my niece Dr Ragini Tharoor Srinivasan read the manuscript attentively and offered invaluable suggestions and criticisms. Ragini's searching comments and criticisms were especially helpful in making me think through my own assumptions and arguments, and I am most grateful. My sisters Shobha and Smita offered thoughts on an early draft and have remained strongly supportive throughout.

While many minds have therefore contributed to the contents of this volume, the final responsibility for the arguments and interpretations in this book rests with me. If, after reading this book, Hindu and non-Hindu alike come away with a new appreciation of the faith I cherish, and the challenges it is currently dealing with in contemporary India, *Why I Am a Hindu* would have served its purpose.

Shashi Tharoor
January 2018
New Delhi

PART ONE

MY HINDUISM

1

MY HINDUISM

Why am I a Hindu?

The obvious answer to this question is, of course, that it's because I was born one. Most people have little choice about the faith they grow up with: it was selected for them at birth, by the accident of geography and their parents' cultural moorings. The overwhelming majority of Hindus in the world were born Hindu. A small handful, inspired by marriage, migration or philosophical conviction, have adopted the faith, usually by a process of 'conversion' unknown to most Hindus. Unlike that small minority, I was never anything else: I was born a Hindu, grew up as one, and have considered myself one all my life.

But what does being a Hindu mean? Many of us began having to interrogate ourselves in the late 1980s, when the world media first began to speak and write of 'Hindu fundamentalism'. This was odd, because we knew of Hinduism as a religion without fundamentals: no founder or prophet, no organised church, no compulsory beliefs or rites of worship, no uniform conception of the 'good life', no single sacred book.

My Hinduism was a lived faith; it was a Hinduism of experience and upbringing, a Hinduism of observation and conversation, not one anchored in deep religious study (though of course the two are not mutually exclusive). I knew few mantras, just a few snatches of a couple of hymns and practically no Sanskrit: my knowledge of Hindu sacred texts and philosophies came entirely from reading them in English translation. (When I went to a temple, I prayed in an odd combination of English, Sanskrit and my 'mother tongue' Malayalam, instinctively convinced that an omniscient God would naturally be multilingual.)

As a student of history I had always been curious about ancient Indian traditions and beliefs, and I had amassed a rather decent collection of books on the subject of Hindu thought, including multiple translations of the Bhagavad Gita. I had also been a passionate follower of the thoughts and speeches of Swami Vivekananda (as will be apparent in what follows). I had read widely in English about my faith, absorbing the wisdom of Dr Sarvepalli Radhakrishnan and Ananda Coomaraswamy, learning about the lives of such notable figures as Swami Vivekananda, Ramakrishna Paramahamsa and Paramahansa Yogananda, and delving into a variety of scholarly studies, from the old classics by A. L. Basham and R. C. Zaehner to the brilliantly interpretative translations and exegeses of Raimon Panikkar and Dr Karan Singh. From these, and others, notably my own father, I had acquired a set of personal convictions that made up 'my' Hinduism. But was that enough, and what did it amount to in the face of a violent new assertion of Hinduness in a form I could not recognise as bearing any relation to my own faith?

DEFINING HINDUISM

The first challenge, of course, was definitional. The name 'Hindu' itself denotes something less, and more, than a set of theological beliefs. In many languages, French and Persian amongst them, the word for 'Indian' is 'Hindu'. Originally, *Hindu* simply meant the people beyond the River Sindhu, or Indus. But the Indus is now in Islamic Pakistan; and to make matters worse, the word 'Hindu' did not exist in any Indian language till its use by foreigners gave Indians a term for self-definition. Hindus, in other words, call themselves by a label that they didn't invent themselves in any of their own languages, but adopted cheerfully when others began to refer to them by that word. (Of course, many prefer a different term altogether—Sanatana Dharma, or eternal faith, which we will discuss later.)

'Hinduism' is thus the name that foreigners first applied to what they saw as the indigenous religion of India. It embraces an eclectic range of doctrines and practices, from pantheism to agnosticism and from faith in reincarnation to belief in the caste system. But none of these constitutes an obligatory credo for a Hindu: there are none. We have no compulsory dogmas.

This is, of course, rather unusual. A Catholic is a Catholic because he believes Jesus was the Son of God who sacrificed himself for Man; a Catholic believes in the Immaculate Conception and the Virgin Birth, offers confession, genuflects in church and is guided by the Pope and a celibate priesthood. A Muslim must believe that there is no God but Allah and that Muhammad is His Prophet. A Jew cherishes his Torah or Pentateuch and his Talmud; a Parsi worships at a Fire Temple; a Sikh honours the teachings of the Guru Granth Sahib above all else. There is no Hindu equivalent to any of these beliefs. There are simply no binding requirements to being a Hindu. Not even a belief in God. I grew up in a Hindu household. Our home always had a prayer-room, where paintings and portraits of assorted divinities jostled for shelf- and wall-space with fading photographs of departed ancestors, all stained by ash scattered from the incense burned daily by my devout parents. I have written before of how my earliest experiences of piety came from watching my father at prayer. Every morning, after his bath, my father would stand in front of the prayer-room wrapped in his towel, his wet hair still uncombed, and chant his Sanskrit mantras. But he never obliged me to join him; he exemplified the Hindu idea that religion is an intensely personal matter, that prayer is between you and whatever image of your Maker you choose to worship. In the Hindu way, I was to find my own truth.

MY TRUTH

I think I have. I am a believer, despite a brief period of schoolboy atheism (of the kind that comes with the discovery of rationality and goes with an acknowledgement of its limitations). And I am happy to describe myself as a believing Hindu: not just because it is the faith into which I was born, but for a string of other reasons, though faith requires no reason.

One reason is cultural: as a Hindu I belong to a faith that expresses the ancient genius of my own people. I am proud of the history of my faith in my own land: of the travels of Adi Shankara, who journeyed from the southernmost tip of the country to Kashmir in the north, Gujarat in the west and Odisha in the east, debating spiritual scholars everywhere, preaching his beliefs, establishing his mutths (monasteries). I am reaffirmed in this atavistic allegiance by the Harvard scholar Diana Eck writing of the 'sacred geography' of India, 'knit together by countless tracks of pilgrimage'. The great philosopher–president of India, Dr Sarvepalli Radhakrishnan, wrote of Hindus as 'a distinct cultural unit, with a common history, a common literature, and a common civilisation'. In reiterating my allegiance to Hinduism, I am consciously laying claim to this geography and history, its literature and civilisation, identifying myself as an heir (one among a billion heirs) to a venerable tradition that stretches back into time immemorial. I fully accept that many of my friends, compatriots and fellow-Hindus feel no similar need, and that there are Hindus who are not (or are no longer) Indian, but I am comfortable with this 'cultural' and 'geographical' Hinduism that anchors me to my ancestral past.

But another 'reason' for my belief in Hinduism is, for lack of a better phrase, its intellectual 'fit': I am more comfortable with the tenets of Hinduism than I would be with those of the other faiths of which I know. I have long thought of myself as liberal, not merely in the political sense of the term, or even in relation to principles of economics, but as an attitude to life. To accept people as one finds them, to allow them to be and become what they choose, and to encourage them to do whatever they like (so long as it does not harm others) is my natural instinct. Rigid and censorious beliefs have never appealed to my temperament. In matters of religion, too, I found my liberal instincts reinforced by the faith in which I was brought up. Hinduism is, in many ways, predicated on the idea that the eternal wisdom of the ages and of divinity cannot be confined to a single sacred book; we have many, and we can delve into each to find our own truth (or truths). As a Hindu I can claim adherence to a religion without an established church or priestly papacy, a religion whose rituals and customs I am free to reject, a religion that does not oblige me to demonstrate my faith by any visible sign, by subsuming my identity in any collectivity, not even by a specific day or time or frequency of worship. (There is no Hindu Pope, no Hindu Vatican, no Hindu catechism, not even a Hindu Sunday.) As a Hindu I follow a faith that offers a veritable smorgasbord of options to the worshipper of divinities to adore and to pray to, of rituals to observe (or not), of customs and practices to honour (or not), of fasts to keep (or not). As a Hindu I subscribe to a creed that is free of the restrictive dogmas of holy writ, one that refuses to be shackled to the limitations of a single volume of holy revelation.

A Hindu can be *astika* (pious) or *nastika* (impious): the terms are said to relate more to orthopraxy (action) rather than orthodoxy (belief), but action proceeds from a set of convictions. As an *astika* he can accept the sacredness of the Vedas, the existence of *atman* (the soul) and belief in God, or he can reject one or more of these credos and still be Hindu, an adherent of the *nastika* variant of Hindu philosophy. As an *astika* Hindu he can subscribe to any of the six major schools of philosophy, the Shad Darshanas (which I describe later); as a *nastika* Hindu he can declare allegiance to one of five schools, including Buddhism and Jainism, which after arising as reform movements against the ritualistic Hinduism of their day, were practically re-absorbed into the parent faith (though their adherents may not see it that way). Or the *nastika* can attach himself to the materialist Charvaka School, whose followers denounced most religious practices and devoted themselves to wealth and profit. The palette of options available is as colourful as the most inventive artist's.

At the same time, as a Hindu, I appreciate the fact that Hinduism professes no false certitudes. Its capacity to express wonder at Creation and simultaneously scepticism about the omniscience of the Creator are unique to Hinduism. Both are captured beautifully in this verse from the 3,500-year-old *Rig Veda*, the Nasadiya Sukta or Creation Hymn:

7

Then there was neither non-existence nor existence,
Then there was neither space, nor the sky beyond.
What covered it? Where was it?
What sheltered it? Was there water, in depths unfathomed?

Then there was neither death nor immortality
Nor was there then the division between night and day.
That One breathed, breathlessly and self-sustaining.
There was that One then, and there was no other.

In the beginning there was only darkness, veiled in darkness,
In profound darkness, a water without light.
All that existed then was void and formless.
That One arose at last, born of the power of heat.

In the beginning arose desire,
That primal seed, born of the mind.
The sages who searched their hearts with wisdom,
Discovered the link of the existent to the non-existent.

And they stretched their cord of vision across the void,
What was above? What was below?
Then seeds were sown and mighty power arose,
Below was strength, Above was impulse.

Who really knows? And who can say?
Whence did it all come? And how did creation happen?
The gods themselves are later than creation,
So who knows truly whence this great creation sprang?

Who knows whence this creation had its origin?
He, whether He fashioned it or whether He did not,
He, who surveys it all from the highest heaven,
He knows—or maybe even He does not know.

— *Rig Veda*, X.129[1]

'Maybe even He does not know!' I love a faith that raises such a fundamental question about no less a Supreme Being than the Creator of the Universe Himself. Maybe He does not know, indeed. Who are we mere mortals to claim a knowledge of which even He cannot be certain?

Hindu thought also makes a virtue out of the unknowability of God. There is a marvellous story in the Upanishads about a sage who is asked to define the nature of God; the wise man, normally loquacious, falls silent. He is pressed by his disciples for an answer, and he replies that that *was* his answer, for the Absolute is silence; the mystery of the divine reality cannot be reduced to words or speech. Neither thought nor words can suffice: 'It is not understood by those who understand it,' says the Kena Upanishad, 'it is understood by those who do not understand it.' The final words of the Upanishads are '*neti, neti*'—'not this, not this'—signifying the indescribability of the Absolute. For many sages, their consciousness of the Divine is untranslatable to others, for those who have not attained the same realisation cannot grasp it through word or sign: it is 'that of which nothing can be said'.

And while I am, paradoxically, listing my 'reasons' for a faith beyond understanding, let me cite the fundamental point: above all, as a Hindu I belong to the only major religion in the world that does not claim to be the only true religion. I find it immensely congenial to be able to face my fellow human beings of other faiths without being burdened by the conviction that I am embarked upon a 'true path' that they have missed. This dogma lies at the core of the 'Semitic faiths', Christianity, Islam, and Judaism. The Bible contains the words 'I am the Way, the Truth and the Life; no man cometh unto the Father [God], but by me' (John 14:6); 'There is no God but Allah, and Muhammad is His Prophet', declares the Quran, denying unbelievers all possibility of redemption, let alone of salvation or paradise. Hinduism asserts that all ways of belief are equally valid, and Hindus readily venerate the saints, and the sacred objects, of other faiths. I am proud that I can honour the sanctity of other faiths without feeling I am betraying my own.

After all, as the philosopher Raimon Panikkar put it so brilliantly in his *The Vedic Experience*, 'It is precisely faith that makes thinking possible, for faith offers the unthought ground out of which thinking can emerge. It is faith that makes moral and other decisions possible, opening to us the horizon against which our actions become meaningful.' As a Hindu I seek meaning in my actions within the context of my religious beliefs.

A FAITH WITHOUT DOGMA

And yet, Hinduism is a civilisation, not a dogma. There is no such thing as a Hindu heresy. Hinduism is a faith that allows each believer to stretch his or her imagination to a personal notion of the creative god-head of divinity. Hinduism is also a faith that uniquely does not have any notion of heresy in it: you cannot be a Hindu heretic because there is no standard set of dogmas from which you can deviate that make you a heretic. Indeed, not even what one might think of as the most basic tenet of any religion—a belief in the existence of God—is a pre-requisite in Hinduism. As I have noted, an important branch of Hindu philosophy, the Charvaka School, goes so far as to embrace atheism within the Hindu philosophical framework.

The Charvakas were an interesting example of the intellectual heterodoxy of ancient Hinduism. Not only were they unabashedly materialist, but they challenged the most cherished assumptions of the astikas. The sage Madhvacharya summarised the Charvaka School in his *Sarvadarsana Sangraha* as arguing that 'there is no heaven, no final liberation, no soul (which continues to exist) in another world, nor any ceremonies of castes or orders which are productive of future reward'. The Charvakas were in fact contemptuous of holy men and their practices: 'The Agnihotra sacrifice, the three Vedas, the mendicant's triple staff (*tridanda*), and the practice of smearing oneself with ashes, are only means of livelihood ordained by the creator for men who have neither understanding nor energy.' And they were also scathing about the theological claims of astika philosophers: 'If [it be true that] an animal slaughtered at the Jyotistoma sacrifice is [in consequence] exalted to heaven', they asked, 'why does the worshipper not immolate his own father?'[2]

Hinduism, in other words, incorporates almost all forms of belief and worship within it; there is no need to choose some or reject others. Mahatma Gandhi famously appreciated this quality of Hinduism: 'Its freedom from dogma makes a forcible appeal to me,' he wrote, 'inasmuch as it gives the votary the largest scope for self-expression.'[3] It is therefore a timeless faith, populated by ideas at once ancient and modern, hosting texts, philosophies, belief systems and schools of thought that do not necessarily all agree with each other. But none has ever been rejected by some supreme authority as beyond the pale; there is no such authority in Hinduism. There can be no Hindu Inquisition because there is neither an exacting theology that everyone must subscribe to as holy writ, nor an exalted authority empowered to appoint an Inquisitor. Hindu thought is like a vast library in which no book ever goes out of print; even if the religious ideas a specific volume contains have not been read, enunciated or followed in centuries, the book remains available to be dipped into, to be revised and reprinted with new annotations or a new commentary whenever a reader feels the need for it. In many cases the thoughts it contains may have been modified by or adapted to other ideas that may have arisen in response; in most, it's simply there, to be referred to, used or ignored as Hindus see fit.

Inevitably, though, the question 'who is a Hindu?' has been asked, and, equally inevitably, political figures have entered the definitional fray. The fighter for Indian independence, 'Lokmanya (accepted by the people)' Bal Gangadhar Tilak (1856–1920), suggested, in a meeting of the Sanatana Dharma Sabha (Association of Hindus), that 'a Hindu is he who believes that the Vedas contain self-evident and axiomatic truths',[4] thus seeking to create a religious identity, based on sacred texts, that would be eligible for special consideration from a British colonial regime that had already extended recognition to Muslims (as members of a defined religious community following the dictates of the Quran). Two decades later Mahatma Gandhi added to Tilak's basic view, writing that Hindus are people who believe in the Vedas, the Upanishads, the multiple Hindu scriptures, the various incarnations of God, rebirth or reincarnation, *varna* (caste) and *ashrama* (the four stages of life, which I describe later), and veneration and protection of the cow, and do not express disbelief in idol worship. This is a rather long and contentious list, since many Hindus (myself included) do not subscribe to some of these requirements and do not consider themselves any less Hindu for not doing so. The foundational theorist of the political philosophy of Hindutva, V. D. Savarkar (whose ideas are discussed more fully below), asserted in the 1920s that one could be a Hindu even if one did not recognise the religious authority of the Vedas.[5] To him, the various religious disputes within Hindu religious thought—between monism and pantheism, between Dvaita and Advaita, between the Vedas and the Upanishads and even including agnosticism and atheism—were irrelevant to the issue of Hindu identity. Savarkar saw 'Hindu-ness' or 'Hindutva' as opposed to 'Hinduism' as a uniting cultural construct that underlay the identity of all those who belong to 'Bharatvarsha', the ancient land of India. Unsurprisingly, then, India's first prime minister, Jawaharlal Nehru, observed that 'Being a Hindu means all things to all men'.[6] British civil servant and historian Sir Alfred Lyall described Hinduism as a 'tangled jungle' full of paradoxes and contradictions, 'a religious chaos' spread all over India, difficult to comprehend and define. No wonder Dr Sarvepalli Radhakrishnan began his celebrated 1926 Upton Lectures on Hinduism by asking of his own faith: 'Is it a museum of beliefs, a medley of rites, or a mere map, a geographical expression?'.[7]

As I have argued, one corollary of this eclecticism is the willingness of Hindus to accept other faiths and modes of worship—indeed often embrace them for themselves. It is quite common for Hindus to show reverence to the religious places of other faiths, and to carry relics or sacred objects of other faiths. History is replete with accounts of Hindus thronging Sufi dargahs, Sikh gurudwaras and Christian shrines (notably the Basilica of Our Lady of Good Health in Velankanni town in Tamil Nadu, which has been described as the 'Lourdes of the East', or Mount Mary Church in Mumbai's Bandra) with the same reverence they might express in their own temples. My late father was a devout Hindu who prayed faithfully twice a day, after his baths. He regularly went on pilgrimages to all the major temples and religious sites in our land. When a fire engulfed the Guruvayur temple in the 1960s, he led a fund-raising drive in Bombay that saw much of his meagre savings diverted to the rebuilding of that shrine. Yet, when a Catholic friend— his life insurance agent, who had made a trip to the Vatican—presented him with an amulet of the Virgin Mary that had personally been blessed by the Pope, he accepted it with reverence and carried it around with him for years. That is the Hinduism most Hindus know: a faith that accords respect and even reverence to the sanctified beliefs of others.

This inclination to revere the Divine, whatever its source, is a notable Hindu trait, reflecting a traditional unwillingness to succumb to doctrinal absolutism. In his historic speech at Chicago's Parliament of the World's Religions on 11 September 1893, Swami Vivekananda spoke of Hinduism as teaching the world not just tolerance but acceptance. The Swami believed that Hinduism, with its openness, its respect for variety, its acceptance of all other faiths, was one religion that should be able to spread its influence without threatening others. At the Chicago Parliament, he articulated the liberal humanism that lies at the heart of his (and my) creed: 'I am proud to belong to a religion which has taught the world both tolerance and universal acceptance. We believe not only in universal toleration, but we accept all religions as true.'[8]

He went on to quote a hymn, the Shiva Mahimna Stotram, which he remembered from his formative years at school: 'As the different streams having their sources in different places all mingle their water in the sea, so, O Lord, the different paths which men take through different tendencies, various though they appear, crooked or straight, all lead to Thee...the wonderful doctrine preached in the [Bhagavad] Gita echoes the same idea, saying: "Whosoever comes to Me, through whatsoever form, I reach him; all men are struggling through paths which in the end lead to me".'[9]

This was a profoundly important idea, and central to the philosophy Vivekananda was preaching. Tolerance, after all, implies that you have the truth, but will generously indulge another who does not; you will, in an act of tolerance, allow him the right to be wrong. Acceptance, on the other hand, implies that you have a truth but the other person may also have a truth; that you accept his truth and respect it, while expecting him to respect (and accept) your truth in turn. This practice of acceptance of difference—the idea that other ways of being and believing are equally valid—is central to Hinduism and the basis for India's democratic culture.

'I challenge the world to find,' Vivekananda proudly declared in a different speech in Chicago, 'throughout the whole system of Sanskrit philosophy, any such expression as that the Hindu alone will be saved and not others. Says Vyasa, "We find perfect men even beyond the pale of our caste and creed".'[10]

One of Hinduism's great strengths—though there are some who see this as a weakness—is its lack of prescriptive tenets. The faith assumes that different people require different pathways to the Ultimate; even within Hinduism, there is no desire to require the same things of all people, it being accepted that people of different spiritual and intellectual attainments will employ different routes in seeking the Divine.

MULTIPLE DIVINITIES

As a result, Hindus allow themselves to worship the divine in multiple forms; the 333 million gods of legend (some versions say 33 million, 300 million and 330 million: even here we are flexible!) are in fact merely a reflection of the infinite aspects of divinity. While other faiths tend to personify the idea of God, seeing Him in anthropomorphic terms as a man-like Being, the Hindu idea of God is both simpler and more complicated. God, to the Hindu, is everywhere, a presence and an absence, within us and outside us. God transcends both time and space. God has no beginning and no end, but equally has no shape and no form. God can therefore be imagined in myriad ways, and in all conceivable shapes and forms, since there is nowhere that God is not, and nowhere that God cannot be. The highest form of God is the Brahman, the Absolute, the universal soul that suffuses all creation.

As a verse in the *Maitreya Upanishad* puts it:

> In the beginning everything was Brahman. He was one, and infinite; infinite in the East, infinite in the South, infinite in the West, infinite in the North, above and below and everywhere infinite. East and the other regions do not exist for him, nor across, nor below, nor above. The Highest Self is not to be fixed, he is unlimited, unborn, not to be reasoned about, not to be conceived. He is like the ether (everywhere), and at the destruction of the universe, he alone is awake. Then from that ether he wakes all this world, which consists of thought only, and by him alone is all this meditated on, and in him it

is dissolved. His is that luminous form which shines in the sun, and the manifold light in the smokeless fire, and the fire in the stomach which consumes the food. Thus it is said:

'He who is in the fire, and he who is in the heart, and he who is in the sun, they are one and the same.'[11]

One of the most famous dialogues in Hindu philosophy, from the *Chandogya Upanishad*, relates to a discussion between a *rishi* (sage) and his son about the existence of God. The young man, Svetaketu, asks his father, Uddalaka Aruni, how he can demonstrate that God exists when there is no visible proof of God's existence. In the typical Hindu manner of instruction, Uddalaka asks his son to fetch a fruit from the banyan tree and cut it open. Inside the fruit, the son finds a small seed. The father asks him to break it apart and see what there is in it, but the seed is all there is. Uddalaka tells his son that all he can see is a small seed; yet something exists in that seed that is so powerful that an immense banyan tree can grow out of it. Similarly, God is not visible, but exists, and the world has grown out of God.

The son is only partly persuaded, so the father asks him to mix salt and water in a bowl. Now, he tells Svetaketu, taste the water and the salt in different parts of the bowl, and once you have done so, separate the salt from the water. The son does as instructed, and points out that the water in every part of the bowl tastes equally salty, and that once dissolved, the salt cannot be separated from the water. Aha, says Uddalaka: you find the salt all-pervasive in the bowl; so too is the universal spirit, which is all-pervasive in creation. When, at the end of our lives, we human beings merge with Brahman, we cannot be separated from it any more than the salt can from the water in your bowl.

Since God is everywhere and in everything, this all-pervasive Universal Spirit is *nirguna*, without qualities, without shape and without gender; Hindus cannot refer to *nirguna* Brahman as 'He', since God can be and is also 'She' and 'It'. The Vedas use the interrogative pronoun '*ka*' (who?), or more precisely *kasmai* (to whom?) for the unknowable God. The impersonal pronoun often used in Sanskrit for God is '*tat*', 'that' in English; in other words, that which exists. Hindu meditation begins with the words '*Om tat sat*': *Om*, the primordial sound that encompasses past, present and future; *tat*, that which exists; *sat*, Truth. The *Chandogya Upanishad* tells the story of Svetaketu, who is taught metaphysics by his father in a series of lessons that each end with the statement '*Tat tvam asi*'—'That you are'—that you are the same as the Brahman that pervades the cosmos.

As the *Hiranyagarbha* hymn in the *Rig Veda* asks:

> *O Father of the Earth, by fixed laws ruling*
> *O Father of the Heavens, pray protect us,*
> *O Father of the great and shining Waters!*
> *What God shall we adore with our oblation?*

— *Rig Veda*, I.121.9[12]

But the sages realised that all this was rather abstruse, and would be difficult for the average human being to comprehend. The *nirguna* Brahman was a philosophical concept at the heart of Hinduism, but people needed to worship something they could imagine and visualise. Hence the idea of the *saguna* Brahman—the Absolute given form, qualities and attributes, also known as Ishvara or Bhagavan. Strictly speaking, Ishvara is the best translation of God in the Christian or Allah in the Muslim sense of these terms, since those faiths have no equivalent for God in the sense of Brahman. But the Hindu Ishvara takes multiple forms: there is the trinity of Brahma (the Creator), Vishnu (the Preserver) and Shiva or Mahesh (the Destroyer), all different manifestations of the God Principle, and their myriad manifestations, plus their *avatara*s, consorts and companions, who may all be worshipped depending on the preferences of the devotee. The *avatara* doctrine—under which these gods manifested themselves in different, recognisable human-like forms, such as Rama or Krishna—also had the distinct advantage of permitting the worshipper to venerate a personal god without this involving any rupture with the mainstream corpus of Hindu thought, which emphasised the impersonal formless aspect of divinity and insisted on '*neti, neti*'. The unknowable *nirguna* Brahman, after all, becomes all the more knowable when it takes human form as an *avatara*; the abstraction of Hindu philosophic thought becomes more accessible in the form of a recognisable figure. The idea of the *avatara* responded to the popular demand for devotion to personal gods, and to their recurrence in the life of the believer. As Krishna says in the Gita (4. 7–8): 'Whenever righteousness declines in the world and unrighteousness arises, I return to earth. For the deliverance of good, the destruction of evil and the re-establishment of dharma, I am reborn from time to time.'

At the same time it is remarkable how the ten avataras of Vishnu, the Dasavataras, seemingly chart the course of human evolution two millennia before Darwin, starting with Matsya (the fish), and proceeding successively through Kurma (the tortoise), Varaha (the boar), and Narasimha (the half man-half lion) to more recognisable human forms, Vamana (the dwarf) and Parasurama (who wields a great axe), then perfect men who are worshipped as divine (Sri Rama and Sri Krishna), then the Buddha (an interesting inclusion, of which more later) and finally Kalki, who is yet to be born, a brilliant youth on a white steed with a devastating sword, encircled by flames, who represents the destruction of the world as we know it.

Some speak simplistically of the holy trinity of Brahma, Vishnu and Shiva as three separate gods, but all three are in fact three sides of one complex being: aspects of the *uttama purusha*, the perfect personality. There is a God who created the gods (and the demons): Prajapati, Lord of all Creatures. There are multiple further manifestations of the divine in popular Hindu iconography: a myriad of gods and goddesses. This might well have resulted from the Vedic civilisation's absorption of the tribal and folk deities it found being worshipped in India before its advance through the country; each local manifestation of a god or a goddess was included in the all-embracing Hindu pantheon, so that as Hinduism spread, it accommodated earlier forms of worship rather than overthrowing them. Similarly, many tribes revered animals, but instead of disrespecting them, Hinduism absorbed the non-humans too, by making them the companions or vehicles (*vahanas*) of the gods. So Vedic gods found themselves riding a lion, mounting a peacock, reclining on a swan, or sitting on a bull. It was part of the agglomerative nature of Hinduism that it neither rejected nor dismissed the faiths it encountered, but sought to bring them into the fold in this way.

Hinduism, therefore, has given birth to a rich iconography, varying according to the specific divine form and further according to the role in which that divinity is depicted, whether at a peaceful moment or in an attack upon evil, for instance, or whether as 'Himself' or transformed for a specific purpose (Vishnu, for instance, became half-man half-lion, Narasimha, to kill a demon who could not be killed by a human). While the iconography of Shiva, Vishnu and the 'remover of obstacles', the elephant-headed Ganesha, is well known, every depiction of Ishvara (in whichever form) involves certain symbolic images and attributes, and the images of these gods were configured to embody profound conceptions of the universe, from the subduing of ignorance and the defeat of evil to the harmonies of destruction and regeneration.

Thus Brahma, the Creator, is always shown with four heads, facing all four directions, as befits the creator of the universe; he holds the Vedas in his hand, a prayer-vessel beside him, and sits on a lotus, the favoured flower in Hindu iconography since it remains pure and unsoiled by the mud and dirt from which it emerges. His consort is Saraswati, goddess of learning and wisdom, who is always depicted holding the musical instrument the *veena*, symbolising the music of the cosmos, the inner sound of Om from which the universe emerged. She has rosary beads in one hand to signify the importance of prayer and meditation, and palm leaf scrolls in another, to epitomise learning. She too sits on a lotus, but sometimes on a peacock, a symbol of the ego that should be suppressed in the pursuit of true knowledge, and her *vahana*, or vehicle, is the graceful swan.

Brahma is rarely worshipped—there are barely a handful of temples dedicated to him, the most remarkable at Pushkar in Rajasthan—but Saraswati is ubiquitous, widely honoured and portrayed, and there is a specific day devoted each year to her exaltation, Saraswati Puja, whereas there is none to Brahma. That she is merely a consort to one of the holy trinity is irrelevant to her importance. Hinduism cannot entirely be absolved of gender bias, but its reverence for the female principle in the godhead is exemplary.

No better example of this exists than the many manifestations of the goddess in the form of Shakti, which literally means strength—the power of the life-force that creates, nurtures, sustains and also destroys the world. The goddess is seen as a source of energy, without which the male aspect of the godhead would be ineffectual. This female energy takes many forms. As Saraswati, she embodies learning; as Lakshmi, wealth and prosperity. As Uma or Parvati, she is Shiva's gentle *ardhangani*, his half, as inseparable from the Lord as fire and heat, or *purusha* (the spirit) and *prakriti* (matter), are inseparable. As Kamakshi or Rajarajeshwari, she is the Great Mother. As Durga, she rides a tiger, bearing weapons to fight the eight evils of humankind— greed, hate, envy, contempt for others, passion, vanity, jealousy and illusion. In her most frightening form she is Kali, the personification of time (*kala*), dark, angry and armed, weapons flailing, her body dripping with blood, wearing the skulls of her victims, sometimes holding aloft the severed head of one or grinding her foot into the prone body of another.

If that sounds macabre, there are fifty-one Shakti-peethas (temples to the goddess) across India, each consecrated to a body part of Shiva's first wife, Sati, whose body was said to have been dismembered in fifty-one pieces by the flying Sudarshana Chakra weapon of Lord Vishnu. (Sati had killed herself during a fire sacrifice conducted by her father, and her disconsolate husband was carrying her body around in grief and mourning; Vishnu's act was intended to get Shiva to snap out of it. Sati was duly reincarnated as Parvati.) There are temples where the goddess retreats into seclusion for three days a month to menstruate, as in Chengannur in Kerala; others where Devi's footprint (on stone) alone is worshipped. My home state of Kerala overflows with temples to the goddess, often referred to simply as Devi or Bhagavathi (both of which simply mean the goddess), though the most popular form of Bhagavathi-worship is of the goddess as Bhadrakali, a form of Kali. One temple in Thiruvananthapuram, the Attukal Bhagavathi temple, is listed in the *Guinness Book of World Records* for the largest gathering of women in one place at one time: millions (2.5 million in 2009, a record that is broken every year, with 4.5 million reported in 2017) assemble each February for the Pongala, at which offerings are cooked and prepared for the goddess.

There is a marvellous Puranic story about the birth of Durga. It is said that a terrible buffalo-headed demon, Mahishasura, had succeeded in conquering all the gods (or *devas*) and established himself as the master of all creation. The gods, despairing in defeat, retreated to a conclave under Lord Indra to find a solution. They decided to pool their strengths, each contributing a particular weapon or personal attribute, and when they had made their contributions and due rituals had been conducted, a dazzling light engulfed the universe from which emerged a fierce female warrior, riding a snarling tiger, wielding a weapon in each of her eighteen arms. She engaged in furious and bloody battle with Mahishasura for nine days and nine nights, at the end of which she vanquished him. These nine days and nights are celebrated annually by Hindus as the nine-day Navaratri festival, which celebrates the defeat of terrible evil by the forces of good—though interestingly, some fringe groups have started to commemorate Mahishasura instead, claiming he is the symbol of the indigenous Adivasis (Tribal peoples) vanquished by the 'civilising' onslaught of the mainstream Hindus.

The various manifestations of Devi suggest that Hinduism took on board multiple goddess-worshipping cults; Kali seems to have been a pre-Vedic goddess converted by the Hindus into one more form of Shakti. Sometimes the same figures in Hindu texts have different genders: Vishnu famously adopted a female form for specific purposes. A female form of Ganesha, now little worshipped, was depicted as Vinayaki or Ganeshvari. In the *Mahabharata*, Arjuna becomes Arjuni (female) and Brihannala (of the third gender) without losing his masculine valour; indeed, the Madurai temple has sculptures of him in all three forms.

Similarly Hanuman, a monkey-god, was enlisted in the service of Lord Rama in the epic *Ramayana*; scholars see in his appearance the absorption of animist nature-worship into Vedic theism, and the accommodation of south Asia's indigenous peoples into the Hindu fold. Characters depicted in the epics as animals with anthropomorphic characteristics may in fact have been Adivasis: Hanuman was perhaps the leader of a monkey-totem Adivasi tribe, Jatayu that of a vulture-totem tribe and Jambuvan of a tribe using bear totems.[13]

Another interesting example is that of the god Jagannath in Odisha, famous for his *ratha* or chariot. It's a beautiful, elaborately carved wooden vehicle used for a sanctified purpose—to wheel an image of a deity worshipped by millions to a temple in full public view—but it has given its name to the English word, 'juggernaut'.

The word is a colonial mangling of Jagannath (Sanskrit for 'Lord of the World'), a manifestation of the god Krishna. Legend has it that in ancient times, King Indradyumna chanced upon the corpse of Lord Krishna, who had been slain by a hunter, and was informed by the god Vishnu that he should make a wooden statue of the Lord and inter his bones in it. The great sage Vishwakarma, the architect of the gods, undertook the task on condition that he not be disturbed while carving the statue. When, after fifteen days, the impatient king went to enquire about the progress of the sculpture, the irritated sage abandoned it unfinished, without hands or feet. King Indradyumna prayed to Brahma, the Creator, who breathed life into the statue by giving it eyes and a soul, though He could do nothing about the stumps where the deity's limbs should have been. This consecrated statue is worshipped at the Jagannath temple in Puri, in the eastern state of Odisha.

The legend almost certainly masks a different story. As I have noted, as Hinduism spread through the subcontinent, it absorbed local animist and tribal faiths it encountered, by accommodating their images of worship into the Hindu pantheon. Jagannatha was probably a Tribal god who was reimagined, through this legend, as a manifestation of Krishna (himself an incarnation of Vishnu), his somewhat rough and limbless appearance explained through an elaborate story that fits within Hindu lore. One of the ways of ensuring the new deity's acceptance by the people was by parading Him four times a year in elaborate *yatras* (journeys) on land and water, of which the most famous is the *ratha* (chariot)-*yatra*, or chariot procession, in the month of Ashadha, according to the Hindu calendar (roughly mid-June to mid-July in the Gregorian). This is when the idol is wheeled to the temple in an enormous chariot as devotees line the streets in a frenzy, hailing the lord with chants and prayers and craning their necks for a glimpse of the deity seated in the chariot, followed by lesser chariots bearing statues of his brother Balarama and sister Subhadra.

How did the deity transported in this devotional procession become transmogrified into an English term for a relentless, remorseless, unstoppable force that destroys anything in its path? Orientalism began early, alas: four centuries before the British conquest of India, fantastical tales about India were propagated in the fourteenth-century travelogue of Sir John Mandeville, who described the festival in his *Travels* and depicted Hindus throwing themselves under the wheels of the enormous Jagannath chariots as a religious sacrifice and being crushed to death. Hinduism, in fact, has no concept of such human sacrifice; if Sir John really saw a Hindu killed under the wheels of a chariot, it can only be because a poor devotee stumbled and fell accidentally upon the path in the tumult and the enormous chariot could not easily stop or turn on the narrow road. Still, the tale, the false image of the faith it portrayed, and the unfortunate associations of the word persisted. By the eighteenth century 'juggernaut' was in common use as a synonym for an irresistible and destructive force that demands total devotion or unforgiving sacrifice—the sense in which it pops up in the novels of Charlotte Brontë and Charles Dickens, and even Robert Louis Stevenson, who applied it to Dr Jekyll's foil, Mr Hyde. It was only Mark Twain, in his *Autobiography*, who described Juggernaut as the kindest of gods; and a look at the lovely model of an eighteenth-century ratha in the British Museum's collection shows you why, for such an exquisite piece of art would only have been used to transport a figure of reverence, not of fear. But alas, by then the damage had been done.

But I digress. Hinduism did not stop with the absorption of earlier animist or tribal religions. It accepted the precepts of Mahavira, the founder of Jainism, treating his followers as a special sect of Hindus rather than as a separate faith. When Buddhism sought to reform Hinduism, Hinduism turned around and sought to absorb it too, by including the Buddha as a reincarnation of Vishnu and his agnostic teachings as merely a *nastika* form of the mother faith. As a result Buddhism has hardly any strength or presence in the land of its birth, having been absorbed and overtaken by the religion it sought to challenge. Hinduism could well have tried the same with Christianity and Islam, too, had it been allowed to do so; but these faiths were not interested in being embraced by Hinduism, since they saw themselves as the revealed Truth rather than as one among multiple versions of truth.

Hinduism is also unusual in seeing God, Man and the universe as co-related. As the philosopher Raimon Panikkar has explained, in Hindu thought, God without Man is nothing, literally 'no-thing'; Man without God is just a 'thing', without meaning or larger purpose; and the universe without Man or God is 'any-thing', sheer chaos, devoid of existence. In Panikkar's explanation, nothing separates Man from God: 'there is neither intermediary nor barrier between them'. So Hindu prayers mix the sacred with the profane: a Hindu can ask God for anything. Among the tens of thousands of sacred verses and hymns in the Hindu scriptures are a merchant's prayer for wealth, a bankrupt's plea to the divine to free him of debt, verses extolling the union of a man with a woman, and even the lament of a rueful (and luckless) gambler asking God to help him shake his addiction. Prayer and worship, for the Hindu, are thus not purely spiritual exercises: they enhance the quality of his life in the material world, in the here and now.

GANESH, MY ISHTA-DEVTA

Hindus are often asked, during certain ritual prayers, to imagine their *ishta-devta*, their personal God, or rather that way of imagining the abstraction of the Absolute in an anthropomorphic form that most appeals to them. I pick Ganesh—or Ganapathi, as we prefer to call him in the South—myself, not because I believe God looks like Him, but because of the myriad aspects of the godhead, the ones He represents appeal most to me.

> *Om maha Ganapathe namaha,*
> *sarva vignoba shantaye,*
> *Om Ganeshaya namaha...*

Every morning, for longer than I can remember, I have begun my day with that prayer. I learned it without being fully aware what all the Sanskrit words meant, knowing only that I was invoking, like millions of Hindus around the world, the name of the great elephant-headed god to bless all my endeavours to come.

Ganesh sits impassively on my bedroom shelf, in my office, in my living-room and my dining-room, as well as my prayer alcove, in multiple forms of statuary, stone, metal and papier-mache. There is nothing incongruous about this; he is used to worse, appearing as he does on innumerable calendars, posters, trademarks and wedding invitation cards. Paunchy, long-trunked (though with one broken tusk), attired in whatever costume the artist fancies (from ascetic to astronaut), Ganesh, riding his way across Indian hearts on a rat, is arguably Hinduism's most popular divine figure.

Few auspicious occasions are embarked upon without first seeking Ganesh's blessing. His principal attribute in Hindu mythology—a quality that flows from both his wisdom and his strength—is as a remover of obstacles to the fulfilment of desires. No wonder everyone wants Ganesh on their side before launching any important project, from starting a factory to acquiring a wife. My own student-day courtship violated time-honoured Indian rules about caste, language, region, age and parental approval; but when we got married, my then wife-to-be and I had an embossed red Ganesh adorning the front of our wedding invitations.

I have since developed an even more personal connection to Ganesh. The great 2,000-year-old epic, the *Mahabharata*, was supposedly dictated by the sage Veda Vyasa to Ganesh himself; since then, many a writer has found it helpful to invoke Ganesh in his epigraph. When I recast the characters and episodes of the *Mahabharata* into a political satire on twentieth-century Indian history, *The Great Indian Novel* (1989), I had it dictated by a retired nationalist, Ved Vyas, to a secretary named Ganapathi, with a big nose and shrewd, intelligent eyes, who enters with elephantine tread, dragging an enormous trunk behind him. Such are the secular uses of Hindu divinity.

For in my Hinduism the godhead is not some remote and forbidding entity in the distant heavens. God is immediately accessible all around us, and He takes many forms for those who need to imagine Him in a more personalised fashion. The Hindu pantheon includes thousands of such figures, great and small. Ganesh is the chief of the *gana*s, or what some scholars call the 'inferior deities'.[14] He is not part of the trinity of Brahma, Vishnu and Shiva, who are the principal Hindu gods, the three facets of the Ultimate First Cause. But he is the son of Shiva, or at least of Shiva's wife, Parvati (one theory is that she shaped him from the scurf of her own body, without paternal involvement).

As a writer I have always been interested in the kinds of stories a society tells about itself. So part of the appeal of Ganesh for me lies in the plethora of stories about how this most unflappable of deities lost his (original) head and acquired his unconventional appearance.

The most widely-held version is the one my grandmother told me when I was little, about the time that Parvati went to take a bath and asked her son to guard the door. Shiva arrived and wished to enter, but Ganesh would not let him in. Enraged by this effrontery, Shiva cut off the boy's head. Parvati, horrified, asked him to replace it, and Shiva obliged with the head of the first creature he could find, an elephant.

This was a salutary lesson in the perils of excessive obedience to your parents, though I don't think my grandmother intended me to take it that way. My mother, who always tried unsuccessfully to resist the temptation to boast about her children, had another version: a vain Parvati asked Shani (Saturn) to look at her perfect son, forgetting that Shani's gaze would reduce the boy's head to ashes. Once again, an elephant's was the head that came to hand.

Growing up in an India where loyalty seems all too often on sale to the highest bidder, I could not but be impressed by Ganesh's rare quality of stubborn devotion to duty. However he may have lost his head, it was Ganesh's obduracy as a guard that, in my grandmother's telling, cost him a tusk. 'The powerful avatar Parasurama,' she recounted, as we little ones gathered round her at dusk, 'possessor of many a boon from Shiva, came to call on the Great Destroyer at his abode of Mount Kailash. Once again, Ganesh was at the door, and he refused to let the visitor disturb the sleeping Shiva. Parasurama, furious, tried to force his way in, but found Ganesh a determined opponent.' (My eyes widened in excitement at this part.) 'Ganesh picked Parasurama up with his long trunk, swung him round and round till he was dizzy and helpless, and threw him to the ground. When his head cleared, Parasurama flung his axe at the obstinate Ganesh. Now Ganesh could have easily avoided the axe, but he recognised the weapon as one of Shiva's. He could not insult his father by resisting his weapon. So he took the axe humbly upon his tusk.' Ever since, Ganesh has been depicted with only one full tusk, the other half-amputated by the axe.

The thrill of that story did not diminish for me when I learned the more prosaic version which says that Ganesh wore down one tusk to a stub by using it to write down the epic verse of the *Mahabharata*. For this reason, the missing tusk signifies knowledge. As I grew older, I learned of more such symbols associated with Ganesh. Scholars of Hinduism tell us that Ganesh's fat body represents the hugeness of the cosmos, its combination of man and pachyderm signifying the unity of the microcosm (man) with the macrocosm (depicted as an elephant). Some suggest it has the less esoteric purpose of demonstrating that appearances mean little, and that an outwardly unattractive form can hide internal spiritual beauty. In any case, his looks do not prevent Ganesh, in most popular depictions, from being surrounded by beautiful women, including his twin wives, Siddhi and Buddhi. Siddhi represents spiritual power and Buddhi intellect; in some versions there is a third wife, Riddhi, embodying prosperity (though she usually replaces Buddhi—perhaps making the point that you can have either brains or wealth but not both!) Further, Ganesh's trunk can be curled into the symbol 'Om', the primal sound; and the snake found coiled around his waist represents the force of cosmic energy.

'But Ammamma,' I would ask my grandmother, 'why does Ganesh ride a rat?' For in most of the pictures in our prayer room, the deity is shown on this unusual mount. At the simplest level the sight of an elephantine god on a tiny mouse visually equates the importance of the greatest and smallest of God's creatures. And, as my grandmother explained, each animal is a symbol of Ganesh's capacities: 'like an elephant, he can crash through the jungle uprooting every impediment in his path, while like the rat he can burrow his way through the tightest of defences.' A god who thus combines the attributes of elephant, mouse and man can remove any obstacle confronting those who propitiate him. No wonder that many worship him as their principal deity, despite his formally more modest standing in the pantheon.

And what is the secret of his appeal to a twenty-first century urbanite like myself? As his unblinking gaze and broad brow suggest, Ganesh is an extremely intelligent god. When I was very young I heard the story of how Parvati asked her two sons, Ganesh and Kartikeya, to go around the world in a race. Kartikeya, the more vigorous and martial-minded of the two, set off at once, confident he would encircle the globe faster than his corpulent brother. Ganesh, after resting a while, took a few steps around his mother and sat down again. Parvati reminded him of her challenge. 'But you are my world,' Ganesh disarmingly replied, 'and I have gone around you.' Needless to say, he won the race—and my unqualified admiration.

So it is no surprise that Ganesh is worshipped in India with not just reverence but enthusiasm. Sometimes this can be carried to extremes, as when Ganesh devotees in Western India in the 1890s allowed the bubonic plague to take many lives rather than co-operate with a British campaign to exterminate the rats that carried it (for the rats were also, after all, Ganesh's mounts). Or when, in late September 1995, word spread around the world that statues of Ganesh had begun drinking milk. In some cases, statues of his divine parents, Shiva and Parvati, were also reported to be imbibing these liquid offerings, but Ganesh it was who took the elephant's share.

In India, the rationalists were quick to react. It was, they averred, a matter of simple physics. Molecules on the rough stone and marble surfaces of the statues had created a 'capillary action' which sucked in the droplets of milk. (*Om capillary actioneyeh namaha?*) These were not really absorbed into the statue but formed a thin layer of droplets on the surface which would be visible if the statue were dark. A team of government scientists proceeded to demonstrate this on television, placing green powder in the milk and showing a green stain spreading over the face of a white marble statue. Mass hysteria was alleged; Indian priests (who live off the offerings of devotees in the temples) were merely trying to whip up more custom, said some; it was all politics, said others, pointing to the need for the then-flagging Hindutva movement to attract the credulous to their credo. *The Pioneer* newspaper published a photograph of a spout emerging from the back of a temple from which milk poured into a bucket;[15] the implication was that it was chicanery, not divine ingestion, that accounted for the disappearing milk in the temples. Still, millions of devotees who flocked to temples worldwide saw in the phenomenon a simple message from the heavens that the gods remained interested in the affairs of ordinary mortals.

But Hindus have always believed that to be the case; the 'milk miracle' merely reinforced an unstated assumption about the nature of the godhead. Our gods crowd the streets, smile or frown on us from the skies, jostle us for space on the buses; they are part of our daily lives, as intimate and personal as the towels in which we wrap ourselves after a bath. As MP for Thiruvananthapuram (Trivandrum, in Kerala), I was struck by the fact that my constituency is the one place in the world where even the airport runway shuts down twice a year for a few hours so that Lord Padmanabhaswamy can be escorted on his usual traditional route across the airfield for His ritual seaside bath. And none in the city, of any faith, considers this remotely unusual.

So the intrusion of the gods into our lives through the milk-drinking episode is no great aberration. They are part of our lives anyway; we see ourselves in them, only idealised. My own affection is for Ganesh himself, a god who—overweight, long-nosed, broken-tusked and big-eared—cheerfully reflects our own physical imperfections. After all, a country with many seemingly insurmountable problems needs a god who can overcome obstacles.

When I was a child in Bombay, I was enraptured once a year by the city's great Ganesh Chaturthi festival, in which India's bustling commercial capital gives itself over to the celebration of this many-talented deity. Hundreds of statues of Ganesh are made, decorated and lovingly dressed; then they are taken out across the busy city streets in amid endless processions of followers, who collectively number over a million, before being floated out to sea in a triumphant gesture of release. As a little boy I stood on the beach watching the statues settle gradually into the water while the streams of worshippers dispersed. It was sad to see the giant elephant heads disappear beneath the waves, but I knew that Ganesh had not really left me. I would find him again, in my wall-calendars, on my mantelpiece, at the beginning of my books—and in the prayers with which I would resume my life the morning after the festival:

MY HINDUISM

Om maha Ganapathe namaha,
sarva vignoba shantaye,
Om Ganeshaya namaha...

Om, I invoke the name of Ganapathi;
Bringer of peace over all troubles,
Om, I invoke the name of Ganesh...

2

THE HINDU WAY

The sage Yajnavalkya was once asked to list the number of gods; it is said he began with the number 3,300 and ended by reducing them all to one—Brahman, the pervasive spirit of the cosmos that underlies all creation. The Rig Veda say '*ekam sat vipra bahudha vadanti*'. This was also Swami Vivekananda's favourite phrase about spirituality: 'That which exists is One; the sages call It by various names.'

Hindus therefore understand that all worship of God reflects an effort to reach out to that which cannot be touched or seen; since God is, in that sense, literally unknowable, one may imagine Him/Her/It in any form, since each form may be just as valid as another and none can be guaranteed to be more accurate than the next one. The various forms of God in Hinduism, reducing the abstract to the specific visual form, reflect the limitations of the human imagination rather than any shapes within which the divine must be confined. Indeed, Hindu legends have the gods manifesting themselves in so many shapes and forms that the notion of one agreed image of God would be preposterous. Thus one can imagine God as a potbellied man with an elephant head, and also as a ten-armed woman with a beatific smile; and since both forms are equally valid to the worshipper, why not also imagine God as a bleeding man on a cross? All are acceptable to the Hindu; the reverence accorded to each representation of the unknowable God by worshippers of other faiths is enough to prompt similar respect from the Hindu. Acceptance is always the name of the game.

As I have remarked at the outset, the key to understanding Hinduism is that it is one faith that claims no monopoly on the Truth. Hindus understand that theirs may not necessarily be the only path that leads to salvation; they are taught to respect all other paths that seek the Truth, knowing that these will vary depending on the circumstances of each individual's life, the culture in which they are born or live, their values and motivations. In the *Gita*, Lord Krishna says, 'Whosoever follows any faith and worships me under whatsoever denomination in whatsoever form with steadfastness, his faith I shall reinforce'.[1] The acknowledgement of multiple paths to the ultimate truth of creation is implicit in the philosophical disputes and arguments that have marked the faith for millennia.

One consequence of this acceptance of difference is that it flies in the face of the certitudes most other religions assert. The French traveller François Bernier, on his well-documented journey through India in the seventeenth century, tried to introduce some Brahmins in 1671 to Christianity, and was startled by their response: 'They pretended not [that] their law was universal; that God had only made it for them, and it was, therefore, they could not receive a stranger into their religion: that they thought not our religion was therefore false, but that it might be it was good for us, and that God might have appointed several different ways to go to heaven; but they will not hear that our religion should be the general religion for the whole earth; and theirs a fable and pure device.'[2]

We respect your truth, the Brahmins were saying; please respect ours.

Some scholars have described Hindus as henotheists, that is, people who worship their God but do not deny the existence of other gods. Every Hindu worships some god, but it may not be the same god worshipped by every other Hindu either. As Radhakrishnan puts it: 'God is more than the law that commands, the judge that condemns, the love that constrains, the father to whom we owe our being, or the mother with whom is bound up all that we can hope for or aspire to.'[3] God is all that, and infinitely more.

This henotheistic attitude means, however, undifferentiated respect for all the various possible ways of worshipping God, whether Hindu or not. A Hindu can accept the worship of the Abrahamic God as another practice of the same kind as he sees pursued by other Hindus. For him, someone worshipping Christ is essentially no different from himself worshipping Vishnu or Shiva. The acceptance of difference starts here for the Hindu. This was why it was possible for a large community of Jews, the Bene Israel, after arriving on the shores of western India around the time of Christ, to practise their faith for centuries in rural Maharashtra without being seen by their Hindu neighbours as practitioners of a different religion; Hindus used to seeing various Hindus pursue their own modes of devotion found nothing odd in a people with their own different practices, assuming them to be just another kind of Hindu, until a wandering rabbi from Jerusalem arrived in India centuries later and identified them as the Jews they were.

It didn't matter to the Hindus around them. The *Haristuti* has a prayer that says: 'May Vishnu, the ruler of the three worlds, worshipped by the Shaivites as Shiva, by the Vedantins as Brahman, by the Buddhists as the Buddha, by the Naiyayikas as the chief agent, by the Jainas as the liberated, by the ritualists as the principle of *dharma*, may he grant our prayers.'[4] This cheerful eclecticism was the attitude that enabled Swami Vivekananda, concluding the presentation of a paper at Chicago's Parliament of the World's Religions in 1893, to call upon the blessings of 'He who is the Brahman of the Hindus, the Ahura Mazda of the Zoroastrians, the Buddha of the Buddhists, the Jehovah of the Jews, and the Father in Heaven of the Christians.' To him they were one and the same: 'That which exists is One; the sages call It by various names.'

SEEING LIFE WHOLE

The British, who in their two centuries of imperial rule over India struggled to understand and come to terms with Hinduism, did a great deal to explore and debate its meanings as best they could. Some saw it, in E. M. Forster's notorious phrase, as 'a mystery and a muddle'; others tried to reduce it to terms they could relate to. Whether

Hinduism was polytheistic or monotheistic was a question that agitated many British minds. After the Census of 1911, one senior British official concluded that 'the great majority of Hindus have a firm belief in one supreme God—Parameshwara, Ishvara or Narayana.' The chief British census official in India, Sir Herbert Risley, observed that 'these ideas are not the monopoly of the learned: they are shared in great measure by the man on the street.' An 'intelligent Hindu peasant', he claimed, not only was familiar with Hindu concepts like the *paramatma* (supreme soul), *karma* (loosely translatable as 'fate'), *maya* (illusion), *mukti* (salvation) and so on, but had 'a rough working theory of their bearing upon his own future'.[5]

A few basic ideas were deeply ingrained into every Hindu, whether he lived up to them or not. Among these commonly-held beliefs were two four-fold divisions. The first was the organisation of life into four stages, or *ashrama*s: these were *brahmacharya*, the bachelor existence, a time to be spent learning and acquiring mastery over the essential disciplines needed to lead a meaningful life; then *grihastha*, the life of a householder, when one married, procreated, and assumed the responsibilities of family life; then *vanaprastha*, when one retired and retreated to the forest to lead a life of contemplation in harmony with nature; and finally, sannyas, the stage of renunciation of all worldly ties, at which one seeks one's ultimate merger with Brahman, the spirit suffusing the cosmos.

The four stages of life also related to the four ends of life, the Purusharthas, that every Hindu had to pursue: *dharma*, the moral code (discussed more fully later), *artha*, prosperity or material well-being, *kama*, desire for pleasure and gratification, and ultimately *moksha*, or the salvation that comes from ultimate self-realisation, the fulfilment of which is the purpose of each individual life.

These stages and ends of life in Hinduism embraced an all-encompassing idea of human needs in a comprehensive vision. Every person needs to learn and to earn; to have sex, food and money; to love, to nurture, to assume responsibility; each individual also has a shared concern for the common good and an indefinable curiosity about the unseen, about that which can only be experienced and not understood through words. All of these urges coexist in all of us; they overlap and interact with each other; we pursue them systematically or randomly, or we stumble across them, but they are present in each of our lives in an interdependence of which we are barely conscious but which the Hindu *rishi*s fully appreciated. The common expression '*mata, pita, guru, daivam*' encapsulates the human journey—one is first, from birth, totally dependent on the mother, then exposed to the outer world by the father, then taught and guided by the guru, until one finally finds God.

The Hindu appreciation of life saw it whole, recognised the supreme ends of life and the stages needed to progress towards their achievement. It did not seek to suppress or deny the normal lust for sex, wealth or possessions, but sublimated these in a larger purpose. (Kama even has its own *shastra*, Vatsyayana's Kama Sutra). Hinduism accommodated the acknowledgement of worldly desires within the quest for the eternal. As Radhakrishnan postulated, Hinduism 'binds together the kingdoms of earth and heaven'. Indeed, it is no coincidence that Hindu gods are all married; they are depicted with consorts, each of whom, like the gods and goddesses themselves, have multiple aspects and manifestations. It is a striking feature of Hinduism that our gods can be susceptible to desire; they are depicted falling for *apsara*s and seducing sages' wives. Lord Shiva even fell for Vishnu in the transformed appearance of the ethereally beautiful Mohini. Prudery appears to have been imported into Hindu social attitudes only in reaction to the Muslim invasions and Victorian colonial rule.

Hindus pursue their quest for the eternal—the search for 'the light beyond the darkness'—through three types of activity: *jnana* or the quest for knowledge, not merely theoretical learning but in the form of realised experience which leads to wisdom; *bhakti* or devotion, expressed principally through prayer, fasting, temple rituals and sacrifice, but also through meditation and self-interrogation; and karma or action and service in the fulfilment of *dharma*. (Karma is a concept that is variously translated as action, fate or destiny, and causality; it means all three, though the meaning depends on the context in which the phrase is used.)

Bhakti is of course the most popular path, and the easiest for most people to pursue, since a capacity for worship comes inborn in all of us. Purists categorise Hindu worship in a taxonomy that runs like this: the most simple Hindus worship spirits and animist forces; the next level of ordinary Hindus worship their own ancestors, popular deities and gurus or godmen; the level above that worships incarnations like Rama, Krishna, or Buddha; above this level are those who worship a personal god, or *ishta-devta;* and highest of all are those Hindus who worship the Absolute, in the form of Brahman. Those who worship the *ishta-devta* or personal *bhagavan* (in other words those trying to reach Brahman through a divine intermediary) must settle for a somewhat lower place in the hierarchy of spiritual yearning than those who seek Brahman for itself, in the quest for ultimate self-realisation. A verse from the *Kena Upanishad*[6] captures some of the exquisite literary talents of the ancients along with the profundity of their philosophical enquiry:

> Who sends the mind to wander afar? Who first drives life to start on its journey? Who impels us to utter these words? Who is the Spirit behind the eye and the ear?

> It is the ear of the ear, the eye of the eye, and the Word of words, the mind of mind, and the life of life. Those who follow wisdom pass beyond and, on leaving this world, become immortal.

> There the eye goes not, nor words, nor mind. We know not, we cannot understand, how he can be explained: He is above the known and he is above the unknown. Thus have we heard from the ancient sages who explained this truth to us.

> What cannot be spoken with words, but that whereby words are spoken: Know that alone to be Brahman, the Spirit; and not what people here adore.

> What cannot be thought with the mind, but that whereby the mind can think: Know that alone to be Brahman, the Spirit; and not what people here adore.

> What cannot be seen with the eye, but that whereby the eye can see: Know that alone to be Brahman, the Spirit; and not what people here adore.

What cannot be heard with the ear, but that whereby the ear can hear: Know that alone to be Brahman, the Spirit; and not what people here adore.

What cannot be indrawn with breath, but that whereby breath is indrawn: Know that alone to be Brahman, the Spirit; and not what people here adore.

Into all of this, great variations and choices enter. Some critics have described Hinduism as animism tempered by philosophy, or mysticism leavened by metaphysics. They are not wholly right, but they are not wrong either. Ultimately, all such worship is merely a means to an end. Some look for God in nature, in forests and rivers, some in images of wood or stone, and some in the heavens; but the Hindu sage looks for God within, and finds Him in his own deeper self.

THE BANYAN TREE OF HINDUISM

As a result of this openness and diversity, Hinduism is a typically Indian growth, a banyan tree. It spreads its branches far and wide, and these in turn sink back into the earth to take fresh root in the welcoming soil. In the shade of the vast canopy of this capacious banyan tree, sustained by multiple roots and several trunks, a great variety of flora and fauna, thought and action, flourishes.

The multiplicity of places of worship in India gives Hindus plenty of choice, and affords religious-minded temple-goers opportunities for extensive pilgrimages. Most Hindu families embark on these quite often; for some, the only holidays they undertake are to temple towns, to worship at the shrine of a powerful deity. While some pilgrimages, especially to well-established temple towns, take on the characteristics of a religious holiday, others can be quite arduous. The annual *yatra* to the ice-cave at Amarnath in Kashmir involves a major trek; that of Mount Kailash and Lake Mansarovar in Tibet, renowned as the abode of Shiva, has cost the lives of many of who have attempted it across the narrow and treacherous Himalayan passes. Pilgrimages to Kedarnath and Badrinath, and to the sources of the Ganga and the Yamuna at

Gangotri and Yamunotri respectively, are other Himalayan journeys that are not for the weak or faint-hearted. Other religious trips are to sites where large numbers of Hindus gather for a special occasion: from the Thrissur Pooram, an annual festival which involves the largest pro-cessional of caparisoned elephants in the world (usually up to a hun-dred pachyderms decked up to the hilt), to the *ratha-yatra* at the Jagannath temple in Puri, Odisha and the Kumbh Melas described below. *Utsava*s (religious festivals, from the Sanskrit '*ut*', to let go or remove, and '*sava*', worldly sorrows, hence an occasion to release one's burdens or cares) abound across the country. Regional festivals witness throngs of worshippers in different parts of the country on different occasions at fixed times of the year—Bengalis celebrating Durga Puja, Maharashtrians Ganesh Chaturthi, the Ram Leela across north India, Onam in Kerala, Pongal in Tamil Nadu. Holi, the festival of colours, is famously the most fun-filled of all *utsava*s, while an occasion like Makar Sankranti, marking the transit of the sun into the Makara rashi (Capricorn—sign of the zodiac) in Hindu astrology, is observed with due solemnity. The largest crowds gather during the Kumbha Melas that take place every twelve years in Haridwar, Allahabad (Prayag), Nasik, and Ujjain: the Allahabad Kumbh, at the confluence of the Ganga and the Yamuna, is an extraordinary sight, attracting some twenty mil-lion people each time.

Sometimes a pilgrimage may consist of a regular visit to one favou-rite temple: the Kerala political leader K. Karunakaran travelled to the fabled Krishna temple in Guruvayur on the first of every month (according to the Malayalam calendar) throughout his long life, and thousands do the same to the hilltop shrine to Ayyappa at Sabarimalai, or to Balaji at Tirumalai. Sometimes it is to a particular area where many temples abound: the temples to the nine planets at Kumbakonam, for instance. But quite often it can be an extensive circuit, such as the one my family undertook by car across southern India when I was fourteen, a three-week journey that enabled us to pray at Tirupati, Madurai (whose famed Meenakshi temple, dedicated to a warrior queen who became a consort of Shiva, boasts 33,000 sculptures), Thanjavur, Kanchipuram, Palani, Rameswaram and innumerable smaller towns in Tamil Nadu and Kerala, halting at each place just to worship at the principal temple, and moving on to the next one. My parents found this profoundly satisfying; for their children, it was all a bit of an adventure, though we learned a little about Hinduism at each stop.

The striking thing to a young boy during this journey was the remarkable variety of these places of worship, the differences in their architectural styles and physical appearances, the different manifestations of god being worshipped at different temples, the variety of rituals and the behaviour of the priests, the different materials presented as *prasadam* (offerings) to the gods, and the idiosyncratic practices associated with each shrine, most famously the shaving of the head at the Venkatachalapathi temple in Tirumalai, Tirupati (Andhra Pradesh), the richest temple in India,[7] where my fourteen-year-old locks were duly shorn as an offering to Lord Balaji.

The Hindu acceptance of variety goes much farther than this, however. Foreigners sometimes politely ask if Hinduism requires vegetarianism or abjures alcohol, and are puzzled when different Hindus give them different answers to the question. Versions of the faith come with their own prescriptions and proscriptions, but there is no universal requirement. There are Hindus, particularly Vaishnavas in the north, who recoil in horror at the very thought of consuming meat and others who will not touch even garlic or onion (considered *tamasik*[8] foods by purists), while there are Hindus who eat all of these and would consider it mildly uncivilised not to do so. Goats are routinely sacrificed at the Kalighat temple in Kolkata and other animals at Kali temples across the land, but most Hindu religious occasions are marked by ostentatious vegetarianism. My children's mother is half-Bengali, half-Kashmiri, descended from a long line of carnivorous Brahmins on both sides who were alternately horrified and mournful about my vegetarianism (some tried to excuse it on the grounds that I must be a 'Vaishnava', a worshipper of Vishnu, though I was too eclectic to be so typecast and had actually been named for Shiva, having been born on Maha Shivaratri. But then in Tamil, the word for vegetarian is 'shaiva'. Go figure!). We brought up our sons to 'eat everything', but their mixed genetic inheritance prevailed: one twin took to meat-eating with relish, while the other, at age seven, with no persuasion whatsoever from his father, turned staunchly vegetarian.

Alcohol offers its own contradictions. There is a strain of prohibition in some aspects of Hindu thought, but this coexists with the use of alcohol in some religious rituals (such as at the Kal Bhairava temples) and indeed with the routine habit, of some *sannyasis*, of consuming marijuana and other hallucinogens in the pursuit of spiritual experiences. In the Vedas, *soma* (or *som-ras*) was a favourite beverage of the Vedic deities, and much alcohol flowed during religious ceremonies and sacrifices; in the *Rig Veda*, Mandala IV, Hymn 18, the god Indra is said to have drunk three lakes of *soma* to fortify himself before slaying the dragon Vritra, who had imprisoned all the waters of the world.[9] The *Mahabharata* is replete with details of alcohol consumed by those who are worshipped as incarnations of Vishnu. In Puranic mythology, there is a Hindu goddess of wine, Varuni, who emerged from the primordial Churning of the Ocean, the Samudra Manthan, as one of fourteen 'ratnas' bestowed upon the world, including the moon. Sanskrit literature, including the poetry and plays of Kalidasa, India's greatest literary figure (even though only a fraction of his sublime work has survived), is replete with references to intoxicating drinks. Yet other texts also offer Dharmashastric objections to Brahmins consuming liquor, and Brahminical Hinduism has tended to disapprove of alcohol consumption.

There is doctrinal variety, as well. Those Hindus who are steeped in the *Upanishads* and the *Bhagavad Gita*, suffused with a sense of Brahman (the Ultimate Reality underlying all phenomena) pervading the cosmos and debating its unity with atman (the Universal Soul also present in each of us) would consider themselves monotheists; the 'common man', innocent of such texts, might think of the multiple deities he sees around him as different gods, and have no difficulty with being considered a polytheist. The truth is that it doesn't matter. These are all equally valid ways of being a Hindu.

This pervasive multiplicity of practices and beliefs makes it difficult to conceptualise Hinduism as one might other religions. As a term of

description, indeed, 'Hindu' implies no monolithic identity; to speak
of the 'Hindu community' as one might the 'Muslim ummah' is contestable, since Muslims are bound to each other by credos, convictions
and rules of which Hindus are innocent. The absence of standard practices and belief systems, and the absence of ecclesiastical hierarchies
and universal religious institutions, adds to the difficulty. When
Christians disagree amongst each other, they disagree with reference
to the interpretation of one single book, the Bible, whose teachings
remain the fountainhead of their faith. The same is true of Muslims,
though the room for interpretation is less, since the Quran is seen as
the revealed word of God, though the Hadith offers more room for
discussion. Hinduism has no such handy volume; when Hindus seek
guidance, it is rarely to textual authority that they turn (though often
to spiritual guides or gurus, whose knowledge, at least in theory, may
be derived from their understanding of various scriptures).

In recent times, the *Bhagavad Gita* has become the equivalent of a
'sacred book' for the Hindus, due to its frequent use by twentieth-
century gurus such as Swami Chinmayananda and political leaders like
Mahatma Gandhi. The *Gita* subsumes the ideals of the Vedas and
Upanishads in the words of the popular deity Krishna, and its exhorta-
tion to do one's duty irrespective of the consequences has been cited
as an inspiration by various figures on the world stage, from Turkish
Prime Minister Bulent Ecevit to justify his country's invasion of
Cyprus, to my failed candidacy for the Secretary-Generalship of the
United Nations.

But Hinduism cannot be reduced to the *Bhagavad Gita*, or any single
holy book. Dr Radhakrishnan put it best: to him, Hinduism is 'not a
definite dogmatic creed, but a vast, complex, but subtly unified mass
of spiritual thought and realisation.' The spiritual leader Dada Vaswani
calls Hinduism variously 'a fellowship of faiths', 'a federation of philosophies', and 'a league of religions'. Note the plural in that last word.

Indeed, the writer Rutvij Merchant adapted a phrase of mine to
make the point. I had written in my book, *India: From Midnight to the
Millennium*, that any truism about India can be immediately contradicted by another truism about India. He observed that 'Hinduism

appears to be very much like India; an essential paradox, as any attempt at a truism about Hinduism can be immediately contradicted by another truism about Hinduism.' Remarking that there are as many Hinduisms as there are adherents, he goes on to add: 'Interestingly, Shashi Tharoor's statement about India "that the singular thing about the country is that you can only speak about it in the plural", applies to Hinduism perfectly; if religion is seen as a technology that can be leveraged to grow spiritually and eventually achieve union with the Supreme, there appears to be no uniformity or synchronisation to the Hindu way; indeed the term "the Hindu way" is in itself a fallacy as there is no one Hindu way.'[10]

Merchant interestingly defines a Hindu as one who is an ardent seeker of Truth: 'An individual who strives to actively discern the existence of the objective Reality otherwise termed as God and attain Him if convinced of His existence, using means that are inherently subjective and dependent on the individual's own proclivities, beliefs and values, is a Hindu.' This definition of Hinduism, if it can be called that—since it could apply to almost anyone of any culture or religious faith—emphasises the individualist nature of the quest for truth, the role of reasoning in the process, and the ultimate yearning for God (whether one uses that term or speaks of the soul's merger with Brahman, the idea is the same).

Some Hindus reject the term 'Hindu' altogether as a description of their faith, preferring to speak of 'Brahmanism', though this is used by some Dalits and others as a term of abuse against the Brahmins who have dominated the faith. But in its origins, the expression refers to the ideal of attaining the Brahman, the Universal Spirit that suffuses the cosmos. Many use the Sanskrit-Hindi phrase, 'Sanatana Dharma', or 'eternal faith' (though 'faith', as I explain shortly, is an inadequate translation of 'dharma'). Sanatana is eternal in the sense that it refers to a *dharma* that is old and new at the same time, ever-present and ever-evolving. In Hinduism, there is no difficulty in accepting that some aspects of *dharma* will be rendered irrelevant over the aeons and that other ideas, innovations and reforms will be infused into the faith and rejuvenate it. The essence of *dharma*, however, remains unchanged throughout eternity.

The Hindu concept of time is very different from Western ideas. In Hindu thought, the world has no beginning and no end, but only experiences endless repetitive cycles of time in four *yuga*s (aeons or ages): Satya Yuga, the age of truth, Treta Yuga, Dvapara Yuga and Kali Yuga (the age of destruction and untruth, the one in which we are all living now). Each Kali Yuga ends with a great flood (*pralaya*) that destroys the world, only to start afresh with a new Satya Yuga. Some Hindus argue that Vaishnavites and Shaivites differ in their perception of time; after all, Vishnu is reincarnated in various *avatars*, while Shiva simply 'is'. Vaishnavites, in this reading, are constantly changing through time, while Shaivites are focused on the annihilation of the self. Though the distinction is interesting, both sets of Hindus relate to time very differently from followers of other faiths, whose temporal existence on this earth culminates, after death, in paradise or hellfire.

I mentioned earlier that *dharma* is often translated as faith, and that this is an inadequate translation. The concept of *dharma* is much broader, embracing an entire system of social ethics covering law-abiding conduct. Indeed, in an afterword to *The Great Indian Novel* in 1989, I listed a whole series of meanings that have been ascribed to the term '*dharma*', an untranslatable Sanskrit word that is, nonetheless, breezily defined as an unitalicised entry in many an English dictionary. (The *Chambers Twentieth-Century Dictionary*, for example, defines it as 'the righteousness that underlies the law'.) A passable effort, to be sure, but no one-word translation in English ('faith', 'religion', 'law'), can convey the full range of meaning implicit in the term. 'English has no equivalent for *dharma*,' writes P. Lal, defining *dharma* as 'code of good conduct, pattern of noble living, religious rules and observance'. Nanditha Krishna, author of several popular books on various aspects of Hinduism, translates *dharma* as 'law of righteousness'. In his book *The Speaking Tree*, Richard Lannoy actually defines *dharma* in nine different ways in different contexts. These include moral law, spiritual order, sacred law, righteousness, and even the sweeping 'totality of social, ethical and spiritual harmony.' Indeed, *dharma* in its classic sense embraces the total cosmic responsibility of both God and Man. My late friend Ansar Hussain Khan, author of the polemical *The Rediscovery of India*, suggested that *dharma* is most simply defined as 'that by which we live'.

The word *dharma* is formed from the Sanskrit root 'dhr', to hold. *Dharma* is therefore that which holds a person or object and maintains it in existence; it is the law that governs its being. To live according to *dharma* is to be in consonance with the truth of things. A moral life, for a Hindu, is a life lived in accordance with his *dharma*, which in turn must be in conformity with the absolute truth that encompasses the universe.

A POLYCENTRIC FAITH

Hinduism is a polycentric faith. Since it admits multiple centres of belief and practice, there is no single structure of theological authority or liturgical power. When there is no centre, there is no periphery either; Sanatana Dharma is inclusive, since there is no basis for excluding any belief. Radhakrishnan argues that Hindu tolerance is not indifference: Hindus understand that not all self-declared truths are of equal value. Still, they are all welcome in that gigantic buffet table of spiritual options the Hindu feels empowered to dip into. Of course, the flip side of the coin is that Hindus tend not to see non-Hindu religious traditions as 'other'; and in particular, they do not see them as challenging or putting into doubt Hindu beliefs and practices, which, after all, are timeless and eternal.

Unlike Hinduism, however, as we have seen, the Semitic (or Abrahamic) faiths believe themselves to be of divine origin. The True Faith was revealed by God to Abraham and was therefore beyond contestation, even if its three major variants, Judaism, Christianity and Islam (in order of appearance!) relied on different texts; and in Muslim belief, God revealed Himself further to Muhammad, who became the definitive Prophet of His Word. Since the word of God cannot be false, all three Semitic religions came to revolve around ideas of absolute truth; they were the only way to reach God, and those who chose other paths were doomed to hellfire or damnation. Many saw it as their duty to show the absolute truth they had found to those who were still in darkness but unaware of the error of their ways. If you resisted their truth, you were wrong and if you were unwilling to correct yourself, you must be either misguided, evil or blind—the only possible explanations for those unable or unwilling to see the truth laid before them by these 'revealed' religions. For this reason it was permissible, for some 'true believers', to convert you to the 'right' path by force or inducement.

Sanatana Dharma, however, saw its adherents engaged in a permanent quest for truth, which was not something revealed from on high by God or a prophet, but something that had to be searched for by prayer, meditation, good conduct and experience, and could well be attained only at the very end of one's life, if at all. Religion is, after all, experience; ideally, it is an experience of God. The *Svetashvatara Upanishad* says: 'God, the maker of All, the great spirit ever seated in the hearts of creatures, is fashioned by the heart, the understanding and the will. They who know that become immortal.' The heart, the understanding and the will each play their part; all are indispensable. This also means that religious experience is personal experience; self-realisation will vary from individual to individual. After all, the Divine, as Radhakrishnan argued, reveals itself to men within the framework of their intimate perceptions and prejudices. The Western faiths largely look outward to the heavens for their revealed truths; the Hindu looks within himself.

A Hindu could live his faith at one or more of several levels: the quotidian, with its temple rituals, religious observances, social customs and good deeds (the path of religious performance); the spiritual, with extensive prayer, meditation, worship of and service to a deity, penance and austerities (the path of devotion); and the intellectual, with a serious study of philosophy and theology (the path of knowledge). Most Hindus never get beyond the first stage; their Hinduism is a religion of temple visits, fasts to propitiate favourite gods, the observance of specific festivals according to the tradition in their geographic regions. But even for the others, who demand more from (and look for more in) their faith, their quest for the truth, their enquiry into the mysteries of Creation, would not end with a blinding flash of realisation from the pages of a sacred book. After all, unlike the Bible, the Dialogues of the Buddha, and the Quran, all the unchallengeable principal texts of their religions, even the *Vedas* are merely the first in a substantial corpus of scriptural works.

It is also true that in a religion as vast, capacious and evolving as Hinduism, there is much in the religious texts that contradict themselves, and each scholar can find scriptural justification for a point of view diametrically opposed to that of another scholar, also with his own scriptural justification. Take, for example, the place of women in Hindu society, which has undoubtedly undergone much transformation, for better and for worse. The epics, the *Manusmriti* and the dicta of Yajnavalkya, putative author of the *Yajnavalkya-smriti*, all contain much material that is bloodcurdlingly misogynist in relegating women to a place of inferiority in relation to men. Bhishma in the Anushasana Parva of the *Mahabharata* declares: 'Women have one eternal duty in this world: dependence upon and obedient service to their husbands.' And yet this is the faith that regarded wives as *ardhangini*, half of the whole, and *sahadharmini*, the partner of the man in the fulfilment of *dharma*. The sage Sayana, in his commentary on the *Rig Veda*, wrote: 'The wife and the husband, being the equal halves of one substance, are equal in every respect; both should join and take equal part in all work, religious and secular.' A warrior queen like Kaikeyi strode on to the battlefield alongside her husband. Swami Vivekananda pointed out with pride that some of the most exalted *rishi*s of the Hindu faith, the most learned and respected authorities on the scriptures, are women. (Twenty-one of the original *rishika*s to whom the *Vedas* were revealed were women: the names of Gargi and Maitreyi today adorn colleges in Delhi University; Vishavara, Ghosha and Apala were also prominent seers.) Adi Shankara, in a theological debate with his famous critic Madana Mishra, appointed as the judge between them the latter's learned wife Sarasavani. Even Manu declared, 'where women are honoured, there the gods rejoice, but where they are not honoured, there all rituals are useless.' Of the 210 Shiva-worshipping Lingayat saints, thirty-five are women. In other words, there is authority for different approaches in the ancient texts; the Hindu is invited to take his pick. If the Hindu chooses wrongly, or unwisely, among the opinions offered to him, it is not Hinduism's fault.

The Hindu understands that all scripture requires interpretation, and cannot be taken literally. In particular, there has long been an acknowledgement that what is laid down in ancient texts may not necessarily have been what was, or is, practised in the faith. The strong position held by the polyandrous, property-owning Nair women in Kerala's matrilineal society, the honoured position of Rajput women, who killed themselves en masse after their husbands fell on the battlefield, and the reverence accorded to women mystics like Mirabai and social reformers like Savitribai Phule, show Hinduism as accepting of women as figures of authority and respect. The fact that the *Manusmriti* is both misogynist and casteist does not preclude the possibility that throughout the ages, it was honoured in the breach.

Hinduism offers the believer much to choose from: what you choose to follow is your Hinduism, while others might find scriptural justification for a contrary view. Hindu philosophy testifies to the extent to which reasoned debate amongst the believers—in dialogue with but not restrictively bound by their scriptures—has allowed Hindu religious philosophers throughout history to reform themselves and their faith.

MANY SACRED BOOKS

As I have asserted, Hinduism has not one sacred book, but several, both complementary and contradictory to each other. The Hindu scriptures are commonly divided into Srutis, Smritis, Itihasas, Puranas, Agamas and Darshanas.

The Srutis are that which has been heard or revealed. The four *Vedas*—*Rig Veda, Sama Veda, Yajur Veda* and *Atharva Veda*—are Sruti, having been revealed to, or heard by, the *rishis*, codified by Veda Vyasa and passed down through generations of disciples. But they are not revealed texts in the Christian or Muslim senses of the term; the *rishi* is a Mantra-Drashta, a seer of mantra or thought; the thought is not his own, but he 'hears' or 'sees' it. It is interesting that the Sanksrit word for philosophy is *darshana*, literally 'seeing': the perception of the seer is as important in Hinduism as his intellectual enquiry. In this, too, Hindu philosophy differs considerably from its Western counterparts.

In fact the *RigVeda* is estimated to have taken perhaps half a millennium to attain its corpus of 10,552 mantras in verse, and in the course of these five centuries at least fifty poet-*rishis* had a hand in its composition. Their sacredness comes from their divine inspiration and sustained quality, not from having been handed down fully composed by God like the Quran. The story is no different with the later Vedas; the four Vedas are believed to have been created between 1500 BCE and 500 BCE, a period of one thousand years. In that period we see enormous evolution from the nomadic faith of the *RigVeda*, in which animal sacrifices, including those of cattle, were offered to the gods[11] and the healthy scepticism in some of its verses, to the evidence in the later Vedas of adjustment to new social realities, such as the *YajurVeda*'s references to new gods, clearly taken into Hinduism from prevailing local faiths—including Pashupati, Lord of the Beasts, and Aushadi, Lord of Medicinal Herbs.

Similarly the 108 *Upanishads*, which distil the essence of the Vedic philosophy, are also Sruti (revealed literature). They were also written over centuries: it is believed that the first eight go back to the period between the eighth century BCE to the fourth century BCE, congruent with the Age of the Buddha. The next three *Upanishads* are post-Buddhist and date from 300 BCE to 200 CE, whereas the remaining 97 *Upanishads* belong to the Puranic period—from the second century CE to the tenth century CE. The chronological gap between the earliest verses of the Rig Veda and the bulk of the *Upanishads* was greater than the time that separates us today from the life of Jesus Christ. An entire *Upanishad* (the *Mandukya Upanishad*) is devoted to the primal sound, Om. In the reckoning of many Hindus, the Upa-Vedas, or subsidiary vedas, include Ayurveda, the science of wellness, Dhanurveda, the science of weapons and the rules of warfare, GandharvaVeda, the science of the performing arts (including the classic text on music, dance and theatre, the *Natya Shastra*), and the Arthashastra, the treatise on statecraft that in many respects anticipated Machiavelli's *The Prince* by nearly two millennia. The Vedangas, the explanatory 'limbs' of the Vedas, deal with such matters as grammar, phonetics, etymology, the art of poetry, the science of rituals and (in the famous *Jyotisha Vedanga*) astronomy and astrology. All these again are the product of centuries of writing and reflection.

The Smritis are that which is remembered; they are composed by human beings without any specific divine inspiration and passed on to guide ordinary people in the conduct of their lives and the performance of their spiritual and worldly duties. The eighteen Smritis, written down largely over the five centuries between 300 BCE and 200 CE, are often referred to as the *Dharmashastras*, since they explicate how *dharma* must be observed, and these are seen as practices that must change with time and place. The Smritis describe the daily life of individuals, prescribing rituals and rules which vary according to each *varna* or social class and are collectively known as *varna-ashrama-dharma*. The Smritis also lay down the rules of governance, known as Raj Dharma, and adumbrate the earliest ideas of what may be considered a Hindu constitutional order, headed by a king. Among the most famous of the *smritis* is the Arthashastra, an ancient treatise on statecraft, economic policy and military strategy, composed between the 2nd century BCE and the 3rd century CE, and attributed by many to Chanakya or Kautilya, principal counsellor to the Emperor Chandragupta Maurya (though this is disputed). In its unsentimental explication of the duties and responsibilities of kings and states, and its ruthless advocacy of amoral policies including alliance-making, coercion and suborning of rivals, it anticipates by several centuries the prescriptions of Machiavelli.

Since the Smritis are purely man-made and mutable, Hinduism does not aver that laws laid down a millennium ago must be followed to the letter today. The foundational laws of Yajnavalkya and the Code of Manu, often cited as the source of 'Hindu law', are Smriti; no Hindu seriously argues that they must be observed to the letter today. (Indeed, it is debatable whether they were strictly followed even in the times it which they were propounded.) In fact, the Smritis were not all internally consistent:

> *A profusion of arguments! The Smritis differ among themselves.*
> *No one's opinion is final or conclusive.*

The essence of dharma is hidden and elusive.
The right path is the path followed by great men.

— *Yaksha Prashna*, Sloka 114[12]

The *Itihasas*, the epics, respond to the human need for instruction through story: the profound philosophical enquiries of the Srutis and the *Smritis* are more easily digested by the common people in the form of parables and epic narratives (which in turn easily lend themselves to theatrical form, dance and music, all the better to communicate their message to the masses). *Itihasa* literally means 'the way it was' and many take the epics literally, though they have been embroidered with mystical and fantastic elements, and it is quite probable that divinity was ascribed to their principal personages only in later retellings. Their principal purpose remains to impart the values of the *Dharmashastras* in story form. The *Ramayana* tells the story of a kingly figure, Rama, who upholds both his personal *dharma* and his raja *dharma*: in the earliest versions he was not portrayed as a god, but as an ideal man devoted to upholding truth. Indeed there is impressive evidence for the historicity of Rama in Valmiki's text, which is replete with astonishingly accurate geographical, botanical and zoological details about his journey from Ayodhya to Lanka and back.[13] He makes enormous sacrifices in his personal life, including giving up his beloved wife, in order to fulfil his *dharma*. The *Mahabharata* was told and retold, with countless interpolations and additions, till about 400 CE; it incorporates the classic poem, the Bhagavad Gita, the Song of the Lord, which distils the essence of the *Upanishads* and is to many Hindus the core religious text of their faith.

The two great Hindu epics, the *Ramayana* and the *Mahabharata*, tell stirring stories accompanied by digressive meditations on values, morals and principles. They are polycentric and fundamental texts about such key issues in society as what constitutes ethical conduct; how a just society is made and sustained; and the duties and obligations of kings, counsellors, warriors, women and sages. They deal with great moral dilemmas and issues of right conduct, justice and fidelity, violence and redemption; they give voice to a range of actors and concerns; they provide models for social and political action; and because they are told and retold as stories, they have embedded themselves in the popular consciousness of Hindus.

The *Ramayana*, the epic tale of an exiled prince's conquest of the demon kingdom where his wife is held hostage, is a stirring saga, intimately familiar to all Indians and most Southeast Asians. Lord Rama's ultimate triumph and his return to rule his own kingdom as a just and benevolent king is the archetypal story of the victory of good over evil; yet in many of its episodes, including what becomes of his queen, there are complex moral dilemmas unveiled that do not lend themselves to simplistic interpretations.

The *Mahabharata* deals much more with *adharma*: it is a tale of the real world, one whose heroes have feet of clay, whose stories have ambiguous ends, whose events range from great feats of honour and valour to dubious compromises, broken promises, dishonourable battles, expedient lies, dispensable morality. It asks profound questions about the nature of *dharma*: Yudhishthira says 'dharma is subtle' and each episode in the epic appears to be a case study of what this means—is *dharma* derived from the *shastras*, from precedents, from *nyay*, from *niti*? Is it determined by caste or gender? The *Mahabharata* offers much ground for reflection on weighty ethical and moral dilemmas. When the low-born Ekalavya becomes a master archer by eavesdropping on lessons offered by Dronacharya to his caste betters, the teacher asks for the boy's thumb in tribute, which would destroy his ability to practise what he has learned. When Draupadi, wife of the Pandavas, is 'lost' in a wager in a fixed game of dice, she questions the right of her husband to stake her and the propriety of the winners to seize her. By raising these questions, the epic obliges Hindus to interrogate themselves about their beliefs. The *Mahabharata* has come to stand for so much in the popular consciousness of Indians: the issues the epic raises, as well as the values it seeks to promote, are central to an understanding of what makes India India. Its characters and personages still march triumphantly in Indian minds, its myths and legends still inspire the Indian imagination, its events still speak to Indians with a contemporary resonance.

While the *Ramayana* (composed from around the 200 BCE to perhaps 200 CE) and the *Mahabharata* (said to be composed between about 400 BCE and 400 CE, after some eight centuries of retellings and interpolations)[14] are the two best-known epics whose core story (and many subsidiary tales) are widely known to practically every Indian, the Itihasas also include the *Yogavasishtha*, stories and fables imparted by the sage Vasishtha to Lord Rama, and the *Harivamsha*, which tells stories of creation and of the origins of Lord Krishna. When the *Ramayana* and the *Mahabharata* were retold in the vernacular languages, they acquired immense popularity and impact. The Kamban *Ramayana* in Tamil in the twelfth century CE, and Tulsidas's *Ramcharitmanas* in Awadhi in the sixteenth century, exalted Rama to his present place in the Hindu pantheon.

The *Mahabharata* incorporated the Bhagavad Gita, an extraordinary, inspirational and profoundly philosophical text which addresses in powerful and poetic language a basic conundrum of human existence: what human beings should do when they are pulled in contradictory directions by equally important but incompatible obligations. We are all faced in life with having to make hard choices; the Gita presents us with the searingly hard choice confronting the heroic warrior Arjuna, who finds himself on the battlefield, about to go to war, in the name of a just cause, whose triumph will involve the killing of several members of his own family. His duty and his moral commitment to one side of the battle stands against his love for his own kith and kin, whose blood he must shed, and that too in violation of the universal moral duty not to take life. But if, for this reason, he refuses to fight, his absence from the battlefield could allow the forces of unrighteousness to prevail; it would mean the victory of those who have committed wrongs, and it would violate his own duty and obligation as a warrior to deploy his martial skills in fulfilment of his duty and in defence of the right. Arjuna confesses his agonising dilemma to Lord Krishna, whose counsel makes up the bulk of the Gita. Perform your *dharma*, Krishna tells Arjuna: do your duty regardless of the outcome. The right action in conformity with your *dharma* is your only obligation; its consequences, even its success or failure, should have nothing to do with the moral motivation for your action. Your own feelings, or prospects of reward, are irrelevant to the need to act. Krishna's philosophical advice is essentially to do what is right regardless of the consequences. Implicit is an acknowledgement that doing the right thing is not always easy, that it can cause pain and grief to others, even others one loves or is bound to. But the path of *dharma*, leading a life of good conduct—what a Westerner might call a moral life—is a complicated and ambiguous task, not to be reduced to simple calculations of defeat or failure, life or death, reward or punishment. Armed with this advice, and with Krishna as his charioteer, Arjuna goes forth to sanguinary battle, and prevails, leaving the battlefield littered with the blood-soaked bodies of his own cousins.

The *Gita* is an amazing text, full of wisdom and philosophical reason, but also a call for action, an exhortation to fulfil one's duty with conviction and courage. It has probably inspired more commentaries per line of text than any other work in the vast canons of Hinduism. Swami Vivekananda and Mahatma Gandhi swore by it; each found different aspects of its poetic brilliance and profundity to live by.

The eighteen *Puranas* (composed roughly between 250 CE and 1000 CE) convey the truths of the Vedas and the Dharmashastras in short stories as well, and have formed the basis of religious education in rural India for millennia. They differ from the Itihasas since they do not comprise a grand epic narrative but several different stories featuring non-recurrent characters. The moral code conveyed through Puranic stories is still the basis for Hindu ethics, and the characters in many Puranic tales have come to epitomise the virtues of faith, chastity, obedience, loyalty, constancy, generosity and so on. Their names are often cited, whether in conversation or even political discourse, as emblematic of those virtues: Prahalada the faithful believer, Savitri the devoted wife, Dhruva the constant, Harishchandra the truthful, and so on. The *Puranas* also tell the stories of the ten incarnations of Vishnu; and the *Srimad Bhagavatam*, or *Bhagavata Purana*, focusing on the life and times of Lord Krishna, is still recited in temples and homes across India.

The *Puranas* mark a significant development in Hinduism, with a much greater emphasis on the worship of Gods in human form, unlike the earlier Vedic faith; where the latter had relied on rituals and sacrifices in which *homams* (prayer rituals around a fire), usually involving the fire god Agni, played a major role, the Puranic practice principally involved idol-worship and *pujas*. (It is suggested that while the Vedic era saw only the worship of a formless and imageless God, the conduct of rituals and the propitiation of the river and mountain and tree gods of local tribes—all of which were 'portable' and not confined to a fixed spot—it was the arrival of the Greeks under Alexander in the fourth century BCE that brought into India the idea of permanent temples enshrining stone images of heroes and gods.) Again, while the Hinduism of the Vedas emerged from mantras and rituals, including elaborate sacrifices, the *Puranas* promoted their values entirely on the basis of myths and stories. By developing the concept of the saguna Brahman to go with the exalted idea of the nirguna Brahman, the Puranic faith integrated the Vedic religion into the daily worship of ordinary people. Using the seductive power of *maya* (illusion), the *nirguna* Brahman of the Vedas took the form of *saguna* Brahman or Ishvara, the creator of *prakriti*, the natural world and the God or Bhagavan of all human beings. Vishnu and Shiva were recognised as Ishvaras; the followers of the former, the Vaishnavas, worshipped Him in several *avatars*, while the followers of Shiva, the Shaivites, confined their worship to Shiva alone, though in several aspects (the dancing Nataraja, the powerfully symbolic *lingam*), and his immediate family (his consort Parvati, his sons Ganesh or Vinayaka, and Skanda or Murugan). Puranic Hinduism witnessed the absorption (even 'Sanskritisation') of the existing local cultures and the adoption of their deities and heroes into Hindu mythology; it is in the Puranic age that both Vaishnavites and Shaivites accepted idol worship, which was earlier absent from the Vedic faith. The *Puranas* offered a bridge between the Vedic religion and local folkways, between highbrow philosophers and vernacular cultures, assimilating both in a narrative of inclusive ethics. It is in the *Puranas* that much of what we today understand by popular Hinduism is anchored.

Not quite fitting into any of these categories is another magnificent work of early Hinduism, authored in the South by Thiruvalluvar (born around 300 CE) whose *Thirukkural*, a collection of 1,330 couplets or *kurals* containing profound aphorisms and imparting moral lessons, has been called by some 'the Veda of the Tamils'.

By the sixth century CE India and Hinduism had a rich mythology, a corpus of elaborate rites and rituals, extraordinary heroic poetry, a well-developed system of popular ethics, an evolving religious architecture and a spiritual literature for the masses. It also had non-religious texts of universal significance, notably the fables of the *Panchatantra*, which imparted practical advice on worldly matters (and on the foibles of human character) in the form of entertaining tales featuring both humans and animals. There is cynicism, including about kings and political leaders; violence, often unfortunate; and humour, sometimes at the expense of the vainglorious. 'We are told quite frankly,' observes the historian Upinder Singh, 'that conventional virtues can lead to ruin. Truthfulness, kindness, and helpfulness to others lead to disaster. The idea of self-sacrifice (even feigned) is mocked. Cunning, quick thinking, and hard-headedness are valorised. The only social relationship that is celebrated is friendship, and even that does not emerge unscathed.'[15]

With idol worship came temple construction, a feature of Hinduism only since the fifth century CE, and reaching its apogee in the magnificent Chola temples of the eleventh to the thirteenth centuries, many of which are still in use today. The 108 Agamas lay down the disciplines and doctrines for the worship of specific deities, notably Shiva, Vishnu and Shakti, which in turn have given birth to cults focused on each of these manifestations of the divine. They also specify the rules for constructing temples in honour of each of these, and for observing related rituals and rites. They are meticulously detailed, ranging from the ablutions to be performed by the worshipper to the adornments on the idol, the timing and order of prayers and so on, and also replete with devotional songs and verses. However, most people worship daily in the privacy of their own homes: instead of idols consecrated in temples, they have portable idols installed in an alcove or puja-room. This practice is sanctified in the *Srimad Bhagavatham* or *Bhagavata Purana* (Part 11, Chapter 27, Sloka 12), which specifies that eight types of material engender permissible forms of idol worship: stone, wood, metal, clay, sand, crystal, a drawing or even just a mental image. Some of the prominent temples were located on the banks of sacred rivers—notably the Ganga, Yamuna, Narmada, Godavari, Krishna, and Kaveri—whose flowing waters were said to have cleansing properties that could purify those who immersed themselves in them.

The Darshanas are the texts of the six principal schools of Hindu philosophy, drawing from many, and are unabashedly intellectual and abstrusely academic in nature. The six (the Shad Darshanas) include three lesser-known schools of Hindu philosophy: the Nyaya School, which emphasises logic and debate; the Vaisheshika School, which sees the universe as made up of countless atoms, each with its own distinctive quality; and the Mimamsa School, which emphasises the role of sacrifice and ritual in seeking salvation (some scholars describe the Vedic religion as Mimamsa Hinduism to distinguish it from the Puranic Hinduism of later years). A fourth, the Yoga School, is better known around the world for its physical practices, but in fact principally focuses on the control of the mind, the breath and the body as the means to attaining the divine samadhi (a state of trance-like meditative consciousness). The central debate in Hindu philosophy is, however, between the two other schools, the oldest, the Sankhya School (so old that it is mentioned in the *Mahabharata*), based on reasoning, which argues the case for dualism or Dvaita (the idea that there is a clear distinction between spirit and matter, between the divine and the worldly) and the newest (founded just over a millennium ago), the Vedanta School, which rejects dualism (Advaita) and sees spirit and matter as essentially one. Vedanta, or 'the end of the Vedas', has, thanks to the initial efforts of Adi Shankara and the nineteenth-century preaching of Swami Vivekananda, become the principal school of Hindu philosophy today, as well as the most influential internationally, and is discussed more fully in the next chapter.

Hindus trust the Vedas, but most do not see them as immune to analysis or criticism; it has been axiomatic in Hinduism that what was valuable to its forefathers might be valuable to us today, but each generation is allowed to enquire into its own spiritual patrimony. The Vedas have a sanctified place in the Hindu consciousness, but the *Upanishads*, the *Puranas*, the epics, and other works of spiritual and philosophical enquiry are also counted among our most basic scriptures. The three prasthanas or divisions of the Vedanta—the *Upanishads*, the *Brahma Sutras* (555 aphoristic verses attributed to Badarayana and written down some time between 450 BCE and 200 CE, which summarise the spiritual and philosophical ideas in the *Upanishads*) and the Bhagavad Gita—correspond roughly, according to Hindu philosophers, with the three stages of faith, knowledge and discipline. Each has value and each can be understood and practised alone or in combination with the others.

That said, as we have seen, Hindus, unlike Muslims and Christians, do not see their religious texts as claiming to embody the ultimate truth. Indeed, it would be a problem if they did, because then different texts would offer contradictory truths and men might be obliged to fight each other to demonstrate the superiority of their truth. Instead, a work of scripture is, to a Hindu, a means of self-realisation; the words, and the insights they contain, are devices through which a diligent Hindu approaches self-transformation. A religious text is a breach in the fog of ignorance that enshrouds the human mind. Allow its insights, the magic of its words, the music of its mantras, to penetrate through the fog, and a transformation might follow. The transformation is not merely in understanding the words of the text as in an Abrahamic holy book, but in opening the mind to new possibilities—including the possibility that the literal claims of the text might be false. The purpose of the religious text is to enter the mind of the reader and help constitute the self.

As Swami Vivekananda put it: 'To the Westerners their religious books have been inspired, while with us our books have been expired; breath-like they came, the breath of God, out of the hearts of sages they sprang, the mantra-drashtas.'

Given this attitude to the Hindu holy texts, the Sanatana Dharma's attitude to the Bible, the Torah or the Quran is the same. Hindus do not look for the literal meanings of these holy books; and since they do not read them literally, they do not argue over them literally either. The Hindu has historically refused to pick a fight over the meaning of other people's religious texts; since they cannot literally be true, to the Hindu, they can either help in self-realisation or not, but they are not worth quarrelling about. You say your holy book is the word of God? Fine; if it helps you understand your true self, if it opens your mind's eyes to the ultimate truth of Creation and helps you merge your soul into the cosmos, it will have served its purpose. Ah, you say, that's not what your holy book is supposed to do? What use is it to you then? Come, let me read it; perhaps it will help open my eyes.

This approach to theological disputation left the honest Christian missionary in colonial times somewhat confused.

THE HINDU LIFE EXPERIENCE

As a result, Hinduism occupies a unique place among the world's faiths. In it, as Dr Radhakrishnan explained:

> 'Intellect is subordinated to intuition, dogma to experience, outer expression to inward realisation. Religion is not the acceptance of academic abstractions or the celebration of ceremonies, but a kind of life or experience. It is insight into the nature of reality (*darshana*) or experience of reality (*anubhava*).'

Hindus dislike people being drafted into truth-armies firing cannons of certitudes; their instinct is to remain sceptical, open, questioning. Reason and intuition must go together. Blind belief in dogma is absent in Hinduism; all spiritual teachings are subject to disputation, and perceptions must be tested through logical thought. The Hindu sacred texts 'are not so much dogmatic dicta as transcripts from life.'

This is all very well, one might say, but what of the vast majority of Hindus, who have not read most of these sacred texts, who are unaware of the glorious capaciousness of their faith, who are inured to theological heterodoxy and scriptural eclecticism? What of those who only know Hinduism as a cultural identity, who go to their temples to pray to their *ishta-devta* (their favourite gods) when they are in trouble or distress, who observe fasts for specific deities, celebrate joyously the major festivals in their area and are conscious of their difference from those who practise other faiths? Is the Hinduism I am describing their Hinduism too?

I would claim it is. Because ultimately the nature of any religious faith is not determined by its scholars, theologians and scriptural exegetes. It is precisely the ordinary believer, the worshipper who is indifferent to theories about his faith but believes in God and values his religion as his way of reaching his hands out to his Maker, who demonstrates the essence of his faith in his own practice of it. In Hinduism, there is an understandable tendency to see the faith through its remarkable Sanskrit scriptural and philosophical writings. But just as important to the practice of Hinduism are the non-Sanskritic, oral, vernacular and regional traditions of worship and ritual, which are indispensable to the way the faith is experienced in different parts of the country. And it is precisely because Hinduism has been practised in a certain way for millennia that is has survived as long as it has with its essential nature unchanged, even as it has faced the vicissitudes of reformist movements like Buddhism and Jainism, military assaults from Muslim invaders, conquest and Islamic rule, the conversion activity of Christian missionaries, reformist challenges like those of Ramananda, Chaitanya and Kabir (of whom later), syncretic movements like Sikhism and the Brahmo Samaj and attempts at conversion of its adherents to other faiths. Every Hindu may not be conscious of the finer points of his faith, but he has been raised in the tradition of its assumptions and doctrines, even when these have not been explained to him. His Hinduism may be a Hinduism of habit rather than a Hinduism of learning, but it is a lived Hinduism for all that.

These 'habits' vary enormously from place to place, caste to caste, and community to community. In South India it is entirely common to see celebrations and practices completely unfamiliar to a north Indian, and vice-versa. The Thaipusam festival, taking place in the Tamil month of Thai, in which devotees carry ceremonial offerings on wooden planks called kavadis and many pierce themselves through the body and march in excruciating processionals to demonstrate their devotion to Lord Murugan, is unknown in other parts of India. Pongal is a huge festival in Tamil Nadu and southern Kerala but a north Indian Hindu will have no clue what it signifies. While Diwali, the Festival of Lights, has over the years become, in popular perception, the standout Hindu festival, it is observed fairly modestly in the south; in Kerala, on the other hand, the festival of Onam is celebrated with enormous gaiety and piety unlike in the north, where it is not celebrated at all.

Onam, in fact, offers another striking example of Hindu diversity. It celebrates the annual return to earth of the *asura* King Mahabali, a wise and benevolent monarch under whose egalitarian rule the people of Kerala flourished in mythical times. The gods, jealous of his overweening power and popularity, sent Lord Vishnu to earth in the form of a Brahmin dwarf, Vamana, who asked the king for as much land as he could cover in three steps. The king, surprised by the modesty of his request, granted his wish; whereupon the dwarf grew to his celestial size as the Lord. With one step he covered the earth, with his second the heavens; and when he had nowhere left to place his third step, he turned to the king to fulfil his promise. King Mahabali humbly offered his own head; Lord Vishnu placed his foot on the monarch's head, driving the king through the ground into the netherworld. Onam commemorates Mahabali's annual return to earth to see how his people are getting on. Rather like Santa Claus, he is largely portrayed as a jolly rotund figure happy to see his subjects enjoying a good time, and Onam is an occasion for holiday cheer, gift-giving and enormous feasts. As I have noted, it is, however, not celebrated by north Indian Hindus, who instead observe, the day before Onam, a minor festival called Vamana Puja in which they worship Vishnu in the form of a dwarf. A Malayalam tweet by a north Indian politician, Bharatiya Janata Party (BJP) President Amit Shah, wishing Keralites well on the occasion of Vamana Puja, caused great offence to its intended audience, since it was portrayed as celebrating the ill-treatment of the popular local king vanquished by Vamana!

As a result of its huge diversity, and the multiple folk religious practices it has absorbed over the millennia, mainstream Hinduism abounds in festivals. There is no day in the calendar which is not associated with some auspicious occasion, or dedicated to a specific god, or assigned to a particular religious practice. The importance and significance of each day will again vary depending on which part of India one is in, and which community one belongs to. In Delhi it is entirely possible to see

Punjabis celebrating Lohri while Bengalis go about their business, Biharis enveloped in Chhath Puja while Maharashtrians remain ignorant of it and Malayalis in Onam holiday spirit while northerners are just gearing themselves up for Diwali.

Rituals are undoubtedly a precious part of religious practice for most Hindus. Some are conducted by priests in arcane Sanskrit while the devotee, having paid his fee, stands with hands folded and listens in incomprehension. (There is a distinction in many scriptural texts between the priest who performs the ritual and the *yajamana* or the person for whom it is performed, whose only role consists of offering a *dakshina* or gratuity to the priest.) Some—particularly the rituals associated with birth and naming, the first feeding of grain to a baby, the first instruction in the alphabet, and of course marriage, death and cremation—are full of inescapable meaning for every participant and bind the worshipper to his faith, family and community. Most often the rituals require a visit to a temple; sometimes they are performed at home. My sisters, who live abroad, do not go as often to temples as our mother, who lives in India, though they strive to keep up certain religious traditions and practices even in foreign lands. But they tell me that they are deeply comforted by the knowledge that on every special occasion in their family, our mother is going to an ancient temple to pray for them, to seek the Lord's blessings for their families, and to distribute alms to the poor in their name. In turn, whether in damp London or sunny California, they remember to light a lamp at dusk in their prayer-rooms, as Hindus have done for centuries.

Hindu rituals almost always require a priest, in most parts of India; however my own community, the Nairs of Kerala, dispenses with the services of a priest on the occasion of marriage, seeing it as a social contract to be performed under the guidance of family elders in the presence of large numbers of usually well-fed witnesses, which would be enough to seal a marriage in the eyes of the world. The eyes of a representative of God they consider much less important; whereas in the north, it would be unthinkable not to have a priest officiating— indeed the wedding might well be considered null and void if a priest didn't turn up to conduct it.

Given this dislike of priestly intermediaries in my gene pool, it is no wonder that as a young boy I asked my father why it was necessary to go to temples. If God is everywhere, I reasoned, isn't He (or She) at home, at school, at work? Why do we need to go to a temple to find Her? My father patiently explained that while God is everywhere, He was especially powerful in certain places, especially those where He had manifested himself through the spontaneous appearance of an idol (as in the Krishna idol in Guruvayur) or other miracles. Such places then became sanctified by the devotions of millions of worshippers over hundreds of years, and thus acquired even more religious significance. It was a self-perpetuating phenomenon: a temple became famous because of something associated with it, usually a legend involving the deity in question, then worshippers came and testified to its powers, saying their prayers at that place had been answered by the Goddess, for instance, and then more worshippers came and the more devotion the temple attracted, the more were the stories of miracles and blessings accruing from worship there, and the more people kept coming....

On that south Indian pilgrimage when I was fourteen, I also found myself asking my father about the behaviour of some of the priests at the more famous temples, who openly stuck out their hands for more money after performing the rituals my father had already paid for. He looked somewhat embarrassed at first, then replied softly but firmly that priests had to live too. They were performing a service to us devotees, but they had families they were responsible for, children they had to educate, and it was only fair they asked for help from the people on whose behalf they had interceded with God. After all, they had what today we would call 'domain knowledge'; they knew the scriptures, had mastered the mantras and could recite the appropriate ones with the required fluency. Why shouldn't they be rewarded for their expertise?

This left my teenage mind only partly mollified, and I have not been as enthusiastic a temple-goer as my parents, especially since I rationalised that praying in the privacy of my own home would be just as effective, as long as my heart was pure and my thoughts clear. I maintain an eclectic prayer-alcove in my home, where dozens of pictures, idols and relics of Hindu deities—including a print that reproduces one of my parents' religious pictures, that I saw my father pray before every day as I grew up—all compete for my reverential attention daily.

Still, the passion of other worshippers keeps drawing me back to temples, especially in my constituency, Thiruvananthapuram, which is blessed with more places of worship per square kilometre than any other metropolis in India, and where friends, colleagues and party workers insist on accompanying me, praying for me and promising assorted divinities that I will perform certain rituals in fulfilment of their undertakings. (I have, as a result, been weighed against bananas, coconuts and salt because *they* had sworn that I would be: this is a powerful incentive against weight-loss, since the heavier I was, the more the temples in question benefited from donations of those items). But I am not complaining. I find peace in the temples, and a strengthening of my ties to those who have accompanied me there, as if we have shared something indefinable in that common space where hope and need combine in supplication to the Divine.

* * *

Some have seen in Hinduism a selfish religion, a collection of individuals praying for themselves, with no equivalent of the Muslim Friday prayer or the Sunday Christian Mass with its service and sermon uniting a community in worship. Philosophically, after all, the most important claim the *Upanishads* make is that the essence of each individual is also the essence of all things; the human self, the *atman*, and the cosmic reality, Brahman, are essentially the same. This leads to the view that one only needs to look within to find divinity; one has no need of fellow worshippers or collective sermonising. Hindu religious practice is essentially contemplative, as the seeker turns his gaze inwards in quest of real awareness. The *Mundaka Upanishad* (II.2.3)[16] offers a marvellous metaphor: the Imperishable is the target for the seeker, the *Upanishads* are his bow, constant meditation is his arrow, and the string of the bow is drawn with his mind filled with Brahman. Because of this interiority, some Hindu critics see Hinduism as lacking the unity that strengthens other faiths and helps them to negotiate the modern world and social pressures better. Its focus on self-realisation rather than collective advancement, they say, might allow plenty of room for philosophical thought, but none for collective action. To such critics, this prevents Hindus from constituting a defined 'community' that can withstand external pressures. Such thinking partly animates the Hindutva project we shall discuss in Chapter Five.

The *Atharva Veda* points out that the quest for awareness, the search for answers, the journey towards self-realisation, never ceases:

> *How does the wind not cease to blow?*
> *How does the mind take no repose?*
> *Why do the waters, seeking to reach the truth,*
> *Never at any time cease to flow?*

> — *Atharva Veda*, X.7.37[17]

And yet this process is not purely self-centred individualism, since the real self one discovers in this profound quest is the same self as everyone else's. Self-realisation leads ultimately to merging one's soul into the collective Brahman. So when one goes to a temple to worship, one is finding a common sanctified space to help one travel to the same destination as every other worshipper.

3

QUESTIONING HINDU CUSTOMS

Some of Thiruvananthapuram's old temples, especially the eleventh-century Sree Padmanabhaswamy Kshetram, recently revealed to be one of the richest temples in the world because of all the treasures deposited there by the triumphant Travancore maharajas of yore, are truly beautiful. This is where Vishnu is worshipped as Padmanabha, lying on the great serpent Ananta as he floats on the vast Ocean of Milk, the Kshir Sagar. It is in this posture that he is so revered that the kings of the Travancore kingdom called themselves 'Padmanabhadasa', servants of Padmanabha, and ruled in his name rather than in their own—a curious inversion of the concept of the divine right of kings, since here it was the kingly right of the divine.

If many temples are beautiful, though, not all old Hindu practices sanctified by these temples are. The ancient tradition of caste was one my nationalist parents tried to shield me from for years, and it was only at age eleven, when asked by a schoolmate in Mumbai what my caste was (in an incident I describe below), that I finally demanded an explanation. But caste as an instrument of discrimination was abhorrent to my liberal sensibilities from a very young age.

CASTE AND HINDUISM

It is difficult to pretend that Hinduism can be exempted from the problems of casteism, since the religion has been cited as legitimising this form of discrimination in some of its sacred texts. The *Rig Veda* does not mention caste in its original books and it first appears in the Purusha Sukta verse, a later interpolation that describes the sacrifice by the gods of Purusha, the cosmic man, to create all human life: according to this verse, from his mouth emerged the Brahmin, the priests and scholars; his arms were made into the Kshatriyas, the warriors and rulers; his two thighs were the general populace, the farmers, merchants and traders who made up the Vaishyas; and from his feet the Sudras, the workers, artisans and servants, were born.

The verse has been challenged, especially by the great constitutionalist and Dalit leader Dr Bhimrao Ambedkar, who considered it a fraudulent attempt to legitimise caste discrimination, but there is little doubt that many Hindus believed that the caste system had religious sanction. Ironically, as I have demonstrated in my 2017 book *Inglorious Empire: What the British Did to India*, India had castes, but not a caste system: the rigidities of caste as we understand it today were introduced by the British in their desire to understand, categorise, and classify the people they were ruling, in order to control them all the better. What the writer on Hinduism Devdutt Pattanaik describes as the attempt by the British to 'force-fit' some 3,000 *jatis* (castes, or some say sub-castes, grouped around hereditary professions) into the four varnas established in the Dharmashastras, has given us a complex 'caste system' whose uneven persistence in Hindu society has been the source of both iniquity and confusion.

The language of the Purusha Sukta verse would seem to rule out any but Brahmin priests in Hindu temples, and yet *shudra archakas* (low caste sacerdotes) perform rituals in many Hindu places of worship, and in October 2017 the Travancore Devaswom (temple board) officially appointed thirty-six non-Brahmin priests, including six Dalits (the former 'Untouchables' who were not even admitted to Kerala's temples till 1936 and who are still denied access to the sanctum sanctorum in many temples where that privilege is reserved only for those who wear the sacred thread, namely Brahmins). It is conventional wisdom that the caste system confined all learning to a narrow privileged caste of Brahmins, yet Veda Vyasa, the compiler of the Vedas, was born to a low-caste fisherwoman, and Valmiki, the author of the *Ramayana*, was a low-caste hunter; both are revered today, even by the Brahmins.

Caste may well have originated in Hinduism's desire to accommodate the different racial, sectarian, and occupational groups it encountered, in a social hierarchy: Dr Radhakrishnan called it 'the answer of Hinduism to the forces pressing on it from outside', an instrument to 'civilise' different tribes it absorbed. To this great scholar, caste 'stands for the ordered complexity, the harmonised multiplicity, the many in one which is the clue to the structure of the universe'.[1] That sounds almost admirable, till one understands that this complexity, in practice, ossified into impermeable social barriers that manifested themselves in degrading forms of social discrimination and economic oppression. It was not always the case: there was a famous 'fuzziness' to the operations of caste in the pre-colonial era, and many famous examples of caste mobility (beyond those of Veda Vyasa and Valmiki). Be that as it may, the workings of caste extended into religious worship as well. Many temples forbade entry of the 'lower' castes and the 'outcastes'; the latter became known as 'Untouchables' because of the innumerable social prohibitions and indignities to which they were subject.

There is no excusing such abhorrent practices, and many modern Hindus have grown up rejecting the discriminatory aspects of the caste system, while still observing caste preferences when it comes to arranging the marriages of their children. Their logic is simple: caste is a form of community organisation that has been in place for ever, and we are not about to jettison it. We are comfortable with the affinities it implies, and we would prefer to perpetuate our family by arranging marriages within our caste group. But that doesn't mean we will discriminate against people of other castes, or mistreat them: we are educated people, and we know that's wrong. This may strike many modern Indians as a dubious compromise, but the attitude I have summarised is far more common within the Hindu population than many imagine.

It should also be said that the most impressive of India's movements against caste discrimination, from those of Basava in the twelfth century to Sree Narayana Guru in the nineteenth, came from within Hinduism and retained a Hindu vocabulary and conceptual world, including reverence for Hindu deities. Sree Narayana Guru, forbidden as an Ezhava from worshipping at the Shiva temple, entered a river and unearthed a *lingam* (phallic statue) that he consecrated himself, thereby creating his own Shiva rather than rejecting the god who was denied to him. The fourteenth-century Bhakti saint Chokhamela was a Dalit whose fervour for God continued even though he was not allowed inside the temple. In one of his verses he addresses the deity as he might speak to a man of an upper caste: 'I am so hungry; I have come for your leavings, I am full of hope.' In another verse, he brings a 'bowl for your leftover food'; with no access to the shrine, he seeks to fulfil his devotion by serving the deity, submitting himself completely and eating the scraps left behind. This is alarmingly conformist, yet revealing of the extent to which Chokhamela's abject social condition had no bearing on his spiritual standing nor on the extent of his posthumous sanctification. Among the Lingayat saints, too, there were many of humble origins. While Basava, the founder of the sect, was born a Brahmin, many of his prominent disciples were of humbler origins: as Manu S. Pillai records, Allama Prabhu was a drummer, Siddharama a cowherd, Maccayya a washerman, and Kakkaya, a skinner of dead cows.[2]

Still, social mobility was relatively rare in Hinduism, and the lot of the outcastes was a terrible one. Was this because of the religion or the society that practised it? Arguably, Untouchability was a social practice for which it is impossible to find scriptural sanction. To suggest that to be a good Hindu you had to practise caste discrimination is therefore theologically unsound. As the philosopher Jonardon Ganeri has explained, 'Hinduism contains within itself the philosophical resources to sustain an internal critique of reprehensible and unjust social practices that have sometimes emerged in Hindu societies.' As those who are familiar with Adi Shankara's beliefs will testify, the Upanishadic insistence on the unity of being, a divinity available to everyone, the *atma* residing in everyone, and the idea that all human souls ultimately merge into the same Brahman, for instance, implies the equality of all souls and argues against caste discrimination. So does the Vedantic concept of the welfare of all human beings, irrespective of social or economic distinctions: '*bahujana sukhaya bahujana hitaya cha*'. Adi Shankara himself is said to have met an outcaste, Chandala, who was ordered by his disciples to move out of the path of the great sage. 'Who are you to ask me to move for you?' the outcaste asked the great *rishi*. 'Is the Self within me different from the Self within you?' Shankara was so struck by this enunciation of Advaita wisdom by the low-born Chandala that he prostrated himself before the Untouchable and proclaimed him to be his guru.

Manu S. Pillai recounts a legend from the same period: 'The sage Vararuchi, son of Sankaracharya's preceptor, married a pariah (low caste) woman, and fathered twelve children with her. One became a Brahmin, another a carpenter, and one was even a Muslim. Yet another sibling, when they all met for a feast, brought to the table food that he enjoyed: the udder of a cow, or beef if you will. Of course the story goes on to transform the meat into a plant that everyone then consumed, but the lesson is simply that though they were different in what they did and what they ate, they were all born of the same parents, and children of the same land.'[3]

Still, caste discrimination was widespread and iniquitous. Of course Hindus have long accepted the logic of 'reservations' (government legislated quotas in employment and education) in India as a means of making up for millennia of discrimination based on birth. This is why the Constitution inaugurated the world's oldest and farthest-reaching affirmative action programme, guaranteeing Dalits and Adivasis (Scheduled Castes and Tribes) not only equality of opportunity but guaranteed outcomes, with reserved places in educational institutions, government jobs and even seats in Parliament and the state assemblies. Given the appalling discrimination to which they had been subject for millennia—especially those subject to the unspeakable privations of Untouchability—this seems only fair to most, including many caste Hindus, who have not objected to these (SC/ST) reservations.

These reservations are granted to groups listed in Schedules of the Indian Constitution on the basis of their (presumably immutable) caste identities. The addition of the 'Other Backward Classes' (OBC) category in 1989 after the acceptance by the government of Prime Minister V.P. Singh of the recommendations of the Mandal Commission added more people to the numbers benefiting from such official reservations, but it didn't change the basis on which they benefited: despite the 'C' in 'OBC' referring to 'classes', the OBC lists contained castes and sub-castes just above the Dalits in the social pecking order. People like myself tend to disavow caste loyalties as unworthy relics of a more unequal pre-Independence past, but accept that granting benefits on the basis of caste is unavoidable. As for ourselves, as intellectual heirs of an anti-colonial freedom movement that explicitly rejected caste, and out-lawed caste discrimination, we aren't supposed to admit to caste feeling even if, in some cases, it lurks somewhere beneath the surface.

I am conscious of my own bias in the opposite direction; as the son of a newspaper executive from Kerala who dropped his caste name (Nair) at college in response to Mahatma Gandhi's exhortations to do so, moved to London and brought his children up in Westernised Bombay, I am a product of a nationalist generation that was consciously raised to be oblivious of caste.

I still remember my own discovery of caste. I was an eleven-year-old representing the seventh form in an inter-class theatrical event at which the eighth form sketch featured the scion of a famous Bollywood dynasty (who are Hindu). The boy would later become a successful screen heart-throb. I had acted, penned a humorous poem and organised my class's efforts, and the young man was either intrigued or disconcerted by what he had witnessed, for he sought me out the next morning at school.

'Tharoor,' he asked me at the head of the steps near the toilet, 'what caste are you?'

I blinked my nervousness at the Great Man. 'I—I don't know,' I stammered. My father, who never mentioned anyone's religion, let alone caste, had not bothered to enlighten me on such matters. 'You don't know?' the actor's son demanded in astonishment. 'What do you mean, you don't know? Everybody knows their own caste.'

I shamefacedly confessed I didn't.

'You mean you're not a Brahmin or something?'

I couldn't even avow I was a something. The Great Man never spoke to me again in school. But I went home that evening and extracted an explanation from my parents, whose eclectic liberality had left me in such ignorance. They told me, in simplified terms, about the Nairs; and so it is to that schoolboy, celluloid hero of the future, that I owe my first lesson about my genealogical past.

Despite this enforced awareness, I grew up thinking of caste as an irrelevance. The idea of caste as a badge of identity bothered me hardly at all, because I saw it as one of several such badges, to be donned or taken off according to my convenience. My caste identity was relevant to family holidays in my parents' ancestral villages, but irrelevant to my cosmopolitan schooling, and my parents never mentioned (or asked) the caste or religion of any schoolmate who came home to play with me or attend my birthday parties. I grew up ignorant of caste, married outside my caste, and brought up two children to be utterly indifferent to caste, indeed largely unconscious of it. Until my fifties, when I entered the caste-ridden world of Indian politics, it remained that way. Even then I deliberately abstained from finding out the caste of anyone I met or worked with; I hired a cook without asking his caste (the same with my remaining domestic staff) and have entertained all manner of people in my home without the thought of caste affinity even crossing my mind.

One of the key identities in India is, inescapably, caste. As has been noted, to some, it's an instrument of political mobilisation; as the political ascendancy in parts of north India has repeatedly demonstrated, when many Indians cast their vote, they vote their caste. English-speaking urban Indians may scorn such behaviour even while accepting it as part of political reality. After all, none of us would object if a Dalit leader advertised her pride in being a Dalit, or called for Dalit solidarity. Yet my obliviousness to caste is itself a confession of privilege; no Dalit, my Dalit friends tell me, can afford to be oblivious of caste. Much of the outrage at caste is, of course, when it's not a member of an oppressed community celebrating its achievements, but members of one of the so-called 'upper castes', someone at the top of the heap, celebrating their privileges, power and prominence.

Caste won't disappear from the landscape of Hinduism: too many political and administrative benefits (and disadvantages) derive from one's caste affiliation for that to happen, not to mention that for many Indians, it is still part of their lived reality, even though it doesn't pack the same punch it once used to. If it becomes more and more one of many interchangeable, mutable forms of identity—one fraternity of many that an Indian can lay claim to—it may cease to matter so much. The majority of Hindus aren't there yet, unfortunately. And politics may not let them get there either. In recent years we have witnessed the unedifying (and unwittingly hilarious) spectacle of castes fighting with each other to be declared backward: the competitive zeal of the Meenas and the Gujjars in Rajasthan to be deemed more backward than each other, and the agitations of privileged and powerful castes like the Marathas, the Patels and the Jats for reservations on the same basis, would be funny if all sides weren't so deadly serious. As an uncle of mine sagely observed, 'In our country now, you can't go forward unless you're a backward.' (That may seem a prejudiced remark, but such views are increasingly held by many whose castes are ineligible for reservations). Caste—ironically entrenched in India by British colonial rule, as I wrote in *Inglorious Empire*—has remained an inescapable feature of our lives.

The news that a recent survey has established that 27 per cent of Indians still practise caste Untouchability[4] is not, in many ways, news at all. Most Indians have grown up in an India where we have seen such behaviour, though the kind of people who read English-language books probably think of it as something that happens in rural, backward villages rather than bigger towns and cities.

But this survey also packs a few other surprises. It shows almost every third Hindu (30 per cent) admitted to the practice. That is, they refused to allow Dalits into their kitchen or to use their utensils. But data from the survey showed that Untouchability was also practised by Sikhs (23 per cent), Muslims (18 per cent) and Christians (5 per cent).[5] These are faiths that pride themselves on their enshrining of equality and the brotherhood of faith. Dr Amit Thorat, the survey's lead researcher, was quoted in the Indian media as saying, 'These findings indicate that conversion [to religions other than Hinduism] has not led to the total change of mindset that was hoped...caste identity is sticky baggage, difficult to dislodge in social settings.'[6]

My father's and my response—to be oblivious to caste and indifferent to the caste associations of friends, employees and associates—is no longer enough in today's caste-conscious India. For a long time I assumed this was the modern Indian ideal—the egalitarian spirit in which one judged people not by their caste but (to borrow from Martin Luther King Jr.) by the content of their character or the sum of their abilities. But living in India over the last decade, after thirty-four years based abroad, has taught me I was wrong. As an eighteen-year-old blogger, Tejaswini Tabhane, pointed out recently, 'A Brahmin's caste pride comes with humiliation for other castes'. Caste, she writes, 'is both the base and superstructure of Indian society and both the relations of power as well as the forces of production are mediated through it. Blindness to caste does not take away the social, political and economical privileges one gets because of one's "accident of birth" in a particular ("upper") caste.' In her words, anyone belonging to a hierarchically privileged caste 'is bound to get the advantages of his caste location, willingly or unwillingly, consciously or unconsciously. Caste governs the distribution of resources and opportunities in Indian society. Caste is very much present in your life even if it is not directly visible to you because your social and economic capital is a production of your caste only.'[7]

I have to concede she is right. And that makes her admonition strike home: 'To be born in a privileged caste is not anyone's fault but to refuse to even acknowledge "unearned benefits" accruing due to one's caste and thereby claiming that the very mechanism that enforces them is absent in one's life is not right.' On the other hand, 'For the people belonging to the marginalised lower strata of this system, caste is about humiliation, deprivation, oppression and imposed identity.'

Caste blindness, in other words, is itself an affectation available only to the privileged; the 'lower' castes cannot afford to be indifferent to

caste. Parallels are sought to be drawn to debates over race-blind policies in the West, but these are inexact: race, after all, is visible, whereas
caste is not, which makes it genuinely possible to be caste-blind in
one's social and personal relations in a way that is not feasible in multi-
race contexts (a white person cannot credibly say, 'I didn't realise he
was black', least of all when a white employer rejects a black appli-
cant's job application, but an upper-caste Hindu can plausibly claim, 'I
didn't know she was a Dalit'). Still, the temper of the times demands
consciousness of caste and positive compensatory action for its disabilities, rather than blindness to it. Jawaharlal Nehru had hoped caste
would disappear from India's consciousness, as I had allowed it to from
mine. In today's India, that will no longer do.

The recent official findings confirming the persistence of the iniquitous practice of caste discrimination across India's religious communities
do not exonerate Hindu society. But caste, Swami Vivekananda told us,
has nothing to do with religion: it is a purely social practice, and many
Hindus can and should bring up their children to abhor the idea of caste.
In the *Puranas* there is the story of a debate between the *rishis* Vasistha and
Vishwamitra on whether the Vedic religion could be universalised or
whether it was intended for the Aryan people alone. The *Upanishads*
broadened the appeal of the ritualistic religion depicted in the Vedas, and
sages like Adi Shankara and Ramanuja democratised it further. Indeed,
Adi Shankara declared that any human being, merely by virtue of their
personhood, could attain the Supreme Consciousness through a study of
the scriptures, the *Puranas* and the epics, meditation (*japa*), fasting (*upav-
asa*) and worship (*puja*). Caste was never approved of by Adi Shankara.
The contemporary rejection of caste draws from a long reformist tradition in Hinduism that embraces all of them, as well as Kabir, Nanak,
Shirdi Sai Baba, Sree Narayana Guru and Mahatma Gandhi.

Hindu society may have maintained a distasteful practice, but no one
can credibly argue that it is intrinsic to the religion. There is a marvellous story of Utanga, a childhood friend of Lord Krishna, who had
received a boon from Krishna that the Lord would provide him water
whenever he needed it on his wanderings. On one occasion, overcome
by thirst in a remote place, Utanga called upon his boon. An outcaste

hunter soon appeared before him, clad in skins and dirty rags, offering him water from an animal-skin water bag. Utanga, a fastidious Brahmin, turned down his offer. The hunter continued his attempts to persuade him to drink the water but Utanga was haughtily unmoved, berating Lord Krishna in his mind for not having fulfilled his promise. The hunter, his generosity spurned even by a man in need, duly disappeared. Soon Krishna himself materialised before Utanga, informing him that he had sent Indra, the king of the Devas, in the guise of the hunter, to offer him not just water but *amrit*, the nectar of immortality. 'Since, instead of accepting his generosity, you chose to judge him by external factors like caste, you have forfeited the chance of immortality,' the Lord informed Utanga.

The Hindu who says that caste discrimination is incompatible with his *dharma* is a better Hindu than one who insists her religion does not permit her to engage a low caste cook in her house (as a senior government official recently did) or claims her faith will not allow her to serve a Dalit boss (which somehow no menial employee in India has yet done). Still, the battles over temple entry to Dalits occurred within living memory; and other instances of the pernicious effect of caste discrimination in the practice of religion are not hard to find. India's first artist to achieve mass popularity, Raja Ravi Varma, did so in the 1890s by printing lithographs of his paintings of Hindu gods, which enabled Dalits to worship in their homes images of the very deities they were not allowed to pray to in the temples, from which they were barred. As I've pointed out a few pages earlier, the great social reformer Sree Narayana Guru in Kerala installed a Shiva-lingam in a temple because Hindus of his Ezhava caste were forbidden from entering the area's established Shiva temples. So the Hindu religion has undoubtedly been complicit in caste discrimination, and the faith's identification with caste oppression has long been the principal negative held against it. Is a religion responsible for the worst behaviour of its followers? Perhaps not; but Hindus collectively need to continue doing all that they can to wash the stain of caste discrimination from the face of their faith.

GURUS AND THE 'GOD MARKET'

Another aspect of popular Hinduism that does not reflect well on it is superstition. Hindus are considered prone to believing in assorted signs and soothsayers; our fondness for astrology, for instance, is widely observed. It is true that a Hindu without a horoscope is like an American without a credit card, and is subject to many of the same disabilities. I even have two horoscopes: one cast for me soon after my birth in London by an expatriate Indian doctor there, another by the family astrologer at the village in Kerala. They didn't match, and to this day, it seems, I have been pursuing two mutually incompatible fates, in the worlds of public service and authorship.

Still, is it fair to saddle Hinduism with the burden of being responsible for its astrologers, many of whom are undoubtedly charlatans? Or should the belief of certain Hindus in astrology be seen as an emanation of Indian society rather than of the Hindu faith?

The latter case is undoubtedly strengthened by the Hindu affinity for gurus and godmen, whose claims to religious significance often do not extend much beyond their garb (and their gab). Hindus have flocked to ochre-robed dispensers of spiritual wisdom for centuries. There have been ascetic fakirs like Shirdi Sai Baba, performers of miracles like Sathya Sai Baba, teachers of meditation like Maharishi Mahesh Yogi and practitioners of sexual liberation like 'Bhagwan' Shri Rajneesh (who later transformed himself into the somewhat more austere Osho). The legendary Sathya Sai Baba has multiple millions of followers around the world; I have written elsewhere of the spotless town of Puttaparthi that serves as his spiritual headquarters, and continues to attract devotees years after his death. Among the 'living saints' of Hinduism, Mata Amritanandamayi, the 'hugging saint', is revered as the embodiment of unconditional love. Her ashram and spiritual retreat, Amritapuri in Vallikavu near Kollam, is a beehive of activity, thronged with followers from around the world; like Sathya Sai Baba, she channels the donations of her followers to major social welfare projects, running a university, medical college, hospital and a television studio.

Such revered figures follow in a long-established Hindu tradition. Advaita Vedantist Hindus have traditionally held gurus or teachers in high reverence, since many ancient texts suggest that one should seek a qualified and able guide in the pursuit of one's spiritual quest. Following a guru is thus seen by many Hindus as desirable though not mandatory, a path to an end rather than an end in itself; a guru is a guide towards the fulfilment of self-realisation, not a substitute for it. In the Advaita tradition, a competent teacher is vital to help a seeker attain correct knowledge and freedom from false knowledge; he (or occasionally she) serves as a revered instructor, counsellor, and shaper of their disciples' values. Since Hinduism emphasises *anubhava*, or the knowledge that comes from experience, as much as philosophical knowledge or *jnana*, which comes from study and reading, a guru can share his experience as a guide and model to the disciple. The best kind of guru is usually an inspirational teacher, a source of wisdom and instruction, a guide moulding the spiritual evolution of the disciple, an elder who imparts his values and a philosopher who reveals the meaning of life to the attentive seeker. Guru means 'dispeller of darkness'; the exalted place of the guru in Hindu thinking reflects the fact that while a mother merely gives us physical birth, a guru ensures our spiritual rebirth. Not all self-anointed gurus are, however, worthy of the appellation.

India is full of gurus; some are figures of great learning and erudition in the religious texts, some are capable of performing mystical and magical feats beyond rational explanation, and some merely impart a quiet wisdom that their followers find inspirational. Such gurus attract followings in the millions, and many have established ashrams to which their devotees flock, and in which many live either permanently or for regular periods, either conducting religious and spiritual practices, or performing social services in the name of their guru's order. But there are also, in the same domain yet of a different order, charlatans, poseurs and tricksters, in what has been dubbed 'the God Market', who woo the credulous with simplistic ideas of spirituality and amass huge fortunes at the expense of the gullible. These include a female guru who wears red mini-skirts and offers homilies on love, a baba who sits in a tree and dispenses benediction through a touch of his foot, and another who receives the world in his naked glory and whose ultimate blessing comes in the opportunity to grasp his exposed male member. Much of this has nothing to do with Hinduism, except that it is a manifestation of the Hindu's eternal search for spiritual truth, in whatever form it can be found.

Many of the devotees of these godmen are not Hindus. Equally, some of these godmen are not Hindu but count Hindus among their followers. It is important to note that the hold godmen have on their followers is not purely a function of religious devotion; rather it has a lot to do with a sense of drift in society, an aimlessness and hopelessness that requires a religious anchor. Clinching evidence for this proposition came in the person of a godman who is not strictly a Hindu, but a Sikh—the self-styled Baba Gurmeet Ram Rahim Singh Insan, whose name is a compound of Sikh, Hindu and Muslim names with 'Insan' meaning 'Human', and whose jailing in August 2017 precipitated a crisis across Punjab, Haryana and Delhi.

The flamboyant, jewellery-bedecked Gurmeet Singh had a reputation for sexually exploiting his female followers, but only two of them had the courage to sue. The case took fifteen years and 200 sittings of the court before he was convicted; during this time, numerous efforts were made by the Baba's devotees to pressure the investigators, the police, the judges and the complainants to withdraw the suit, but they did not give in.

Baba Gurmeet Ram Rahim Singh Insan was always a peculiar godman, eschewing spiritual asceticism for gaudy showmanship and ostentatious living. He liked his hair long, his motorcycles powerful, his cars expensive, his attire sequinned and his women clingy. He performed in popular music videos of his own composition—his biggest hit is called 'Love Charger'—and had a feature film made about himself called *Messenger of God*. This unlikely 'Rockstar Baba', however, amassed a mass following of fanatic worshippers estimated at over ten million.

He or his henchmen kept this flock together in ruthlessly effective ways. A crusading small-town journalist who reported the rape complaint against him was murdered in 2002. The Baba's movement, known as the Dera Sacha Sauda, amassed significant landholdings and property assets, and exerted influence over various aspects of life in the states of Punjab and Haryana; its reach extended to Delhi.

And yet the Dera Sacha Sauda fulfilled a genuine need in north Indian society, giving millions an identity and a standing they had not previously known. Sections of people who had long known only oppression found in the dera movement a measure of security, safety and dignity they and their families had not historically enjoyed, as well as (or so the cynics say) a simpler, more 'market-friendly' version of religious faith. The dera movement considerably predates Ram Rahim, and had established itself for valid and even admirable reasons well before he became its best-known exponent.

Dera members are overwhelmingly Sikhs, though there are many Hindus among them. Sikhism is a faith that enjoins equality among its faithful, a message that had in the past inspired conversions of people from the lower Hindu castes, particularly Dalits and the 'Other Backward Classes'. But so deep is the prejudice in Indian society that many converted Sikhs found themselves treated no better by their co-religionists of higher castes, who dominate the official Sikh religious bodies which run the major gurudwaras or Sikh shrines.

Faced with an entrenched status quo, many Sikhs of less privileged backgrounds became disillusioned. Their feelings of anger and helpless-ness, compounded by poor education and soaring unemployment, led them to alcohol and drugs. Punjab became known as the drug capital of India, a reputation underscored in the searing portrayal of mass drug addiction in the recent hit film *Udta Punjab*.

It is in this context that the Dera Sacha Sauda and its charismatic leader emerged as saviours. For all his bling, Baba Gurmeet Ram Rahim Singh Insan exemplified an alternative life. The dera offers free education to its members and their children, free food for the hungry, and meaningful employment in its enterprises; it keeps the faithful off drugs, and more than jobs, it gives them a sense of meaning and pur-pose to their lives. In the process, it gives them that most precious and intangible of human needs—dignity and a sense of belonging.

Politicians played along with the Baba and his dera, and indeed with several other such religious movements; Dera Sacha Sauda is one of the biggest, but far from the only, of several deras dotting Punjab and Haryana. The deras, after all, helped keep social peace, tamp down discontent, and channel frustrations towards constructive activity. Rather than disapprove of them as dangerous cults, successive governments rushed to embrace them. Their religious nature offered a far safer alternative to drugs and crime. The deras ended addiction, replaced anomie with community and redirected despair to divinity, even if it came attired in flashy silver jackets and drove a Range Rover.

The intense loyalty the deras in turn inspire cannot be underestimated. Their fulfilment of people's basic needs is suffused with the religious fervour that comes along with affiliation to a spiritual guru. And most of them are led by figures less ostentatious and controversial than Gurmeet Ram Rahim Singh Insan. But social and economic insecurity is at the heart of a dera's religious appeal and its fanatic following. Where government and civil society failed, a seeming charlatan with an insatiable lust succeeded, and his success mattered far more than his flaws. People who were willing to lend their wives and daughters to their guru could not understand why the same 'blessing' extended to two girls should land him in jail. As an anonymous posting on social media pointed out, 'a lost man doesn't care if a rapist gives him direction. A hungry man will take food from a murderer's hand'.

The mass upsurge by dera followers on their guru's conviction revealed their fears that without him and his organisation, they might once again slide back into the margins. This explains the intensity of their identification with him, whatever he does. They are literally willing to kill for him or, as they might see it, for themselves. Many Indians lamented that such blind religious devotion should thrive in their country in the second decade of the twenty-first century. But the violence that followed the jailing of this particular godman raises far more troubling questions than that.

The episode shows that India's much-vaunted economic growth and development has shallow roots indeed: that it has failed to deliver caste equality and social justice to the underclasses. It shows official institutions of governance all-too-readily subcontracting their responsibilities to religious orders, and enabling their leaders to live above the law. It shows the fragility of law and order systems, which failed so spectacularly in the face of mass fury. And it shows the hold of religious leaders on the loyalties, and the passions, of vast sections of people who find validation for their lives in such unthinking followership.

HINDU FATALISM

One unavoidable issue to be dealt with relating to popular notions of Hinduism is that of 'Hindu fatalism'. Does not our belief in destiny, in karma and predestination, make us inured to our lot in life and accepting of Fate, rather than seeking to change it?

There is an old story, from our ancient *Puranas*, the kind of story Hindus have often told to illustrate larger points about themselves.

A man—the quintessential Hindu, one might say—is pursued by a tiger. He runs fast, but his panting heart tells him he cannot run much longer or faster. He spots a tree. Relief! He accelerates and gets to it in one last despairing stride. He climbs the tree. The tiger snarls beneath him, but he feels he has at least escaped its snapping jaws. But no— what's this? The branch on which he is sitting is weak, and bends dangerously. That is not all; termites are gnawing away at it. Before long, they will eat through it and the branch will snap and fall.

The man realises this, sees the tiger below him waiting for him to tumble into its grasp. But as the branch bends, it sags over a well. Aha! Escape? Our hero looks hopefully into the well. Perhaps he can swim! But the well is dry. Worse, there are poisonous snakes writhing and hissing on its bed, waiting for prey.

What is our hero to do? As the branch bends lower, he perceives a solitary blade of grass growing on the wall of the well. On the tip of the blade of grass gleams a drop of honey.

What action does our Puranic man, the archetypal Indian, take in this situation?

He bends with the branch, and licks up the honey.

This story is at least 2,000 years old, but it could be told today. It speaks of what the Orientalists saw as Hindu fatalism, a tendency for us to be resigned to our lot and to accept the world as it is ordained to be. The story speaks of our self-absorption in the face of impossible circumstances, and our willingness to make the best we possibly can out of those impossible circumstances.

That is the Hindu answer to the insuperable difficulty. One does not struggle against that which one cannot overcome, but seeks instead to find the best path, for oneself, to live with it. In many ways, it explains what the West has regarded as Hindu fatalism, and to which V. S. Naipaul referred as a tendency for 'non-doing'.

And yet this is a very partial understanding of Hinduism. The *Bhagavad Gita* asks Hindus to raise themselves by the self; that is, to use whatever elements Fate has dealt them—the circumstances of their birth, their location, their access to wealth, the opportunities for education and so on—as best they can to move towards self-realisation. The fact that circumstances are what they are does not deny the Hindu the freedom of will to seek to change them. The position of the planets at the time of a Hindu's birth may have determined some of his or her possibilities, charting good phases and bad ones in their lives, but then it is up to them to make what they can of them. It is wrong to suggest that everything is willed by Fate for the quiescent Hindu, that his destiny is decreed. The Hindu works with God to fulfil his potential. God is not just above and beyond us; to the Hindu, He is also within us. He struggles with us, suffers with us, strives with us. To that degree, the Hindu knows he shapes his own fate, in partnership with God.

Early in my United Nations career, my first boss, a lay preacher in his native Denmark, asked me a pointed question: 'Why should a Hindu be good?' Not, I replied, in order to go to heaven or avoid hell; most Hindus do not believe in the existence of either. If heaven is a place where a soul should sprout white wings and sing the praises of God, it must be rather a boring place, hardly worth aspiring to, and God must be a rather insecure Being. And as for hell, the very notion of hell is incompatible with Hindu cosmology, since it suggests there is a place where God is not, and that, to the Hindu, is impossible to conceive, for God is everywhere or He would not be God.

If Hinduism is, indeed, a *manava dharma*, an ethical code applicable to the whole of humanity, then it is legitimate for a non-Hindu to ask: why indeed should a Hindu be good? First, because he is bound by the moral obligation to fulfil his *dharma*, the right action his religion enjoins upon him always to undertake.

The Hindu is taught that there are six principal obstacles to the performance of *dharma*: two are Purusharthas gone wrong, *kama* as lust rather than desire, and *lobha* as greed and avarice for material possessions (beyond *artha* which is the legitimate acquisition of wealth and worldly goods for a worthy life). Four other vices are personal failings that are within an individual's capacity to prevent: *krodha* (hatred), *mada* (vanity), *matsarya* (envy) and *moha* (delusion arising from ignorance or infatuation). These six obstacles are prevented and overcome through the practice of seven essential virtues laid down from the time of Adi Shankara: *ahimsa* (non-violence), *satyam* (truth), *shivam* (piety), *sundaram* (the cultivation of beauty), *vairagyam* (detachment), *pavitram* (purity) and *swabhavam* (self-control). The rejection of these vices and the practice of these virtues are essential for a Hindu to lead a good life.

My boss wanted a more pragmatic reason for why a Hindu should be good. If it was not the promise of a better life in the next world, or a desire to avoid eternal damnation in Hell, what was a Hindu's incentive? I explained that whereas in Christianity the body has a soul, in Hinduism the soul has a body. In other words, we are emanations of a universal soul, the *atman*, which does not die; it discards its temporal form, the body, from time to time. Since the purpose of the soul is ultimately to reach moksha, to attain union with Brahman and stop the endless cycle of birth and rebirth in various bodies, the incentive for a Hindu to be good lay in the desire to progress towards this goal. An amoral Hindu, one who lived in *adharma*, would be in disharmony with the world and be set back in his soul's striving for *moksha*.

I am not sure he was satisfied with my answer, and I am not sure you, the reader, will be. There was, however, a catch in what I was propounding. If the soul is permanent and the body is not, it makes sense that the soul sheds bodies and keeps returning to earth until it has attained *moksha*; from this flows the doctrine of *punarjanmam* (reincarnation), the idea that one will be reborn until one has attained that level of self-realisation.

The idea of reincarnation, emerging from the endless cycle of birth and rebirth, is basic to Hinduism. If in other faiths the individual is a body which has its own soul, in Hinduism the individual is a soul which happens to be in temporary possession of a certain body; the immortal soul occupies a mortal corpus, which it discards at the end of its physical life, only to re-emerge in another form, until it accomplishes true self-realisation and *moksha*, and merges with Brahman. This cycle of birth, death and rebirth is known as Samsara, and it is a belief that addresses one of the central challenges facing every believer in God—if God is all-knowing, all-seeing, all-compassionate and merciful, why does He permit so much suffering, pain, inequality and inequity to bedevil his creations? The Hindu answer is that such suffering is the result of man's own actions in a previous life; our present circumstances are caused or enabled by our past deeds and misdeeds, action and inaction. The soul continues from life-cycle to life-cycle, hopping from body to body as a caterpillar climbs onto a blade of grass and jumps to a new one (the metaphor is Upanishadic, not my own.)

I always considered this deeply unfair: why should a human being, conscious only of himself in his present life, have to suffer for wrongs he does not recollect and misdeeds he has no memory of having committed in previous lives of which he is unaware? Still, I had to accept it was a more coherent explanation than the contradictory ones offered by other faiths, which struggled to reconcile the world's injustices with their theological belief in a merciful God. If you thought of God as, for instance, an old man in a white beard looking down benevolently at you from the heavens, listening to your prayers and interceding when He saw fit, then it was difficult to accept that His benevolence stopped short of your well-being despite your prayers, or that He was indifferent to the cruelty and suffering assailing His creatures. If you stopped thinking of God that way, however, but saw God in everyone and everything, in the bad and the good, in the unfair as well as the just, as an impersonal cosmic force that just *is*—then you can come to terms with the world's tragedies as well as its joys. The idea of reincarnation is related to that of *karma*, or action—the accumulated actions of your life. So the very circumstances of your birth—the home, the place, the nation and the opportunities into which you are born—are determined by your soul's actions in its previous incarnation.

The time and circumstances of your death, too, are beyond human agency; when you have finished enjoying the benefits earned from (and paying for the misdeeds committed in) your previous life, your time on earth ends and your soul discards your body, to enter another. This is known as *prarabdha karma*. Then there are your characteristics, tendencies and aptitudes, themselves emerging from the accumulated learnings of your previous lives; this is called *sanchita karma* and can be changed by your efforts, education and conduct in your present life. Finally there is *agami karma*, those of our actions which will pave the way for our future (reborn) life. Our evil words or deeds in the present life will mar our soul's prospects in the next, whereas good deeds, right actions and the fulfillment of our *dharma* without regard to reward, will ensure our rebirth at a higher stage of the progress towards *moksha*.

To some this suggests another, somewhat simplistic, answer to the question 'Why should a Hindu be good?' Be good so that you are reborn in a better situation in your next life than in the present one; if you are good, you may reappear as a king or a sage, whereas if you are bad, you might come back as an invalid or a mosquito. (Or as Amartya Sen, the Nobel laureate, put it: 'As a Hindu, if you are a good economist in this life, you come back in the next as a physicist. If you are a bad economist in this life, you come back in the next as a sociologist.') Jokes apart, your *prarabdha karma* is established by what your soul has experienced in its previous foray in a human body: your incentive to be good is to improve its chances of a better time in its next innings.

I was never comfortable with this idea, since it seemed to me to have been devised somewhat self-servingly by the upper castes to ensure social peace. Do not rebel if you are born poor or 'Untouchable', the doctrine seemed to imply, since it's merely your soul paying for the sins of your past life; and do not blame us for leading a much better life than you, since we are merely reaping the benefits of our past good deeds.

Behave, conform, accept your lot and serve your betters, the doctrine seemed to suggest, and you will enjoy the rewards next time around. As a philosophy to reconcile people with their lot, and that would help maintain social peace, such a belief-system was of inestimable value. (It also justified human suffering in terms that no other religion's theology could match.) But I found it ethically dubious—and so, no doubt unfairly, looked askance at the idea of reincarnation itself. I was wrong to do so, since the socio-political rationale was irrelevant to the Hindu sages who had advanced the theory of *punarjanmam*. They were less concerned about issues of socio-political conformism than I was; the *rishis'* interest lay in the soul's unsteady and imperfect progress towards self-realisation and merger with the cosmos. Their doctrine was about the divine soul, not the social circumstances of the body it happened to occupy.

4

GREAT SOULS OF HINDUISM

Much of what I believe as a Hindu comes from an early and intense reading of the writings and lectures of Swami Vivekananda (1863–1902), the magnetic-eyed saint with the majestic mien and marvellous oratorical skills, who did more than anyone else to place Hinduism on the world map in the late nineteenth century. Swami Vivekananda was an inspiration to me right from my formative years. One of the few accomplishments I remember from a hyperactive extra-curricular life at college relates to him. I was asked to deliver, at age eighteen in 1974, the annual Vivekananda Memorial Oration at Delhi University. The honour was given to me because of my fondness for his ideas and a willingness to recite them with something approaching the oratorical flourish for which he was famous; any fantasy of association with him, alas, ends there.

To understand Vivekananda's Hinduism one has to go much farther back in time. His ideas emerged from the Advaita Vedanta School of Hindu philosophy, anchored in the oldest *Upanishads* and established by Adi Shankara in the eighth century CE, which as we have seen is undoubtedly the most influential of the multiple schools of philosophy and theology that characterise Hinduism.

HINDUISM: THE EARLY DAYS

It is said that the roots of Hinduism can be traced to the Indus Valley civilisation that flourished around 3300 to 1500 BCE (although some sources claim that it is even older). Since the script of that civilisation has not yet been satisfactorily deciphered, it is difficult to aver this with any certainty, but the ruins of the Harappan cities reveal evidence that suggest a priestly hierarchy and a cult of worship, and Indus Valley seals show a cross-legged figure who seems to represent Shiva. At any rate, the worship of male and female gods clearly existed, as perhaps did a fertility cult, along with the worship of nature, animals and spirits. The doctrines of what we recognise today as Hindu *dharma* were first established (it is said, by the sage Yajnavalkya) in around 3000 BCE (many scholars dispute the historicity of this date, suggesting instead dates a millennia and a half later, 1500 BCE). They were reified in the four Vedas, composed roughly between 1700 and 500 BCE, laying down many of the mantras and benedictions, rituals and ceremonies of the faith, together with commentaries on these. The faith was then replenished by Veda Vyasa (the sage who is said to have codified the Vedas and is credited as the 'author' of the *Mahabharata*).

But despite the richness of the epics such as the *Mahabharata* and *Ramayana*, the religion of the later Vedas became excessively ritualistic and rigidly hierarchical. Other ideas and practices needed to be accommodated. Around 150 BCE, some centuries after Vyasa, Patanjali, a notable scholar of the Sankhya School of Hindu philosophy, compiled the *Yoga Sutras*, a classic text on yoga theory and practice, which laid the foundations of classical yoga. Patanjali's sutras lay down an eightfold path, *ashtanga* yoga, which involves a rigorous set of physical, psychological and moral pursuits, following the strictest discipline, which, if progressively followed under the guidance of a suitable teacher, would lead the practitioner to ultimate self-realisation and pure consciousness. Then the *Upanishads* emerged, throwing the light of sophisticated (and sometimes abstruse) philosophical enquiry on the faith. Building on the sacred Vedas, these were all foundational texts of Hinduism. The *Puranas* were composed, and their stories helped integrate the Vedic religion with the folk religions of India, absorbing them in a shared ethic.

Subsequently, Hinduism became paralysed by its own inflexible practices of orthodoxy, ritualism and formality, and the rise of mutually antagonistic sects locked in interminable conflict. Inevitably, reformers arose to challenge it, notably the ascetic Mahavira Jaina (c. 599 BCE–527 BCE) and the other-worldly Gautama Buddha (c. 563 BCE–483 BCE), whose followers branched out into new religions distinct from the Mimamsa Brahminism practised by mainstream Hindus. Both new faiths flourished for several centuries, as Hinduism descended into esoteric disputes over Sankhya dualism and Charvaka materialism. It was then, in the late eighth century CE, that a youthful South Indian sage rose to heal and rejuvenate a divided religion.

ADI SHANKARA

This was Adi Shankara, whose Advaita Vedanta was the philosophically robust response to that era of confusion, integrating diverse thoughts and Hindu practices into a philosophy based on the Vedic dictum of 'One Truth, Many Expositions'. Advaita Vedanta is only one—and arguably the last—of the six schools known as the 'six systems' (Shad Darshanas) of mainstream Hindu philosophy, but it has proved the most enduring. Shankara emphasised the importance of *pramanas* or methods of reasoning, tempered by *anubhava* or intuitive experience, which empower the seeker to gain the spiritual knowledge adumbrated by the sacred texts. He focused on selected texts—the Bhagavad Gita, the Brahma Sutras and ten of the 108 *Upanishads*—as the key reference works of Hindu *dharma*, illuminating them through his *bhashyas* (commentaries). Reasoning is essential to clarify the truth, according to the Advaita School, and Shankara was a famous debater of his time, challenging and being challenged by those of different philosophical persuasions but triumphing always through the power of his reasoning and the force of his arguments. His *bhashya*s are all written in prose, not verse, with lucidity and sharpness, and employ the Upanishadic question-and-answer format that the West calls 'Socratic'.

Adi Shankara also authored the *Vivekachudamani*, 581 verses spelling out the qualifications required in a student of Vedanta: to be able to discriminate between the real and the unreal; to be able to maintain a spirit of detachment from this world; to have the capacity to control sensory perceptions; and to feel an intense desire to attain self-realisation and *moksha*. The *Vivekachudamani* reviews the entire range of Hindu philosophical thought and argument, from the *Upanishads* to the Bhagavad Gita. More accessibly, and as part of his effort to popularise the faith, Adi Shankara also authored a hundred *stotrams*, verses that can be sung as *bhajans* by the worshipper (or *bhakt*)—many fairly brief but some quite long, like his most famous *bhajan*, the Bhaja Govindam. Most of the *stotrams* (hymns or verses) relate to the worship of the major Puranic gods, though some are devoted to spiritual themes and others are sung in praise of sacred rivers or the holy city of Kashi (Varanasi). To Adi Shankara, *bhakti yoga* (the practice of worship) was an important step towards *jnana yoga* (the cultivation of knowledge). The sage was very conscious of the need to revive the faith of which he was such a master. In Verse 7 of his Bhaja Govindam, he laments the fact that children are interested in play and young men in pretty girls, but the old worry since no one is interested in the Absolute.

Adi Shankara was not merely a philosophical thinker who reconciled the doctrines and traditions of the ancients with a robust interpretation for the future; he was also a practical reformer. He purified the worship of the Goddess, which had become somewhat questionable thanks to dubious practices introduced by the tantrics, and introduced the *samayachara* form of Devi worship, involving hymns of exquisite beauty like the Soundarya Lahari or the waves of beauty, composed by himself. His ready acceptance of many Buddhist principles and practices so narrowed the gap between the two faiths as to make the absorption of Buddhism by the parent faith inevitable in India.

Adi Shankara's extraordinary travels—which began when he was just eight years old and continued till his death at the age of thirty-two—took him to every corner of the Indian subcontinent, from Rameswaram in the extreme south to Srinagar in the Kashmir Valley in the extreme north, from Dwarka in Gujarat to Kamarupa in Assam in the north-east, and various points in between. He established temples almost everywhere he halted, all of which have remained in continuous use since, and left behind five major *mutths* headed by successor Shankaracharyas to this day: Jyotirmath near Badrinath (Uttarakhand), Govardhan Mutth in Puri (Odisha), Kalika Mutth in Dwarka (Gujarat), and two in the south, the Sarada Peetham in Sringeri (Karnataka) and the Kanchi Kamakoti Peetham in Kanchipuram (Tamil Nadu). (Most Hindus count only the first four as his major legacies, though the prominence in the twentieth century of the Shankaracharyas of Kanchi has elevated that *peetham* into a religious seat of equal if not greater significance.) In addition to these 'pontifical' seats, Adi Shankara is credited with the creation and organisation of the order of Dasanami Sannyasis, wandering monks who took the message of the faith across the country. Despite Shankara's skill in debate, Advaita nonetheless believes that pure logic cannot alone lead to philosophical truths; knowledge is all very well, but experience and meditative insights are essential too. Shankara's Advaita Vedanta was based on *shastra* ('scriptures'), *pramanas* or *yukti* ('reason') and *anubhava* ('experiential knowledge'), supplemented by *karmas* ('spiritual practices') and the purity and steadiness of mind achieved in yoga. None was sufficient in itself: the entire package, as it were, allowed the seeker to gain the knowledge and insights required to attain self-realisation.

Shankara also proposed the four '*mahavakyas*' or 'great sentences' of his doctrine—'Prajnanam Brahma' (knowledge is Brahman), 'Ayam Atma Brahma' (this atman is Brahman), 'Tat tvam asi' (that you are), and 'Aham Brahmasmi' (I am Brahman)—as the guiding principles of Hindu spiritual contemplation, all of which underscored his doctrine that the inner immortal soul, atman, and the great cosmic spirit, Brahman, are really one and the same. Atman and Brahman had been regarded by the 'dualist' Sankhya School of thought as separate entities, but Shankara argued that while they might seem different at the empirical level of reality, this is an illusion. Brahman, the spirit that suffuses the cosmos, is the sole reality; other than Brahman, everything else, including the universe, material objects and individuals, is ever changing, transient and illusory (*maya*). (As Radhakrishnan was later to

91

explain, *maya* is not merely illusion, but 'a subjective misperception of the world as ultimately real.') Brahman is Paramarthika Satyam, Absolute Truth, and one's *atman* or self is identical to it. Realising this and accepting the true self, pure consciousness, as the only reality (*sat*), leads to *moksha* or salvation, defined by some as a state of bliss (*ananda*) and by others, more modestly, as the endless but not beginningless absence of pain, the pain all human beings suffer in the course of their ordinary lives. The supreme truth of Brahman is *sat-chit-ananda* (truth-consciousness-bliss), as Shankara wrote in his *Upadeshasahasri*:

> *I am other than name, form and action.*
> *My nature is ever free!*
> *I am Self, the supreme unconditioned Brahman.*
> *I am pure Awareness, always non-dual.*

— Adi Shankara, *Upadeshasahasri* 11.7[1]

As I have noted earlier, the *Manduka Upanishad* explains that Om is the bow, one's *atman* is the arrow, and Brahman the target. The term Advaita ('not-two') refers to the rejection of dualism: as Shankara's follower, the sage Anandagiri, put it, to say that Brahman and *atman* are separate would be like dividing a fowl in two and saying that one half can be cooked while the other half would lay eggs.

Shankara's Hinduism does not see God as external to the universe. God dwells in the universe, but God is not the universe; He is in it and beyond it. The world is in God, and the two are indivisible. Advaita Vedanta emphasises *jivanmukti*, the idea that *moksha* (salvation or liberation, the realisation of the ultimate purpose of each individual) is achievable in the course of our present life. Advaita's adherents seek their spiritual fulfilment in the acquisition of this profound spiritual knowledge and in immersing themselves in the indissoluble union of the true Self (*atman* or soul) with the highest metaphysical Reality (Brahman).

Shankara also asserted that the realisation of self-knowledge required the mind to be purified by an ethical life that observed essential precepts or Yamas such as *ahimsa* (non-injury, non-violence to others in body, mind and thoughts), *satya* (respect for truth, abstinence from falsehood), *asteya* (rejection of theft), *aparigraha* (abstaining from craving possessions) and a simple life of meditation and reflection. These ideas were to have a profound and lasting impact on Mahtama Gandhi twelve centuries later. (Of *ahimsa*, Gandhi wrote: 'Nonviolence is common to all religions, but it has found the highest expression and application in Hinduism.')

From the ancient texts, Advaita Vedanta accepted the idea of the Purusharthas, the four goals of human life. These, as we have seen earlier, are *dharma*, the right conduct of the individual in accordance with his duties and obligations; *artha*, the material possessions required to sustain the individual and those dependent upon him; *kama*, the pursuit of pleasure and comfort, including love and sexual pleasure; and *moksha*, the individual's ultimate salvation, his liberation from earthly bonds and his realisation of union with the divine spirit. This last involves a state of full awareness of the ultimate oneness of the soul, atman, and Brahman; the Hindu realises the Divine within himself, perceives the Divine in other beings, and accepts that Brahman is in everything, and everything is Brahman.

> *Without beginning and end is he; in the midst*
> *Of chaos is he, and brings forth all things. Creator*
> *Is he, and sole pervader, of manifold forms.*
> *When a man knows God he is freed from all fetters.*

— *Svetashvatara Upanishad*, V.13.2[2]

Despite such ideas being seen by many as Brahminical and elitist, Advaita Vedanta, by conceiving of Oneness in this manner, lays the philosophical groundwork for the fundamental equality of all human beings. In the same section of his *Upadeshasahasri*, Adi Shankara posits precisely this ethical premise of equality; any *bheda* (discrimination) based on class or caste or parentage is, Shankara declared, a mistake, a sign of error and of lack of knowledge. Shankara's liberated individual understands and practises the ethics of non-discrimination, since the high-born and the low are all part of the same Oneness. This was all the more significant in a religion on which the pernicious practice of caste discrimination had begun to cast a blight. The Advaita Vedantist recognised all living beings as essentially one, and therefore as essentially equal.

WHY I AM A HINDU

The fully realised self is *sat-chit-ananda* incarnate, as Shankara himself sings:

'Atma Shatakam' (The Song of the Self):

> I am not the mind, nor the intellect, nor the ego, nor the material
>   of the mind;
> I am not the body, nor the changes of the body;
> I am not the senses of hearing, taste, smell, or sight,
> Nor am I the ether, the earth, the fire, the air;
> I am Existence Absolute, Knowledge Absolute, Bliss
> Absolute—I am Shiva, I am Shiva. (Shivoham, Shivoham).
>
> I am not the Prâna, nor the five vital airs;
> I am not the materials of the body, nor the five sheaths;
> Neither am I the organs of action, nor the object of the senses;
> I am Existence Absolute, Knowledge Absolute, Bliss Absolute—
> I am Shiva, I am Shiva. (Shivoham, Shivoham).
>
> I have neither aversion nor attachment, neither greed nor delusion;
> Neither egotism nor envy, neither Dharma nor Moksha;
> I am neither desire nor objects of desire;
> I am Existence Absolute, Knowledge Absolute, Bliss
> Absolute—I am Shiva, I am Shiva. (Shivoham, Shivoham).
>
> I am neither sin nor virtue, neither pleasure nor pain; Nor
> temple nor worship, nor pilgrimage nor scriptures, Neither
> the act of enjoying, the enjoyable nor the enjoyer;
> I am Existence Absolute, Knowledge Absolute, Bliss
> Absolute—I am Shiva, I am Shiva. (Shivoham, Shivoham).
>
> I have neither death nor fear of death, nor caste;
> Nor was I ever born, nor had I parents, friends, and relations;
> I have neither Guru, nor disciple;
> I am Existence Absolute, Knowledge Absolute, Bliss
> Absolute—I am Shiva, I am Shiva. (Shivoham, Shivoham).
>
> I am untouched by the senses, I am neither Mukti nor knowable;
> I am without form, without limit, beyond space, beyond time;
> I am in everything; I am the basis of the universe; everywhere am I.

> I am Existence Absolute, Knowledge Absolute, Bliss
> Absolute—I am Shiva, I am Shiva. (Shivoham, Shivoham).

— Adi Shankara, Nirvana Shatakam[3]

All of this may seem somewhat abstruse to some, a sort of Hindu theological primer of no interest to most Hindus, let alone others. In fact there is far greater complexity to Advaita Vedanta than my simple summary can even begin to hint at. The *Kena Upanishad* makes that clear:

> I do not think that I know it well. Nor do I know that I do not know it.
> Among us those who know, know it; even they do not know that they do not
> know.

— Kena Upanishad, II.2[4]

However, there was the dawning realisation, among many of those who followed in his footsteps in the centuries following Adi Shankara's death in the mountain temple of Kedarnath at the young age of thirty-two, that there was a great need to make his breakthroughs intelligible to the common man. There were other even more compelling reasons for the faith to change and evolve.

REINVENTING HINDUISM

Though they were eclipsed and even reabsorbed into Hinduism, both Jainism and Buddhism had a lasting impact on the religion they had sought to transform. Buddhist monasticism led to the establishment of the concept of *sannyasis* (monks or ascetics) in Hinduism—who, inspired by the Buddhists, wear ochre robes, shave their heads and practise celibacy for life. (There was no pre-Buddhist equivalent of this: Hindu priests were *grihasthas*, married householders, and not *sannyasis*). Similarly the Buddhist monasteries prompted Sankaracharya to establish *mutths*, in which *sannyasis* and lay students could live together and learn in a sort of *gurukul* (or traditional school). As to Jainism, the acceptance of *ahimsa* as a basic principle in Hinduism was clearly a response to Mahavira Jaina's emphasis on this doctrine. The adoption of vegetarianism as a superior form of life by a large number of Hindus, especially Brahmins, is also a Jain contribution to Hinduism.

Hinduism reasserted itself in response to the rise of Buddhism and Jainism, largely supplanting or absorbing these faiths across the country, to the extent that the practice of Buddhism largely ended (so much so that that until the 1950s, the Buddha in Sarnath sported a Vaishnava namam, or holy mark on his forehead), and the Jains began to be regarded by a section of Hindus as a sort of Hindu sect (though many Jains disputed this) rather than as a rival faith. By the tenth century, Hinduism had reasserted its dominance, swallowed up its reformers, reformulated its popular doctrines, equipped itself with a higher philosophy which found acceptance among the intellectuals, accommodated popular forms of idol worship, created major spiritual centres and furnished itself with *sannyasis* to spread the word. Its supremacy in India seemed incontestable.

But around 1000 CE a new challenge arose from the northwest to the dominance of Hinduism in the subcontinent. The raids into India by Mohammed bin Qasim, who invaded Sind in 712 CE, Mahmud of Ghazni (who attacked India seventeen times between 1000 CE and 1027 CE) and Muhammad Ghori (who launched several bloody raids between the 1180s and the 1220s), among others, took many lives, destroyed much property and left deep scars. Hinduism found itself confronting a dynamic force animated by religious zeal in direct contradistinction to everything the faith stood for. Islam challenged the philosophic basis of Hinduism, questioned its social structure, denied its pantheistic beliefs, expressed contempt for its pluralist doctrines and coveted its treasures. It was a challenge of a very different order from that posed by Buddhism or Jainism. The impact of the Muslim invasions, and the proclivity of some Muslim warlords to attack temples for their treasures and demolish them in the process, as well as the inclination of some of the conquered peoples to adopt the religion of their conquerors, made the need for a renewal and revival of the Hindu faith all the more urgent after the eleventh century CE, when Ghazni's success had rung the alarm bells.

The looting of temples and their subsequent destruction—which occurred repeatedly, ranging from historic Somnath on the Gujarat coast to Mathura in the interior—was a direct assault on the Hindus and their faith, and an undeniable challenge to which Hinduism had to rise or succumb. For invaders like Mahmud of Ghazni the attacks had twin motives—the fabled wealth of India was mostly hoarded in its temples, which made them attractive targets, but there was also the zeal of the Muslim warrior to smash the seats of idolatry. The Hindus were left with a stark choice—revive or disappear.

Renewal was the Hindu response. This renewal occurred through a number of processes—the simplification and propagation of Brahminical doctrines; the adoption of some practices and beliefs from Buddhism and Jainism; the accommodation of popular folklore, local deities and regional forms of worship into the master faith; the greater emphasis on the worship of gods in easily accessible human form; the use of music, dance and theatre to propagate religious stories; the universal practice of daily worship at home, so that the temple was not the only locus of sustenance for the faith; and eventually, as I describe below, the rise of *bhakti* worship, in which an almost mystical devotion to a personal god became a hallmark of Hindu religiosity. In addition, there was Hinduism's very lack of a central organisational structure: the knowledge of the Vedas was preserved and perpetuated by being passed on from generation to generation within Brahmin families, or by individual sages or gurus to their disciples. Such a diffused pattern of dissemination was much more difficult to eliminate, or to subsume into a new faith. Another vital factor was the early truce between the spiritual and temporal powers in society: in response to the rise of Buddhism and Jainism, Brahmins (the priestly caste) and Kshatriyas (the warrior and ruling class) came to a mutual understanding that their interests would be best served in alliance, rather than in undermining each other.

All of these ensured that not only did India not turn into a fully Muslim country, as so many other Asian countries—from the Maldives to Malaya and Indonesia—were to do, but that Hinduism survived and thrived even in conditions of political dominance by rulers of another faith.

Indeed, the resilience of Hinduism throughout history is little short of remarkable. It has survived innumerable invasions, raids, attacks and outright conquest; each time, where lesser faiths in other places crumbled before the invader and most of the people adopted the conqueror's faith, Hinduism stood strong and bounced back. In the mid-nineteenth century, Karl Marx marvelled at this phenomenon and found it remarkable. Hinduism remained a non-aggressive faith, but it was extraordinarily strong in its own defence. Hinduism took the blows and battled on; and every time the invader withdrew, Hinduism arose again, sometimes bloodied but always unbowed.

RAMANUJA AND THE BHAKTI MOVEMENT

Key to this resilience was doctrinal openness and flexibility of practice. A thousand years ago in southern India, Ramanuja (said to have lived 1017–1137 CE to the age of 120), a great Vaishnava theologian, who headed the monastery at Srirangam, reinvented and revitalised Hinduism, following in Shankara's footsteps with a qualified form of Advaita. His doctrinal contribution was important: his commentaries on the Gita and on the Brahma Sutras contested Adi Shankara's interpretations of those scriptures. More important were the religious aspects of Ramanuja's teachings, to the effect that the burdens of *karma* can be overcome by Divine Grace, attained through the worship of a loving and just God—an alternative view to the recondite philosophical constructs of Shankara, and thus a vital contribution to Indian spiritual revival. Through this approach Ramanuja popularised worship and brought organisational energy into the faith, conducting daily *puja*s and annual temple festivals, allowing image-worship and more inclusive temple-based rituals at the Srirangam Mutth he headed and in other nearby temples. Strikingly, he permitted women and worshippers of the lower peasant castes (though not, it should be said, Dalits) to participate in temple worship, a privilege they had been denied. Ramanuja also allowed the chanting of the popular Alvar (or Azhvar) hymns, which were sung in demotic Tamil, the language of the people, rather than in the arcane Sanskrit of official temple liturgy. Ramanuja's reforms spread across southern India to other major Vaishnavite temples and can be seen in many ways as a reinvention of Hinduism, taking Shankara's work to the masses.

Ramanuja's innovations prefigured the popularisation of Hinduism in the Bhakti movement, which through prayer and song brought the esoterica of Hindu philosophy in simple language to the ears and the hearts of the common people. In some ways he could be said to be a pioneer of it. The Bhakti movement began in south India and swept northwards, creating a devotional theistic popular Hinduism that expressed itself vividly in the cult worship of different gods and goddesses and flourished across much of India between the twelfth and the eighteenth century CE. The movement started in Tamil Nadu between the fourth and the ninth centuries with the Nayanars and the Alvars, several of whom, notably the poetess Andal, were women. They sang in praise of Shiva and Vishnu respectively in Tamil, and as the Bhakti movement spread, brought more vernacular languages into a faith previously dominated by Sanskrit.

Ramananda, a Vaishnava *sanyasi* from Allahabad, travelled through much of the Indo-Gangetic plain, the land of Aryavarta, in the fourteenth century, preaching the doctrine of Bhakti, urging people to place their trust in, and surrender themselves to, a merciful God. The mysticism of his gospel, its offer of a refuge from the misery of human suffering, its assertion of equality of all before God and its depiction of God as a loving force in the lives of worshippers, gave Ramananda's teachings great appeal. He settled in Varanasi, where among the many disciples he acquired was the remarkable Muslim weaver Kabir, one of a dozen poet-sants (saints), both male and female, who took Ramananda's teachings to the masses.

Bhakti had its stars—poet-saints like Kabir (c. 1440–1510 CE), who wrote some extraordinarily compelling verses distilling the essence of Hindu philosophy, and who was singing in praise of religious harmony at a time when the West was conducting Inquisitions and burning witches and heretics at the stake; Lalleshwari or Lalla Rukh (c. 1317–1372 CE), the great Bhakti songstress of Kashmir, who sang passionately of her devotion to Shiva but as emotionally of her refusal to discriminate between Hindu and Muslim; mystic singers like Mirabai (c. 1498–1597 CE), whose songs transported the singer and her audience into a level of ecstasy reminiscent of some of today's Evangelical

churches; the twelfth-century poet Jayadev, whose *Gita Govindam* revolutionised the worship of Radha and Krishna, and whose ideas were
echoed in the lyrics of the blind bard Surdas (c. 1478–1583 CE), the
man who helped establish the Vrindavan-Mathura area as Krishna's holy
land; and the remarkable writer, poet and saint Tulsidas (c. 1532–1623
CE), author of two of the most popular Hindu texts even today, the
Ramcharitmanas, retelling the story of Lord Rama, and the Hanuman
Chalisa, forty-three devotional verses in praise of the powerful monkey-god. Tulsidas wrote in Avadhi (though initially in Sanskrit); Kabir's
verse can still be understood by Hindi speakers today. Verse and song
became vehicles for Bhakti ideas throughout India.

Mirabai's husband, the Rana of Udaipur, allegedly disapproved so
much of her devotion to Lord Krishna that he tried to poison her, but
miraculously the poison turned into honey as she drank it, and she
danced in ecstasy before her adored Lord. As one of her hymns declares
with the sense of abandonment and ecstatic devotion for which she
is known:

> *Tying anklets upon her feet, Mira dances in ecstasy.*
> *People say Mira has gone mad.*
> *Her mother-in-law says she has disgraced the clan,*
> *The Rana sent her a cup of poison,*
> *Which Mira, laughingly, drank.*
> *I have myself become the eternal maid-servant of*
> *My Narayana.*
> *Mira's God is Giridhar, lifter of the mountain.*
> *O Indestructible One, meet me swiftly in your*
> *Eternal embrace.*[5]

Bhakti's creative effulgence was remarkable, and reached its peak,
perhaps surprisingly, during the rule of the Muslim Mughal monarchs
(1526 to the mid eighteenth century); the movement confirmed
Hinduism's resilience in the face of Islamic conquest. But it was also
much more than that: the Bhakti movement refreshed and strengthened Hindu society at a time when the state was in Muslim hands. It
taught a staunch monotheism, shunned caste distinctions and rules,

preached an absolute surrender to God and offered a religious experience that involved the direct realisation of God through devotion. To that extent, the Bhakti movement's reinterpretation of Hinduism resembled Islam's monotheism and egalitarianism; but its principles could also be found in the *Upanishads*, its personal gods in the *Puranas*, and its religious doctrine was anchored in that of the Bhagavad Gita, which summons the worshipper to surrender all and take refuge in *dharma*. The emotional connection of the worshipper to God that Bhakti expressed brought the devotee to a relationship of profound love for the divine, a love that, as the Gita expressed it, combined that of a father and a son, a devoted friend for another and a lover with their beloved.

The remarkable reach of Bhakti ideas ranged from the great poets, philosophers and preachers Narsi Mehta in Gujarat to Vidyapati in Mithila and Chaitanya Deva in Bengal (who founded the Vaishnava movement in Bengal through his kirtanas, devotional songs to Krishna), Jnaneswara, Tukaram, Eknath and Namdev in Maharashtra, Basavanna in Karnataka and Thyagaraja in Tamil Nadu. The Krishna devotee Shankara Deva, after travelling extensively across India, returned to his native Assam and led a major revival of Hinduism in the north-east of the subcontinent.

In Kashmir in the late tenth century, Acharya Abhinavagupta propounded the doctrines of Kashmiri Shaivism which have profoundly influenced the practice of the faith in that state. Some of the great *acharya*s from the south, like Ramanuja, in effect established their own sects, restoring strength to the religion while transforming its practice in their areas. Basavanna, also known as Basava or Basaveshwara (c. 1131–1167 CE), with his staunch rejection of the caste system, his emphasis on vegetarianism and his abjuring of temple worship, created a sect, the Lingayats or Veerashaivas, who are hugely influential in modern Karnataka. His challenge to caste was uncompromising. 'Loaded with the burden of the Vedas,' he said dismissively, 'the Brahmin is a veritable donkey.'[6] Though born a Brahmin himself, Basava shed his sacred thread at the age of eighteen and dismissed ideas of caste hierarchy: 'The higher type of man is the man who knows himself.' After all, as he pointed out: 'On the same earth stands the outcaste's hovel and the deity's temple. Whether for ritual or rinsing, is not the water the same?'[7] Members of all castes were the same; the Brahmin and the outcaste were born the same way. Or 'is there anybody in the world,' he asked, 'delivered through the ear?'[8]

Basava established a Hall of Experience (Anubhava Mantapa) where men and women from all castes could meet freely and discuss radical ideas. He shook off the established strictures against inter-dining and inter-marriage with 'Untouchables', provoking the social and political repression that extinguished his career; but his ideas, compiled in the form of *vachanas*, survived and have gained in strength to the present day. While the Jain influence is apparent in his establishment of monastery-like *mutths*, Basava's religious belief was in Vishishta Advaita, in which Shiva is equated with Brahman and the worship of Shiva leads to the Absolute. Another reformer, Madhvacharya (c. 1199–1294 CE), revived ideas of dualism and worship of the *saguna* Brahman in the form of Lord Krishna. His commentaries on the sacred texts, together with those of Sayana on the Vedas, are amongst the most significant contributions to Hindu philosophy after Adi Shankara's. Madhvacharya upheld dualism; in his theology the *atman* did not merge with Brahman but dwelt in close proximity to it. He also came closest to a theory of hell in Hinduism, suggesting that some souls were so weighed down by their bad deeds that they were unable to progress to salvation and had to suffer eternal damnation.

It is striking, too, that one offshoot of Bhakti contributed to the emergence of a wholly new religion, namely Sikhism. Its founder, Guru Nanak (1469–1539 CE), was also a poet and singer in the Bhakti tradition; the holy book of the Sikhs, the Guru Granth Sahib, includes large numbers of verses by Bhakti poets, most of all by Kabir. In its monotheism, and its emphasis on brotherhood and social equality, Sikhism derived much from Islam too, but its persecution by the later Mughals, notably Aurangzeb, turned Sikhism into a warrior faith, fighting to protect itself and the larger Hindu community. For many years in Sikhism's heartland, Punjab, Hindu families brought up one son as a Sikh, to fight for the faith.

Had Hinduism not acquired the demotic appeal to the masses that Bhakti provided it, many more might have converted to the religion of the rulers. But by offering an individual-centred path to the Divine, and by making spirituality accessible irrespective of one's caste, gender or circumstances of birth, Bhakti revived and rejuvenated the ancient Vedic traditions. Bhakti took Hinduism far away from the formalism of Vedic rituals, the austerity of asceticism, the abstractions of sages; it transformed the quest for *moksha* to a loving relationship between each individual and his or her personally chosen manifestation of God. Salvation became accessible to the lowest castes, to women and even to those formerly outside the Hindu fold, 'Untouchable' Dalits and Muslims. Bhakti brought vigour to the practice of faith by its conduct of shared religious services, collective *bhajan*-singing, community chanting of the names of the deity being adored, open (indeed some-times extravagant) emotionalism in expressing love for the Divine, and the holding of festivals and pilgrimages. Much of what we regard as popular Hinduism today can trace its roots to the Bhakti movement.

Even something as basic as temple architecture served to reinforce faith in religion. Familiar legends from Hindu mythology are engraved or painted on the walls and pillars of most temples in the form of sculptures. Any available surface is used: the *shikhara*s and *gopuram*s, the outer walls of the sanctum sanctorum, and where possible on interior surfaces as well. As a result a Hindu temple becomes a permanent advertisement for its faith. Devotees who visit the temple recall and appreciate the visual representation of these tales and legends; this adds to their religious experience and reinforces their conviction.

It is clear from the foregoing that Hinduism has hardly been an unchanging religion. It faced major reform movements and embraced them whole—notably Buddhism, of which Swami Vivekananada said: 'Shakya Muni [the Buddha] came not to destroy, but he was the fulfil-ment, the logical conclusion, the logical development of the religion of the Hindus...the Buddhist cannot stand without the brain and philoso-phy of the Hindu, nor the Hindu without the heart of the Buddhist.' The *Matsya Purana* hailed the Buddha as an *avatara* of Vishnu, as did other texts and temple inscriptions. In Vivekananda's telling, both

Buddhism and Sikhism were variants of Hinduism that served to cleanse, purify and ultimately strengthen the mother faith.

The historical evolution of Hinduism testifies to its adaptability. The Vedas gave birth to an excessively ritualistic and formalistic religion; the *Upanishads* then lightened the practice of Hinduism through a spiritual movement based on philosophical enquiry. When the Upanishadic religion itself became mired in disputes over dogma, Buddhism preached a message of simplicity and morality that contrasted with a Hinduism mired in ritual and abstruse disputation. And then Adi Shankara travelled the length and breadth of the country, leading a moral and religious reawakening. Shankara and Ramanuja restored Hinduism to pre-eminence and popularity as the principal religion of India. Sages like Madhvacharya, Chaitanya, Ramananda and Basava (whose followers, the Lingayats, now want to be classified as a separate religion altogether, like the Sikhs); Kabir, Mirabai, Tulsidas, even Guru Nanak, who founded Sikhism, but whom many Hindus, notably Swami Vivekananda himself, see as a Hindu reformer—the names of those who rose to reform, revive and rejuvenate the beliefs of the people in this ancient land are legion. As early as the Gupta period, when Hindu religious revival first occurred in response to the rise of Buddhism, Hinduism came up with creative evidence of its adaptability through its emphasis on the doctrine of *avatara*s. The doctrine is clearly stated in the Bhagavad Gita: 'When religion declines and evil-doers are to be destroyed, I shall be born at different periods,' says Krishna. Some *avatara*s were worshipped as such even in the time of Panini, but it is with Krishna that we first have the idea of an *avatara* of God and not merely a deified human being, a doctrine that was handily adapted to the Buddha himself. Hinduism has never been uniform or unchanging, immovable or unalterable. It is a religion that has abjured the immutable revelation for the growth of human consciousness.

As we have seen, Islam was initially a threat, and the attacks of Muslim invaders on temples and Hindu treasures, as well as the rape and abduction of Hindu women, in a number of episodes in the five centuries from 1000 CE onwards, led to a defensive closing of the ranks and the adoption of protective practices that entrenched restrictions and prohibitions previously unknown in Hindu society. The protection of life, religion and chastity introduced rigidities into Hindu practice: restrictions on entry into temples (to safeguard their treasures from prying eyes), child marriages (to win protection for girls before they were old enough to be abducted by lustful invaders) and even the practice of *sati* (the burning of a widow on her husband's funeral pyre) were all portrayed as measures of self-defence during this turbulent period of Indian history, that devolved into pernicious social practices wrongly seen as intrinsic to Hinduism rather than as a reactions to assaults upon it.

But once Muslims went beyond invading and stayed on to rule, won adherents and made their peace with the country, Islamic precepts also played a part in the reshaping of Hinduism:[9] the Bhakti cults and the rise of Sikhism, both strongly influenced by Islamic ideas of equality and brotherhood, testify to that. Although conversion was not uncommon, forced or voluntary, whether of individuals who found it expedient to adopt the religion of the conquerors, or of entire communities (artisan sub-castes in north India, for instance) who were told that failure to convert would result in the loss of patronage for their products by the Muslim ruling classes, it was never universal, except in some pockets of the subcontinent (notably Kashmir, where most of the population, including many Brahmins, converted en masse to Islam, mostly under duress during the reign of Sultan Sikander [1389–1413 CE]).[10] The overwhelming majority of the populace stayed Hindu.

HINDUISM'S RESPONSE TO THE BRITISH

When the British came, with their peculiar blend of curiosity and contempt for the beliefs and practices of the land they had found so absurdly easy to conquer, Hinduism found itself sharing space with a fiercely monotheistic culture that (unlike its precursor, Islam) claimed the trappings of modernity and progress for itself. The British found a Hinduism which, in reaction to Islamic conquest, had in some ways retreated into a shell, adopting practices to shield it from the hostile faith and searching for security in insularity. Thus a civilisation which had historically sent envoys around the world, trading with the Roman empire and exporting its religious ideas across Asia, became so self-protective that it forbade travel 'across the black water', and insisted on excommunicating those who violated this proscription, or at least forced them to undergo purificatory rituals before they could be read-mitted into the Hindu fold. Most Britons in India sneered at a faith they saw as primitive and mired in superstition. (There were, of course, notable exceptions, but in general the colonial attitude to Hinduism was one of incomprehension and contempt.) The shock of contact inevitably had a catalytic effect, leading to some remarkable reactions on the part of Hindus, including another round of reform.

Some Hindus recoiled in disgust from the British, and retreated into the secure bunker of their faith as they had known it in practice, sealing themselves off from all foreign influence. But a few others looked at their faith in the light of the new intrusion, and were embarrassed by what they saw. The Hinduism they practised seemed, especially if seen through British eyes, mired in superstition and mumbo-jumbo; it was associated with idol worship, with incantations in a dead language, with caste hierarchy and iniquitous social practices. They craved a reformed Hinduism that could hold its own with Western Christianity and even earn the respect of the British.

The most interesting of those who felt this way was Raja Rammohan Roy (1772–1833 CE), an aristocratic Bengali from a prominent and wealthy family, educated in his mother-tongue as well as in Sanskrit, Persian and Arabic before being schooled in English. His view was in direct response to the disadvantageous position that Hinduism found itself in under early British rule. 'The present system of the Hindus is not well calculated to promote their political interests,' he argued shrewdly. 'It is necessary that some change should take place in their religion, at least for the sake of their political advantage and social comfort.'[11]

Accordingly, Roy promoted a rational, ethical, non-hierarchical, and modern Hinduism, committed to ending the worst Hindu social prac-tices of the day and streamlining Hindu theology. He founded a reform movement, the Brahmo Samaj, which was clearly a product of the interaction of his reformist ideas of Hinduism, emerging from a modernistic reading of Advaita Vedanta, with early-Victorian Christianity. The Brahmos rejected the idolatry that Hinduism had become synonymous with in British eyes and professed belief in a formless God, along with a monotheistic theology based on their reading of the *Upanishads* and of the Vedanta, Hindu sacred texts that credibly lent themselves well to such a 'modern' interpretation. Brahmos affirmed their belief in the existence of One Supreme God—'a God, endowed with a distinct personality and moral attributes equal to His nature, and intelligence befitting the Author and Preserver of the Universe.' Brahmos would worship Him alone, and not necessarily in temples or at specific holy days: 'We can adore Him at any time and at any place, provided that time and that place are calculated to compose and direct the mind towards Him.'

In creating the Brahmo Samaj, Roy was strongly influenced by Unitarianism, whose uncompromising monotheism posited the oneness of God (in opposition to the Trinity of the Father, the Son and the Holy Ghost). Roy's attitude to Hinduism was in many ways comparable to the Unitarians' to Christianity, paring the faith of unnecessary accretions and reducing it to its most basic affirmations of deism. (Today, it is impossible to read of the beliefs of the Unitarian Universalists without being struck by their similarities to the central tenets of Upanishadic Hinduism.) Some Hindu scholars refused to consider Roy to be a Hindu at all, seeing in the Brahmo faith a form of Christianity dressed in Indian clothes. Others saw Roy as a staunch reformist within the Hindu faith: he wore a sacred thread all his life. But it would take a Vivekananda, not a Roy, to preach, seven decades later, a robust, modernist and universalist Hinduism, anchored in its own precepts, that could look the rest of the world's religions in the eye and oblige them to blink.

Roy was motivated in large measure by a desire to impress his European acquaintances by proving, as he put it, that 'superstitious practices which deform the Hindu religion have nothing to do with the pure spirit of its dictates'. Accordingly, he combined precept with action. Social reform was crucial to his approach. Roy rejected those Hindu traditions that his education taught him to see as social evils, campaigning against caste discrimination, the denial of equal rights to women, sati, polygamy and child marriage, while arguing that none of these practices had sanction in the scriptures.

Roy passionately believed in modern, British-style education as an indispensable tool to transform society. The East India Company, busily engaged in sending back to England as much money as they could squeeze out of India, had no desire whatsoever to spend funds on creating educational institutions for Indians. So Roy realised an Indian would have to take up the challenge. In 1817, he set up the Hindu College at Calcutta in collaboration with a Scotsman not affiliated to the East India Company, David Hare, following it up with the Anglo-Hindu school in 1822 and the Vedanta College in 1826. Roy founded the Vedanta College to create an institution where his monotheistic doctrines could be taught alongside a contemporary Western curriculum. In a synthesis of Western and Indian learning, Roy maintained a frenetic pace of institution-building: in 1830, for instance, he helped the Revd Alexander Duff to establish the General Assembly's Institution (now known as Scottish Church College). Not only did Roy donate the land on which the institution was built, he personally recruited the first batch of Indian students to study there. He also campaigned for freedom of the press, which was hemmed in with various restrictions in his time.

Roy died, at the age of sixty-one, on a trip to England undertaken with a view to raising the stipend paid by the British to the Mughal Emperor, as well as in the hope of presenting a better account of his country to the British. He is buried in Bristol, amongst the people he had tried to impress, but far from the country he had worked so hard to transform. His influence outlasted him, though the Brahmo Samaj never acquired the prominence or the popularity that he might have hoped for and that he might have been able to give it had he lived a longer life.

Subsequent Brahmo thinkers included Debendranath Tagore, who questioned important Hindu precepts, challenging the authority of the Vedas and belief in reincarnation and *karma*, and Keshub Chandra Sen, who emphasised personal religious experience over doctrine and sought to make spirituality more accessible to ordinary people. Vivekananda's initial beliefs as a teenager were strongly influenced by these thinkers, whom he met and interacted with in his late teens, and the doctrines of the Brahmo Samaj. (But, as we shall see, he moved from the Brahmos as he learned new ideas at the feet of the mystic Ramakrishna Paramahansa.)

Brahmoism was not the only response to British Christianity in the colonial era. The brave and determined Ishwar Chandra Vidyasagar in Bengal led a social movement for widow remarriage, setting an example by marrying a widow himself. He also worked for the teaching of Sanskrit to be offered to all castes. The great Sanskrit scholar R. G. Bhandarkar set up the Prarthana Samaj in Bombay with M. G. Ranade to oppose the iniquities of the caste system. Half a century after Roy created the Brahmo Samaj, a dynamic Hindu sage, Swami Dayanand Saraswati (1824–1883), established the Arya Samaj as a pure but reformed version of the Hindu faith.

Unlike Roy, Dayanand asserted the infallible authority of the Vedas, while also affirming belief in one God and rejecting idol-worship as the Brahmos had done, along with other Puranic accretions to the pure Vedic religion. Arguing that idolatry and polytheism, which so attracted the contempt of the Christian missionaries, were not mentioned in the Vedas, Dayanand Saraswati called on Hindus to terminate these practices. (However, he opposed cow-slaughter, a debatable position for one anchoring himself in the Vedas, which is replete with stories of sacrificial offerings of animal, including at least one reference to the slaughter of cows.)[12] He established *gurukuls* (Vedic schools) as alternatives to English education; these schools emphasised Vedic values and culture, while teaching the Hindu precepts of devotion to, and the pursuit of, truth (*satyam*). The Arya Samajis saw their faith as Sanatana Dharma, and found their almighty Creator (known as Om, the primordial sound) in the *Yajur Veda*, rather than the Ishvaras of the Puranic age. Like some other Hindus, they regarded the text of the Vedas as itself divine, and reciting the Vedas as a sufficient act of worship.

But their belief systems were not purely of ancient origin. The reaction to Christianity in their doctrines is evident not only in the discarding of idol-worship but in the Arya Samaj doctrine that the Vedas are 'revealed' texts, while the other sacred books of the Hindus—the *Puranas*, the epics and even the Gita—are not. They are equally dismissive of the supposedly revealed texts of other faiths, such as the Bible and the Quran. In this respect the Arya Samaj departed from the principle of acceptance of other faiths as equally valid, the principle that characterises Swami Vivekananda's Hinduism.

As a reform movement, the Arya Samaj advocated the equality of all human beings and the empowerment of women; it opened its doors to all Hindus irrespective of caste or sect, performing simple marriages according to the prescriptions in the Brahmanas of the *Yajur Veda*. It also created a conversion ritual called *shuddhi*, complete with formal certification, for non-Hindus wishing to enter the faith, something which had never existed before and which seemed to have been inspired by Christian practices of baptism. In his *The Discovery of India* Jawaharlal Nehru describes the Arya Samaj as thus having introduced religious proselytisation to Hinduism. (Non-Hindus marrying Hindus have found that if they wish to adopt their spouse's faith, the only way they can do so is through the Arya Samaj's conversion route.)

These practices, however, have helped the Arya Samaj version of Hinduism appear more familiar to those exposed to the way the Semitic religions conduct their faith. Unsurprisingly, the Arya Samaj is strongly rooted in many Hindu expatriate communities, offering the equivalent of Christian 'Sunday school' classes in the principles of the faith to Hindu children in suburban America. Yet it remains little more than a sect in its own homeland, adhered to by a modest minority of Indian Hindus.

Greater local success was obtained by three nineteenth-century reformers (and contemporaries) in southern India, Sree Narayana Guru (1856–1928), Mahatma Ayyankali (1863–1941) and Chattampi Swami (1853–1924), whose lives and impact overlapped. Chattampi Swami, an upper-caste Hindu sage, opposed caste oppression and spoke up for the emancipation of women; Mahatma Ayyankali, from an 'Untouchable' community, fought successfully against the iniquitous discriminations that prevented outcastes from using certain roads and public spaces in

Travancore. But the greatest impact was that of Sree Narayana Guru, who overcame the disadvantages imposed upon the 'backward caste' Ezhava community by preaching a modern Hinduism of love, equality and universalism. 'One religion, one caste, one God for all mankind', was his dictum. 'Whatever a person's caste, it is enough that a human be good', he famously declared. He backed up his precepts by establishing educational institutions throughout South India and by setting up ashrams and spiritual retreats to advance his ideas. Mahatma Gandhi called on Sree Narayana Guru in 1925, three years before the latter's death; without a common language (the guru did not know English and Gandhiji had no Sanskrit), the two great souls communed largely in silence and through an interpreter, but the more famous man emerged awestruck from the experience. In 1999, Sree Narayana Guru was voted by the readers of the most popular Malayalam-language magazine the greatest Keralite of the twentieth century.

The mystic sage Ramana Maharishi (1879–1950), and the revolutionary-turned spiritual guide Sri Aurobindo (1872–1950), were two other remarkable contemporaries born in the nineteenth century. Ramana Maharishi's intense spirituality, his quest for self-realisation, his intuitive grasp of Advaita and Bhakti led to him being widely considered a Jivanmukta, one who had attained self-realisation in this life. One can see Ramakrishna as the exemplar of *bhakti yoga*, Vivekananda as the very model of *karma yoga*, and Ramana Maharishi as that of *jnana yoga*. His key question to aid the attainment of self-realisation was '*Who am I?*' Am I the body, the mind, the senses? Ramana Maharishi did not travel to disseminate a message, perform social service or establish a new order of monks, but the simple example of his spirituality made him an object of great popular veneration. It is said that on the night of his death, a comet passed across the sky behind his mountain abode at Arunachalam.

As for the Cambridge-educated Sri Aurobindo, he began as an extremist political revolutionary, and ended as an other-worldly spiritual giant. During his political phase (essentially 1905 to 1910), Sri Aurobindo evolved a philosophy of spiritual nationalism, writing passionately and evocatively of the divinity of the motherland, personified as a goddess, Bhavani Bharati (a forerunner in some ways of the Bharat Mata deified by the Hindutva movement). But during his incarceration in a bomb conspiracy case, Aurobindo realised his spiritual interests outstripped his political ones. He moved to the French enclave of Pondicherry and spent the last four decades of his life (1910–1950) there in spiritual contemplation, writing brilliant exegeses on aspects of Hinduism, including a magisterial commentary on the Gita, and establishing an ashram that thrives to this day. Rather than individual salvation, he was concerned with the spiritual evolution of the human race; his concept of Integral Yoga envisaged a threefold path that involved total surrender to the Divine, the raising of human consciousness to a 'supramental' level, and finally the transformation of the terrestrial human race into a wholly new order of being.

It was said of Sri Aurobindo that he could trace almost every modern Western idea to the ancient Hindu scriptures, and that if one could not find a specific reference upon examination, that was because one was reading the words literally and failing to comprehend that the ancient Hindu sages had elliptical and metaphorical means of conveying the ideas that today we consider modern. The French political scientist (and student of modern Hindu politics) Christophe Jaffrelot has labelled the process of adoption and acceptance of Western ideas, beliefs and values by Indian sages, masked by the claim that these were actually derived from the ancient Hindu texts, as 'strategic syncretism'.[13] Whatever one calls it, it was one more instance of how resilient Hinduism was in the face of Western colonial dominance, and how effectively it adapted to the demands of proving its viability and relevance in the modern era.

SWAMI VIVEKANANDA

Though Ramana Maharishi and Sri Aurobindo achieved their prominence after his death, Swami Vivekananda (1863–1902), who came of age at the culmination of all the developments I have earlier chronicled, was also heir to the grand, diverse and varied traditions of Hinduism, for he had drunk deeply from the well of a faith whose eclecticism he saw as a strength. As he put it, 'sect after sect arose in India and seemed to shake the religion of the Vedas to its very foundations, but [over the years]...these sects were all sucked in, absorbed and assimilated into the immense body of the mother faith. From the high spiritual flights of the Vedanta philosophy, of which the latest discoveries of science seem like echoes, to the low ideas of idolatry with its multifarious mythology, the agnosticism of the Buddhists and the atheism of the Jains, each and all have a place in the Hindu's religion.'

His initial beliefs were influenced by Brahmo concepts of a formless God and the rejection of idolatry, and anchored in a rationalised Hindu theology based on the *Upanishads* and reliant on Advaita Vedanta. But though Brahmoism was an influence, it was by no means the determinant influence; Vivekananda abandoned the Brahmos for the savant who became his guru, the mystic monk Ramakrishna Paramahamsa (1836–1886). Ramakrishna, who was subject to visions, trances and 'intense spiritual rhapsodies' (in the words of Dr Karan Singh), which brought him to purest consciousness, preached a religious universalism in which he urged the thousands who flocked to him to abandon all quarrels over religion and to look for God with a pure heart. He imparted his wisdom in simple parables that won him a devoted following among the masses as well as the elite of his day, as well as deep spiritual attainment that he imparted to his most illustrious devotee. From Ramakrishna, Swami Vivekananda acquired a more profound, as well as broader, familiarity with Hindu doctrines of the oneness of *atman* and Brahman, of the role of spirituality and the quest for self-realisation and liberation, as well as the stories and parables through which these beliefs could be propagated.

Vivekananda explained his sacred texts in terms his Western audience at the Chicago Parliament of the World's Religions could understand: 'The Hindus have received their religion through revelation, the Vedas. They hold that the Vedas are without beginning and without end. It may sound ludicrous to this audience, how a book can be without beginning or end. But by the Vedas no books are meant. They mean the accumulated treasury of spiritual laws discovered by different persons in different times. Just as the law of gravitation existed before its discovery, and would exist if all humanity forgot it, so is it with the laws that govern the spiritual world. The moral, ethical, and spiritual relations between soul and soul and between individual spirits and the Father of all spirits were there before their discovery, and would remain even if we forgot them.'

This led Vivekananda to the ringing affirmation that whereas many Westerners think of the self as a body that possesses a soul, Hinduism sees the self as a soul that possesses a body: 'The Vedas declare,' he said, that 'I am a spirit living in a body: I am not the body. The body will die, but I shall not die.' On the question of the existence of God, again an idea that would make his faith more comprehensible to foreigners, Vivekananda explained: 'at the head of all these laws, in and through every particle of matter and force, stands One, *"by whose command the wind blows, the fire burns, the clouds rain and death stalks upon the earth"*.' (The 'One' was a carefully-chosen word; whereas to the Swami it implied the oneness of Brahman and atman, cosmic spirit and soul, it also embraced the idea of the One God of the Semitic faiths.) 'And what is His nature?' Vivekananda went on. 'He is everywhere, the pure and formless One, the Almighty and the All-merciful. *"Thou art our father, Thou art our mother, Thou art our beloved friend, Thou art the source of all strength; give us strength. Thou art He that beareth the burdens of the universe; help me bear the little burden of this life."* Thus sang the Rishis of the Veda.'

A certain amount of mysticism inevitably came into the message, as his audience expected: 'the Hindu believes he is a spirit. Him the sword cannot pierce; Him the fire cannot burn; Him the water cannot melt; Him the air cannot dry. The Hindu believes that every soul is a circle whose circumference is nowhere, but whose centre is located in the body, and that death means the change of this centre from body to body.... The Vedas teach that the soul is divine, only held in the bondage of matter; perfection will be reached when this bond will burst and the word they use for it is, therefore, *"mukti"*—freedom, freedom from the bonds of imperfection, freedom from death and misery.'

But here Vivekananda had a little surprise up his sleeve for the listening Westerners, particularly for those who thought of their God as a distant vision, or an aged and forbidding figure in the clouds with a white beard. 'And how to worship Him?' he asked of his God. 'Through love. He is to be worshipped as the one beloved, dearer than everything in this and the next life. This is the doctrine of love declared in the Vedas, and let us see how it is fully developed and taught by Krishna whom the Hindus believe to have been God incarnate on earth. He taught that a man ought to live in this world like a lotus leaf, which grows in water but is never moistened by water; so a man ought to live in the world—his heart to God and his hands to work.' For Vivekananda this selfless love for God was implicit in the teachings of the Bhagavad Gita. 'It is good to love God for hope of reward in this or the next world, but it is better to love God for love's sake; and the prayer goes: "Lord, I do not want wealth nor children nor learning. If it be Thy will, I shall go from birth to birth; but grant me this, that I may love Thee without the hope of reward—love unselfishly for love's sake."'

To Vivekananda, the answer to the question 'What is Hinduism?' could be reduced to the idea of realisation, of the union of *atman* and Brahman, the *moksha* taught by Advaita Vedanta: 'the whole object of [Hinduism] is by constant struggle to become perfect, to become divine, to reach God, and see God; and this reaching God, seeing God, becoming perfect even as the Father in Heaven is perfect, constitutes the religion of the Hindus...' He explained: 'There is something beyond even this fine body, which is the Atman of man, which has neither beginning nor end, which knows not what death is...I am already joined—from my very birth, from the very fact of my life—I am in *Yoga* [union] with that infinite life....'

From there, having explained Hinduism in terms that Westerners could grasp, Vivekananda firmly parted from their basic assumptions. He argued that the Hindu religion 'means realisation and nothing short of that. "Believe in the doctrine and you are safe" can never be taught to us, for we do not believe in that; you are what you make your-selves...religion is to be realised, not only heard; it is not in learning some doctrine like a parrot.' This dismissal of Western catechisms enabled Vivekananda to argue robustly that Advaita was science rather than philosophy. Hinduism has always been free of the science versus faith conflicts that have bedevilled other religions. Indeed, in 1896, Vivekananda claimed that Advaita appealed to modern scientists: 'I may make bold to say that the only religion which agrees with, and even goes a little further than modern researchers, both on physical and moral lines is the Advaita, and that is why it appeals to modern scientists so much. They find that the old dualistic theories are not enough for them, do not satisfy their necessities. A man must have not only faith, but intellectual faith too.'

He also argued that 'there is no polytheism in India'. The idol worship one saw in India's temples should not be taken literally:

> By the law of association the material image calls up the mental idea and vice versa. This is why the Hindu uses an external symbol when he worships. He will tell you it helps to keep his mind fixed on the Being to whom he prays. He knows as well as you do that the image is not God, is not omnipresent....To the Hindu, man is not travelling from error to truth, but from truth to truth, from lower to higher truth. To him all the religions from the lowest fetishism to the highest absolutism, mean so many attempts of the human soul to grasp and realise the Infinite, each determined by the conditions of its birth and association, and each of these marks a stage of progress.

And he added that it was not very different in the so-called monotheistic faiths: 'the images, crosses, and crescents are simply so many symbols—so many pegs to hang spiritual ideas on. It is not that this help is necessary for everyone, but those that do not need it have no right to say that it is wrong.' Idolatry in India 'is the attempt of undeveloped minds to grasp high spiritual truths'.

The Swami was certainly not seeking to downplay his own faith: far from it, he spoke proudly in 'the name of the most ancient order of monks in the world' and 'the mother of religions'. Vivekananda was contemptuous of what he called 'kitchen religion', the farrago of taboos and restrictions on diet and conduct that had come to constitute Hinduism for some. But he also made no distinction between the actions of Hindus as a people (embodied by their grant of asylum to people fleeing religious oppression, for instance) and their actions as a religious community (visible in their tolerance of other faiths). He spoke proudly of Hindu India offering refuge to Jews fleeing Roman persecution and Zoroastrians escaping Muslim rule in Persia: 'I am proud to belong to a country which has sheltered the persecuted and the refugees of all religions and all countries of the earth.' For him, there was no real distinction between Hindu believers accepting other faiths and Hindus extending asylum to people of other faiths, because Hinduism was as much a civilisation as a set of religious beliefs.

In a different speech to the same Chicago convention, Swami Vivekananda set out his philosophy in simple terms: 'Unity in variety is the plan of nature, and the Hindu has recognised it. Every other religion lays down certain fixed dogmas and tries to compel society to adopt them. It places before society only one coat which must fit Jack and John and Henry, all alike. If it does not fit John or Henry, he must go without a coat to cover his body. The Hindus have discovered that the absolute can only be realised, or thought of, or stated through the relative, and the images, crosses, and crescents are simply so many symbols—so many pegs to hang spiritual ideas on. It is not that this help is necessary for everyone, but those that do not need it have no right to say that it is wrong. Nor is it compulsory in Hinduism.'

Vivekananda was also, uncommonly for his time, a believer in gender equality: he related well to women, who numbered among his closest devotees, and worked with them to take his message to the world. It is no wonder then that he began those inspiring speeches to the Parliament of the World's Religions with the words, 'Sisters and brothers of America...' The first time he uttered them, it was reported, the phrase, and his voice, had an electrifying effect upon the audience.

In his book *Raja Yoga* Vivekananda introduced the 'four yogas', his interpretation of Patanjali's *Yoga Sutras*, as a practical means for each individual to work towards realising the divine force within himself. The four yogas were raja yoga (psychological and mystical practices as well as spiritual exercises), karma yoga (work and the way of action and social service in the quest for the divine), bhakti yoga (devotional worship and expression of love for the divine), and jnana yoga (the path of knowledge and reason in the pursuit of self-realisation). The four paths were distinct but could be pursued simultaneously or in parallel. Vivekananda tried to combine all these in himself. He pursued his own divinity by discipline and effort, deep study, reading and reflection, and huge physical effort that included walking the length and breadth of India with nothing but a staff, a water pot and his own charisma to sustain him.

He was a profoundly moral figure, with none of the indulgences that modern Indian 'godmen' have become known for; as Adi Shankara preached, he lived by a code of truth, purity, celibacy and unselfishness that anchored his *shraddha* (faith). Although many of his deeply committed followers were women, he treated them as sisters and daughters, irrespective of their age, and lived the celibate life of a *brahmachari*, seeing intimate relations as incompatible with his mission of spiritual service. In this he remained essentially a monk, but unlike his preceptor Ramakrishna he was no other-worldly figure: a compelling speaker and a magnetic presence, Swami Vivekananda was focused on human behaviour in the real world he saw around him. He argued that it is an insult to preach religion to a man with an empty stomach, and for many in India, he said, God will only appear as a loaf of bread.

The Vedanta, interpreted in comprehensible contemporary terms, became the vehicle for his preaching. As Vivekananda explained: 'Each soul is potentially divine. The goal is to manifest this Divinity within by controlling nature, external and internal. Do this either by work, or worship, or mental discipline, or philosophy—by one, or more, or all of these—and be free. This is the whole of religion. Doctrines, or dogmas, or rituals, or books, or temples, or forms, are but secondary details.'

Vivekananda lived up to this precept himself: work, worship, mental discipline and philosophy, he mastered them all. He believed that spiritual realisation needed the awakening of the human will; this required him to adopt a path of pursuing spirituality through service. Worldly success was important, but such success could only be the outcome of focused thought and action. It is important to remember that Swami Vivekananda—despite being a spiritual figure, despite being a disciple of the immortal Ramakrishna Paramahamsa, despite being a *sannyasi* who travelled throughout India and taught the message of Vedanta and the Gita, the message of religion and spirituality as he understood it— was also very much anchored in the real needs of India, of his people at that time and in the future.

Of the many angles from which the social problems of India could be analysed, he proceeded from the religious and spiritual perspectives. Therefore, the Swami founded the Ramakrishna Math, based on the twin ideals of self-realisation and service to the world, and named for his guru, Sri Ramakrishna Paramahamsa. But since a math (or matham or mutth) is essentially a place of contemplation, Vivekananda laid the foundation of the Ramakrishna Mission, also named for his preceptor, as a philanthropic, volunteer organisation to work alongside the religious monastic order to spread his teachings throughout the world. The Mission based its work on the principle of karma yoga, the path of selfless, altruistic service propounded by Vivekananda. Karma yoga preached an ethic of action and doing, not merely of the meditation and reflection that was all that spirituality had hitherto been identified with. Ever since its inception, the Ramakrishna Mission has stayed true to its motto of 'Atmano mokshartham jagat hitaya cha', which translated from Sanskrit means 'For one's own salvation, and for the good of the world'.

Vivekananda undoubtedly revolutionised the traditional image of the Hindu monk, the *sannyasi*, in India by setting the example and making social service an integral part of the *sannyasi*'s life. Initially, after the passing away of his guru, Sri Ramakrishna, he had thought of going on a pilgrimage to the holy places like Varanasi, Ayodhya, Vrindavan, and the ashrams of yogis in the Himalayas. However, after a couple of years spent on such visits, he turned his gaze to the common people for whom the only reality in life was their struggle for survival.

When, around Christmas of 1892, he travelled on foot to Kanyakumari, at the southern tip of India, he meditated on the 'last bit of Indian rock' jutting out into the ocean, on which now stands the Vivekananda Rock Memorial. It was at this juncture in his life that the Swami pondered over his experiences of observing the miseries of the poor in the various parts of the country, which culminated in his

'Vision of One India'. This has now come to be called the 'Kanyakumari resolve of 1892', about which he later wrote:

'At Cape Comorin, sitting in Mother Kumari's temple, I hit upon a plan: we are so many sannyasins wandering about, and teaching the people metaphysics? It is all madness. Did not our Gurudeva once say, "An empty stomach is no good for religion?" That those poor people are leading a life of brutes is simply due to ignorance... Suppose some sannyasins, bent on doing good to others, go from village to village, disseminating education and seeking in various ways to better the condition of all down to the Chandala...can't that bring forth good in time? ... We, as a nation, have lost our individuality, and that is the cause of all mischief in India. We have to give back to the nation its lost individuality and *raise the masses*...' Vivekananda wanted 'to set in motion a machinery which will bring noblest ideas to the doorstep of even the poorest and the meanest'.

These ideas galvanised his followers, in a country that had long been inured to the tyranny and oppression faced by a majority of the people. And thus began a new epoch in his life. Nationalism—not just in the sense of overthrowing the foreign ruler, but in the sense of national reawakening—became a prominent theme in Vivekananda's thought. He believed that a country's future depended on its people, and his teachings focused on what today we might call human development. Our modern systems of governance have a lot to learn from his teachings. His assessment of the social problems of India was realistic, rather than theoretical. He connected with the common man to a degree that would be the envy of most modern politicians, largely owing to the fact that he wandered all over the country with a few followers and a begging bowl in his hand.

What bothered the Swami, even more than poverty itself, was the gulf between the rich and the poor, between the high-placed and the low-born, and further, the ugly sight of the strong regularly oppressing the weak. 'This is our native land', he often bemoaned, 'where huts and palaces exist side-by-side.' Such was the dichotomy of the times that it seemed inconceivable to him that India could have the unity and brotherhood which are preconditions for national greatness. Born, as it were, a 'disunited mob', we could not combine: in our unity would lie the fulfilment of our nationhood.

But this would mean liberation from ourselves and not just from the British. Vivekananda was searingly honest in his criticism of the social practices that kept India backward. He denounced the oppression of the masses by iniquitous social practices, including caste discrimination. He propagated the idea that 'the divine, the absolute, exists within all human beings regardless of social status'. He also voiced his opposition against the manner in which women were kept, in conditions of servile dependence on men, which made them 'good only to weep at the slightest approach of mishap or danger'. He taught us values that actually mandated change in the arrangements of our society. He refused to accept that religion was cited in favour of iniquitous social practices like child marriage: he was a religious reformer as well as a social reformer. Child marriage, which Rammohan Roy had fought against, still persisted across India, since the British were reluctant to outlaw it. 'A girl of eight is married to a man of thirty and the parents are jubilant over it. And if anyone protests against it, the plea put forward is that our religion is being overturned', he lamented. His devotee Sister Nivedita, born in Britain as Margaret Noble, started a girls' school in Calcutta to advance his progressive ideas about the education of women. He wanted a fully educated India, an objective we have not yet fulfilled a century and a quarter later.

These practices, and the dissensions which divided Hindu society, pained Swami Vivekananda all the more because they were being adhered to in the name of religion. He preached that 'seeing the divine as the essence of others will promote love and social harmony', but he had no illusions about how prevalent such attitudes were. He was furious about those who claimed their beliefs were superior to anyone else's. 'Ask a man who wants to start a sectarian fight,' he declaimed, '"Have you seen God? Have you seen the Atman? If you have not, what right have you to preach his Name—you walking in darkness trying to lead me into the same darkness—the blind leading the blind, and both falling into the ditch?"'

121

Vivekananda helped create, in his own lifetime, a band of volunteers to work among the poor, the distressed and the marginalised. Many of these were young people, for Swami Vivekananda personified the eternal energy of Indian youth and awakened in many young people a restless quest for truth. One of his more famous exhortations to young Indians came from his lectures in *Raja Yoga*, in which he memorably said, 'Take up one idea. Make that one idea your life—think of it, dream of it, live on that idea. Let the brain, muscles, nerves, every part of your body, be full of that idea, and just leave every other idea alone. This is the way to success, that is the way great spiritual giants are produced'.

A spiritual giant himself, Vivekananda expressed his mission in disarmingly simple terms: 'What I want to propagate is a religion that will be equally acceptable to all minds; it must be equally philosophic, equally emotional, equally mystic and equally conducive to action'. His own teachings, as well as the work done by the Ramakrishna Math and Mission in the century after his passing, have made Swami Vivekananda a modern day apostle of the ideas that underpin the modern Hindu's conception of the world and of our place in it.

But the fact is that he never considered himself detached from the world; his spirituality was anchored in the world. Swami Vivekananda taught us that a true nationalism that was rooted in both spiritual yearning and a spirit of social service. 'Arise, awake, and stop not till the goal is reached' was his motto, citing a *sloka* (verse) of the *Katha Upanishad*. And that, to my mind, is the great lesson he leaves to those of us in public life: that we must have values, that we must join the quest for attainment of some knowledge of the Divine, for that is ultimately what all spirituality is about, but that spirituality is meaningless if it is not embedded in a genuine concern for the well-being of ordinary people in our country, and a willingness to act on it.

In multiple speeches around the world and in India, Vivekananda continually reiterated a basic message: that the Hindu recognises one supreme spirit that suffuses the universe. He worships the one God while recognising that others see and name Him differently. 'Ekam sat vipra bahudha vadanti': the Truth is One but sages call It by different names.

AFTER THE SWAMI, TOWARDS THE MAHATMA

Two decades after Vivekananda's premature death at the age of thirty-nine, a very different figure, clad not in the saffron or ochre robes of the Hindu sage but in the cap and gown of the Oxford don, rose to explicate the Hindu religion to an audience of academics and theologians. Delivering the prestigious Upton Lectures at the age of thirty-eight, Dr Sarvepalli Radhakrishnan, then the youngest Fellow of All Souls' College, described 'the Hindu view of life' in contemporary terms. For the Hindu, Radhakrishnan explained, God is in the world, though God is not the world, and the world is not God; He is more than the Creator, he preserves, protects, destroys, remakes, and strives continuously, alongside human beings. The *Brihadaranyaka Upanishad* captures this idea beautifully, though Radhakrishnan did not cite it:

> *He who is abiding in the earth, yet different from the earth;*
> *He who is abiding in the water, yet different from the water;*
> *He who is abiding in the wind, yet different from the wind...*

— *Brihadaranyaka Upanishad*, III.7.3–7[14]

In both places, the text uses the same Sanskrit word, '*antara*' which means both 'interior to (abiding in)' and 'different from'. There is no dualism between the natural (the reality we see around us) and the supernatural (the cosmic spirit); each is rooted in the other. As Radhakrishnan brilliantly put it: 'The Hindu spirit is that attitude towards life which regards the endless variety of the visible and the temporal world as sustained and supported by the invisible and eternal spirit.'[15]

Like Vivekananda in Chicago, Radhakrishnan had some startling news for his Western audience: the Hindu did not think in terms of good and evil. 'Evil has reference to the distance which good has to traverse. Ugliness is halfway to beauty. Error is a stage on the road to truth.' After all, he added: 'As every soul is unlike all others in the world, the destruction of even the most wicked soul will create a void in God's scheme.'[16] There was no notion of sin in this philosophy, nor of Heaven nor Hell. (And yet the idea of sin is not wholly absent from the Vedas; the notion that sins can be washed away in holy waters goes back to the *Rig Veda*.) Damnation was not God's way, since the sinner was himself part of the universal cosmic spirit. How could there be a hell, since it was impossible for there to be a place where God was not? Vivekananda had said years earlier that Hindus reject the idea of fear and the idea of sin: 'the Aryans threw it aside as a very primitive sort of idea and went further on... [for] a more philosophical and transcendental idea.' That idea Radhakrishnan expressed in almost poetic terms: 'The cure for error is not the stake or the cudgel, not force or persecution, but the quiet diffusion of light.'[17]

Radhakrishnan spoke as a professor of philosophy; Vivekananda declaimed as a preacher; but their message was the same, rendering the Hinduism of Advaita Vedanta comprehensible to the modern Western mind. It was, however, the charismatic Swami who had the more lasting impact. Vivekananda's overt respect for all other paths and religions was an integral part of what he preached. Part of his appeal lay in the way he combined ancient wisdom with contemporary insights, in spreading his profound message of interfaith harmony and spirituality married to rationalism.

Vivekananda had quoted the Bhagavad Gita to the effect that 'Whosoever comes to me, through whatsoever form, I reach him; all men are struggling through paths which in the end lead to me.' Vivekananda went on to denounce the fact that 'sectarianism, bigotry, and its horrible descendant, fanaticism, have long possessed this beautiful earth. They have filled the earth with violence, and drenched it often with human blood, destroyed civilisation, and sent whole nations to despair'.

His confident belief that the death-knell of these negative forces had been sounded was sadly not to be borne out. But his vision—summarised in the Sanskrit credo 'sarva dharma sambhava'—all religions are equally worthy of respect—is, in fact, the kind of Hinduism practised by most of India's Hindus, whose instinctive acceptance of other faiths and forms of worship has long been the distinctive hallmark of Indianness, not merely in a narrow religious sense, but in a broader cultural and spiritual sense too.

The efforts of Swami Vivekananda and the other Hindu reformers and thinkers served to reassert their faith in the face of the racist notions of Christian superiority peddled by the colonial rulers. Far from the religion of superstitious idol-worshippers caricatured by the imperialists, they demonstrated that Hinduism was sophisticated, monotheistic and inclusive. It was a faith that had undergone several reformations and absorbed them all; the incorporation of Buddhist ideas, for instance, had made the Buddha—a figure familiar to, and respected by, many Westerners—a part of the Hindu faith. Hinduism had survived in even more sophisticated and cosmopolitan a form, and it would see off the threat of colonial modernity as well.

And yet, curiously enough, the nature and content of the Vedanta tradition meant that while it enabled Hindus to stand up with self-confidence against imperial rule, it did not generate a narrow Hindu nationalism. If Hinduism, as Advaita Vedanta taught, was an inclusive faith, the nationalism it animated must also be inclusive. Hindus thus agitated against colonial oppression, but they were happy to pursue the goal of *swaraj* or self-rule through collective action with other Indian religious communities.

MAHATMA GANDHI

The leader who most embodied this approach was Mahatma Gandhi, who called himself a follower of Advaita Vedanta. Swami Vivekananda had preached Advaita Vedanta as an inclusive universal religion; similarly Gandhi did not conceal his own staunch Hinduism, but presented it as a faith that respected and embraced all other faiths. He was immersed in Hindu beliefs and customs, and profoundly influenced by the Yamas of Adi Shankara, particularly *ahimsa* and *satya* to which he gave profound meaning when he applied them to the nationalist cause. But when Gandhi held prayer-meetings at which Hindu devotional bhajans were chanted, so also were songs, hymns and verses sacred to other religions. He actively promoted syncretism: *Raghupathi Raghava Raja Ram*, he chanted, *Ishwara Allah Tero naam*. This practice emerged from his Vedantic belief in the unity of God and all human beings; he believed staunchly that all beings have the same *atman* and therefore should be treated with equality. His conviction that all paths to God should be seen as equally valid led him to respect the beliefs and practices of other faiths and to refuse to impose his own upon them (as he explained when refusing to advocate a ban on cow slaughter that would affect other communities).

Such behaviour did not endear him to every Hindu. Gandhi's assassin, Nathuram Godse, denounced 'Gandhi's betrayal of Hinduism' during his trial. It was an odd charge, since many saw Gandhiji as the quintessential Hindu leader in Indian politics, but it is true that his Hinduism was not particularly religious in the conventional sense. He died with the name of Rama on his lips but there is no evidence that he ever believed in or worshipped a personal god. ('There is an indefinable mysterious power that pervades everything,' he wrote, implying faith in an impersonal, undefinable power: 'I don't regard God as a person.') Gandhi declared his faith in 'all that goes by the name of Hindu scriptures' but, as the scholar K. P. Shankaran points out, he 'immediately qualified it by saying that he also believed in all other religious texts in a similar way'.[18] He also took Hinduism's eclectic and wide-ranging texts and belief structures literally, making it clear that he retained the right to choose what tenets he believed in, to interpret what they taught him, and to reject anything in them that he could not agree with. His emphasis on the ethics of *satya* and *ahimsa*, elevating them above almost any of the other principles of Hinduism, was distinctive: 'Truth for me is God.'

Gandhi was more a reinterpreter of Hinduism than a reformer of it; by drawing from it to suit his beliefs and purposes, he redefined the traditional vocabulary of Hinduism without ever departing from it. He criticised many of the iniquitous social practices of Hinduism without denouncing the faith from which they had emerged, and unlike his contemporary Ambedkar, who denounced Hinduism's distortions and cruelties and eventually left the faith, Gandhi always tried to change it from within. According to K.P. Shankaran, Gandhi's rejection of the vocabulary of the European Enlightenment and modernity (for the reasons he had explained in his 1909 book, *Hind Swaraj)* forced him to fall back on a vocabulary that he was familiar with, that of the Vaishnava tradition of his parents. Gandhi's objective was to create an ethical

Indian state founded on *ahimsa* and *satya*, non-violence and truth, principles he found in Advaita philosophy. The national motto of independent India—*Satyameva Jayate* (Truth Alone Triumphs)—is from the *Mundaka Upanishad*, chosen by Mahatma Gandhi as his guiding credo. His own translation of the Bhagavad Gita portrays the text as a philosophy of Anashakti Yoga, meant for votaries of *ahimsa*. Gandhiji took a text that had traditionally been seen as extolling war and action, and transformed it into a paean to non-violence and truth. It was quite a feat (what some have seen as a creative 'misreading' of the text),[19] that located his Hinduism on a platform of *ahimsa* and *satya*, and at the same time anchored his political strategy in the Hindu faith of the masses.

And even while doing so, Gandhi took care to include Indians of other faiths in his capacious and agglomerative version of Hinduism. He noted that there is ample religious literature, both in the *astika* and *nastika* religious traditions, that supports a pluralistic approach to religious and cultural diversity. Gandhi found support for his Advaitist beliefs not only in the Vedanta but in the Jain concept of 'Anekantavada'—the notion that truth and reality are perceived differently by different people from their own different points of view, and that therefore no single perception can constitute the complete truth—from which he derived the axiom that 'truth is many-sided and relative'. Gandhi often expressed the view that the spirit of synthesis was the essential hallmark of Indian civilisation. This led him to declare once, in response to being classified a Hindu: 'I am a Hindu, a Muslim, a Christian, a Parsi, a Jew'. (To which the Muslim League leader Muhammad Ali Jinnah tartly riposted: 'Only a Hindu could say that.')

As a Hindu, I am proud to lay claim to the legacy of the tradition of thought and action that began with the Vedas and grew under Adi Shankara, flowered through Bhakti, embraced social reformers like Raja Rammohan Roy and Sree Narayana Guru, and has Swami Vivekananda and Mahatma Gandhi as two of its fountainheads.

PART TWO

POLITICAL HINDUISM

5

HINDUISM AND THE POLITICS OF HINDUTVA

When I was a columnist for *The Hindu*, which despite its name has been a secular, even left-inclined, newspaper throughout its existence, I received a number of letters from readers on the subject of Hindu ethics and *dharma*, prompted by some of my writings on the subject. One letter, from the retired Director-General of Police of Tripura State, Mr B. J. K. Tampi, made a challenging point. Arguing that *dharma* 'has a pre-eminently secular meaning of social ethics covering law-abiding conduct,' Mr Tampi sought for *dharma* its due prominence in Hindu life. 'In fact the four ends of human life,' he went on, 'dharma, artha, kama and moksha, are always mentioned in that order. The purport is that the pursuit of wealth and pleasure should be within the parameters of dharma and moksha (the final emancipation of the soul from rebirth through religious practices).' Mr Tampi adds, citing Swami Ranganathananda (1908–2005, the spiritual teacher who was the thirteenth and most famous head of the Ramakrishna Mission): 'the excessive Indian fear of rebirth has led to the neglect of true worldly dharma for the sake of an other-worldly moksha. It has made men unfit both in the worldly (secular) and spiritual spheres.'

Now I have never met the good Mr Tampi—whose theological learning is all the more impressive in one who served in the practical profession of a policeman—but his analysis gladdens my secular heart.

The fact is that, despite having done so much to attract the opprobrium of those who seek to politicise Hinduism, or the Hindutva brigade as I call them, I do believe that propagating *dharma*—and instilling deeply at all levels of society the need to live according to one's *dharma*—can be the key to bridging the present gap between the religious and the secular in India.

The social scientist T. N. Madan has argued that the increasing secularisation of modern Indian life is responsible for the rise of fundamentalism, since 'it is the marginalisation of faith, which is what secularism is, that permits the perversion of religion. There are no fundamentalists or revivalists in traditional society.'[1]

The implication is that secularism has deprived Indians of their moral underpinnings—the meaning that faith gives to life—and religious extremism has risen as an almost inevitable antithesis to the secular project. The only way out of this dilemma is for Hindus to return to the tolerant, holistic, just, pluralist *dharma* articulated so effectively by Swami Vivekananda, which embraces both worldly and spiritual duty.

After all, as Mr Tampi points out, the Hindu's secular pursuit of material happiness is not meant to be divorced from his obedience to the ethical and religious tenets of his faith. So the distinction between 'religious' and 'secular' is an artificial one: there is no such compartmentalisation in Hinduism. When you conduct your life by performing your duties ethically, are you 'secular' or (since you are fulfilling your *dharma* while adhering to a moral code) a 'good Hindu'?

There is also a terminological issue here. The secularism avowed by successive Indian governments, as Professor R. S. Misra of Banaras Hindu University has argued, is based on *dharma-nirpekshata* ('keeping apart from dharma'), which is impossible for any good Hindu to adhere to. BJP politicians like Rajnath Singh and Yogi Adityanath have argued that Indian governments cannot observe *dharma-nirpekshata* but should follow the precept of *panth-nirpekshata* (not favouring any particular sect or faith). In this they are not far removed from my argument—which I have made for several years before my entry into Indian politics—that 'secularism' is a misnomer in the Indian context of profuse religiosity, and what we should be talking about is 'pluralism'. I believe the roots of India's pluralism can be found in the Hindu acceptance of difference, which has become an article of faith for most of Indian society. But many critics of secularism are not terribly enamoured of pluralism either. To Professor Misra, for instance, the problem with *dharma-nirpekshata* is that an authentically Indian ethic would ensure that secular objectives are infused with *dharma*.

I find this view persuasive but incomplete. Yes, *dharma* is essential in the pursuit of material well-being, public order and good governance, but this should not mean turning public policy over to *sants* and *sadhus*, nor excluding any section of Indian society (for instance, minorities who reject the Hindu idea of *dharma* as irrelevant to their lives) from their rightful place in the Indian sun. If we can bring *dharma* into our national life, it must be to uphold, rather than at the expense of, the pluralist ideal of Indian-ness.

Hinduism has always acknowledged the existence of opposites (and reconciled them): pain and pleasure, success and failure, creation and destruction, life and death are all manifestations of the duality inherent in human existence. These pairings are not contradictory but complementary; they are aspects of the same overarching reality. So also with the secular and the sacred: a Hindu's life must involve both. To acknowledge this would both absorb and deflect the unsavoury aspects of the resurgence of Hindutva.

THE RSS AND SAVARKAR

India's current ruling party, the Bharatiya Janata Party, officially adopted Hindutva as its defining credo in 1989. It is the doctrine assiduously promoted by the Hindu nationalist volunteer organisation the Rashtriya Swayamsevak Sangh (RSS), founded in 1925, and its affiliated family of organisations in the 'Sangh Parivar', notably the Vishva Hindu Parishad (VHP, World Hindu Council), set up in 1964 with an avowed intention of protecting and promoting the Hindu religion. The word Hindutva is widely used by all of them, but what does the term actually mean?

The man largely credited with the invention of the concept of Hindutva—literally 'Hinduness'—is Vinayak Damodar Savarkar

(1883–1966), whose *Essentials Of Hindutva* (Bombay: Veer Savarkar Prakashan, 1st edn 1923) laid out the concept. Republished in 1928 as *Hindutva:Who Is a Hindu?*, it is in many ways the foundational text of the Hindu nationalist creed.

Savarkar chose the term 'Hindutva' to describe the 'quality of being a Hindu' in ethnic, cultural and political terms. He argued that a Hindu is one who considers India to be his motherland (*matrbhumi*), the land of his ancestors (*pitrbhumi*), and his holy land (*punya bhumi*). India is the land of the Hindus since their ethnicity is Indian and since the Hindu faith originated in India. (Other faiths that were born in India, like Sikhism, Buddhism and Jainism also qualified, in Sarvakar's terms, as variants of Hinduism since they fulfilled the same three criteria; but Islam and Christianity, born outside India, did not.) Thus a Hindu is someone born of Hindu parents, who regards India—'this land of Bharatvarsha, from the Indus to the Seas'—as his motherland as well as his holy land, 'that is the cradle-land of his religion.'

In keeping with the race doctrines of the times, Savarkar conceived Hindutva as an indefinable quality inherent in the Hindu 'race', which could not be identified directly with the specific tenets of Hinduism. Hindutva, he declared, 'is so varied and so rich, so powerful and so subtle, so elusive and yet so vivid'[2] that it defied such definition. But of course, the concept of Hindutva would have made no sense unless it was explained in relation to the religion of Hinduism. So Savarkar asserted: 'Hinduism is only a derivative, a fraction, a part of Hindutva.'[3] To him, the religion was therefore a subset of the political idea, rather than synonymous with it—something many of its proponents today would be surprised to hear. Savarkar, however, argued that: 'Failure to distinguish between Hindutva and Hinduism has given rise to much misunderstanding and mutual suspicion between some of those sister communities that have inherited this inestimable and common treasure of our Hindu civilisation... It is sufficient enough to point out that Hindutva is not identical with what is vaguely indicated by the term Hinduism. By an "ism" it is generally meant a theory or a code more or less based on spiritual or religious dogma or system. But when we attempt to investigate into the essential significance of Hindutva, we do not primarily—and certainly not mainly—concern ourselves with any particular theocratic or religious dogma or creed...'[4]

In other words, Hindutva is more than the Hindu religion, and as a political philosophy it does not confine itself to adherents of the Hindu faith. Despite this distinction, Hindutva would help achieve the political consolidation of the Hindu people, since Savarkar also argued that a Muslim or a Christian, even if born in India, could not claim allegiance to the three essentials of Hindutva: 'a common nation (*rashtra*), a common race (*jati*) and a common civilisation (*sanskriti*), as represented in a common history, common heroes, a common literature, a common art, a common law and a common jurisprudence, common fairs and festivals, rites and rituals, ceremonies and sacraments.'

Hindus, thus defined, constituted the Indian nation—a nation that had existed since antiquity, since Savarkar was explicitly rejecting the British view that India was just, in Churchill's notorious phrase, 'a geographical expression.... No more a single country than the Equator.' Savarkar's vision of Hindutva saw it as the animating principle of a 'Hindu Rashtra' (Hindu Nation) that extended across the entire Indian subcontinent, and was rooted in an undivided India ('*Akhand Bharat*') corresponding to the territorial aspirations of ancient dynasties like the Mauryas (320 BCE–180 BCE), who under Chandragupta and Ashoka had managed to knit most of the subcontinent under their territorial control. In the words of a later RSS publication, *Sri Guruji, the Man and his Mission*, 'It became evident that Hindus were the nation in Bharat and that Hindutva was Rashtriyatva [nationalism].'[5]

For Savarkar, Hinduness was synonymous with Indianness, properly understood. Savarkar's idea of Hindutva was so expansive that it covered everything that a scholar today would call 'Indic': 'Hindutva is not a word but a history. Not only the spiritual or religious history of our people as at times it is mistaken to be by being confounded with the other cognate term Hinduism, but a history in full... Hindutva embraces all the departments of thought and activity of the whole Being of our Hindu race.'[6]

In turn, the Hindu 'race' was inextricably bound to the idea of the nation. As Savarkar put it, 'We Hindus are bound together not only by the tie of the love we bear to a common fatherland and by the common blood that courses through our veins and keeps our hearts throbbing and our affections warm, but also by the tie of the common homage we pay to our great civilisation—our Hindu culture'. By definition, however, his idea of Hindutva, as mentioned above, excluded those whose ancestors came from elsewhere or whose holy lands lay outside India—thereby eliminating Muslim and Christians, India's two most significant minorities, from his frame of reference. What their place would be in Savarkar's Hindu Rashtra was not made explicitly clear, but the best they could hope for was a sort of second-class citizenship in which they could live in India only on sufferance.

In 1939 Savarkar wrote the foreword to a book by the Nazi sympathiser and European-born Hindu revivalist who called herself Savitri Devi. Savitri Devi (1905–1982), born Maximiani Portas of mixed Greek, French and English parentage, was a remarkable figure who, among other idiosyncratic beliefs, considered Adolf Hitler an avatar of Vishnu. Her book, prophetically titled *A Warning to the Hindus*, is a passionate polemic about the need for Hindu reassertion. Savitri Devi asserted that, 'Hinduism is the national religion of India, and there is no real India besides Hindu India'. Savarkar joined the author in arguing that:

> 'In all walks of life, for a long time, the Hindus have been fed on inertia-producing thoughts which disabled them to act energetically for any purpose in life, other than "moksha," that is to say escape from this world—where to? God knows. And this is one of the causes of the continuous enslavement of our Hindu Rashtra for centuries altogether'.[7]

Not for Savarkar the abstruse metaphysics of Advaita; what he and Savitri Devi were interested in was political power, here and now. For Savitri Devi, political power, defined as 'the power of law with organised military force' is 'everything in the world... We would like the Hindus to remember this, and to strive to acquire political power at any cost. Social reforms are necessary, not because they will bring more "humanity" among the Hindus, as many think, but because they will bring unity, that is to say power.'[8]

DEFINING NATIONHOOD: GOLWALKAR

This logic was taken even farther by M. S. Golwalkar (1906–1973), the *sarsangchalak* or head of the Rashtriya Swayamsevak Sangh (RSS) for three decades (1940–1973), who supplanted Savarkar as the principal ideologue of Hindu nationalism, notably in his 1939 screed *We, or Our Nationhood Defined*[9] and in the anthology of his writings and speeches, *Bunch of Thoughts*.[10] Golwalkar made it clear that India was the holy land of the Hindus. He writes: 'Hindusthan is the land of the Hindus and is the terra firma for the Hindu nation alone to flourish upon...'[11] According to him, India was a pristine Hindu country in ancient times,[12] a place of unparalleled glory destroyed in successive assaults by foreign invaders. He felt that a 'national regeneration' was necessary. He also contended that the national regeneration of this 'Hindu nation' (the 'motherland' for which the 'Hindu people' shed their blood)[13] could only come about through the revival of its Hinduness. Golwalkar rejected the concept of what he called 'territorial nationalism', the modern variant of nationalism which identified a state with its territory and bestowed equal rights of citizenship on all those who lived within it. That, to him, made no sense: a territory was not a nation, a people constituted a nation. Who were this people? In the Indian case, Hindus.[14] Golwalkar and the RSS became passionate advocates of 'cultural nationalism'.[15] This, of course, is directly opposed to the civic nationalism enshrined in the Constitution of India.

India's independence from colonial rule in 1947, Golwalkar argued, did not constitute real freedom because the new leaders held on to the 'perverted concept of nationalism' that located all who lived on India's territory as equal constituents of the nation. 'The concept of territorial nationalism,' he wrote, 'has verily emasculated our nation and what more can we expect of a body deprived of its vital energy? ...[and] so it is that we see today the germs of corruption, disintegration and dissipation eating into the vitals of our nation for having given up the natural living nationalism in the pursuit of an unnatural, unscientific and lifeless hybrid concept of territorial nationalism.'[16]

Golwalkar's *Bunch Of Thoughts* argues that territorial nationalism is a barbarism, since a nation is 'not a mere bundle of political and economic rights' but an embodiment of national culture—in India, 'ancient and sublime' Hinduism. In his tract, Golwalkar sneers at democracy—which he sees as alien to Hindu culture. He also writes approvingly of the Laws of Manu as the work of a 'great soul'; he talks of the high regard in which *Manu Smriti* is held around the world by referring to a statue in the Philippines bearing the inscription: 'The first, the greatest and wisest lawgiver of mankind'. (That Manu's legal prescription is condemned by many for its elitism and casteism, its gender prejudice, its implicitly authoritarian ethos and its disparagement of the lower castes never crosses Golwalkar's mind.) But in all fairness, Golwalkar was only echoing Nietzsche, who wrote of the *Manu Smriti*: 'This absolutely Aryan testimony, a priestly codex of morality based on the Vedas, of a presentation of caste and of ancient provenance not pessimistic even though priestly—completes my conceptions of religion in the most remarkable manner.'[17] For Golwalkar, therefore, salvation lies not in Indian democracy, but in the historian Manu S. Pillai's words, 'in embracing Hindu dharmocracy'.[18]

Pillai's phrase is not entirely tongue-in-cheek: Golwakar intends traditional Hindu practices to prevail in his Hindu Rashtra, including caste discrimination. 'We know as a matter of history,' he writes, 'that our north-western and north-eastern areas, where the influence of Buddhism had disrupted the caste system, fell an easy prey to the onslaught of Muslims…. But the areas of Delhi and Uttar Pradesh, which were considered to be very orthodox and rigid in caste restrictions, remained predominantly Hindu even after remaining the very citadels of Muslim power and fanaticism.'[19] So the more caste-ridden society was, the more robustly it resisted the encroachments of the foreign faiths that sought to erode it: to Golwalkar, 'the so-called "caste-ridden" Hindu Society has remained undying and inconquerable…(while) casteless societies crumbled to dust'.[20]

The alternative to territorial nationalism, to Golwalkar, was a nationalism based on race. In *We, or Our Nationhood Defined*, at the height of Hitler's rise, Golwalkar wrote: 'To keep up the purity of the Race and its culture, Germany shocked the world by her purging the country of the Semitic Races—the Jews. Race pride at its highest has been manifested here. Germany has also shown how well nigh impossible it is for Races and cultures, having differences going to the root, to be assimilated into one united whole, a good lesson for us in Hindustan to learn and profit by.'[21]

This marked an evolution from Savarkar's notion that saw Hindutva as principally a cultural identity and Hinduism as a part of a national Hindu culture. In an important respect, Golwalkar reversed Savarkar's logic: 'With us,' he wrote, 'culture is but a product of our all-comprehensive religion, a part of its body and not distinguishable from it.'[22] From Golwalkar onwards, Hindutva was seen as an ideology seeking to establish the hegemony of Hindus, Hindu values and the Hindu way of life in the political arrangements of India. In this he was building on Savarkar's derisive rejection of Gandhian 'universalism' and 'non-violence' which he considered delusionary opiates. Instead of Gandhi's moral lessons in favour of peace, Savarkar advocated the 'political virility'[23] of Hindutva, an idea which found full flower in Golwalkar.

Golwalkar made no bones about the principal targets of his race-hatred: 'Ever since that evil day, when Moslems first landed in Hindustan, right up to the present moment, the Hindu Nation has been gallantly fighting on to shake off the despoilers. The Race Spirit has been awakening'.[24] The association of Hindutva with an explicitly anti-Muslim agenda can be traced to its unambiguous avowal by Golwalkar. But 'race', fashionable though the term was when Golwakar wrote in the 1930s, especially in the context of Nazi ideology, was not an entirely accurate word for what he meant, not least since many, indeed most, of India's Muslims were descended from Hindu ancestors themselves and therefore were of the same race or ethnicity as the Hindus for whom Golwalkar was speaking.

According to the proponents of Hindutva, despite that common descent, Muslims had cut themselves off from Hindu culture: they prayed in Arabic, rather than the Sanskrit born on Indian soil, turned to a foreign city (Mecca) as their holiest of holies, and owed allegiance to a holy book, and beliefs spawned by it, that had no roots in the sacred land of India. Naipaul echoes this thought in his *Among the Believers*: 'It turns out now that the Arabs were the most successful imperialists of all time; since to be conquered by them (and then to be like them) is still, in the minds of the faithful, to be saved.'[25]

Golwalkar's answer was to seek the assimilation of Muslims and other minorities into the Hindu nationalist mainstream by forcing them to abandon these external allegiances (rather as the Jews were forced to adopt outward signs of adherence to Christianity during the Spanish Inquisition four and a half centuries earlier). The German notion of a volksgeist, a 'race spirit' to which everyone would have to conform, appealed strongly to Golwalkar. To remain in India, Muslims would have to submit themselves to Hindus. Recalling the parable of Muhammad going to the mountain, Golwalkar wrote: 'In the Indian situation, the Hindu is the mountain, and the Muslim population, Mohammed. I need not elaborate.'[26] A few paragraphs earlier I have quoted his approving words about Nazi theories of race. There is more in his writing that is even more chilling.

Golwalkar's hatred for non-Hindus was especially virulent when it came to Muslims and Christians; he regarded Parsis and Jews in India as model minorities who knew their place and did not ruffle any Hindu feathers. In his pungent view: '[H]ere was already a full-fledged ancient nation of the Hindus and the various communities which were living in the country were here either as guests, the Jews and Parsis, or as invaders, the Muslims and Christians.'[27] He added: 'They never faced the question how all such heterogenous groups could be called as children of the soil merely because, by an accident, they happened to reside in a common territory under the rule of a common enemy.'

Golwalkar strongly opposed all talk of a secular Indian state. As he wrote in *We, or Our Nationhood Defined*:

'There are only two courses open to these foreign elements', Golwalkar went on, 'either to merge themselves in the national race and adopt its culture or to live at its mercy so long as the national race may allow them to do so and quit the country at the sweet will of the national race. That is the only sound view on the minorities' problem... [The] foreign races in Hindusthan must either adopt the Hindu culture and language, must learn to respect and hold in reverence Hindu religion, must entertain no idea but those of the glorification of the Hindu race and culture, i.e., of the Hindu nation and must lose their separate existence to merge in the Hindu race, or may stay in the country, wholly subordinated to the Hindu Nation, claiming nothing, deserving no privileges, far less any preferential treatment—not even citizen's rights.'[28]

Golwalkar acknowledged the reality of diversity within Hinduism, but argued that Hindus shared 'the same philosophy of life', 'the same goal' and 'the same holy samskaras',[29] which therefore formed a strong cultural and a civilisational basis for a nation. These values, aspirations and philosophy were not, however, in his view, shared by Muslims and Christians. Though the proponents of Hindutva would not welcome the comparison, Golwalkar's conception of Hindu India is not so very different from the prevailing ideology of a Muslim Pakistan.

While Hindutva has tended to reserve most of its virulence for Muslims, Golwalkar was openly suspicious of Christians too. In *Bunch of Thoughts* he describes how, though the Christians seemed 'quite harmless'[30] at a glance, with their missions, schools, and colleges, they were part of something more sinister. 'So long as the Christians here indulge in such activities and consider themselves as agents of the international movement for the spread of Christianity and refuse to offer their first loyalty to the land of their birth and behave as true children of the heritage and culture of their ancestors, they will remain here as hostiles and will have to be treated as such.'[31]

On the issue of these minorities, *Bunch of Thoughts* goes further than his earlier writings:

> 'We, in the Sangh, are Hindus to the core. That's why we have respect for all faiths and religious beliefs.... But the question before us now is, what is the attitude of those people who have been converted to Islam or Christianity? They are born in this land, no doubt. But are they true to its salt? Are they grateful towards this land which has brought them up? Do they feel that they are the children of this land and its tradition and that to serve it is their great good fortune? Do they feel it a duty to serve her? No! Together with the change in their faith, gone are the spirit of love and devotion for the nation.'[32]

These are sweeping generalisations that admit of no exception in Golwalkar's thinking:

> 'Whatever we believed in, the Muslim was wholly hostile to it. If we worship in the temple, he would desecrate it. If we carry on bhajans and car festivals, that would irritate him. If we worship [the] cow, he would like to eat it. If we glorify woman as a symbol of sacred motherhood, he would like to molest her.'

In a December 1947 speech, four months after Partition, Golwalkar, referring to Muslims, said that 'no power on earth' could keep Muslims in Hindustan. 'They should have to quit this country... If they were made to stay here the responsibility would be the Government's and the Hindu community would not be responsible. Mahatma Gandhi could not mislead them any longer. We have the means whereby [our] opponents could be immediately silenced'.[33]

Golwakar's alternative answer to this problem lay in reconversion. 'It is our duty,' Golwalkar offers, 'to call these our forlorn brothers, suffering under religious slavery for centuries, back to their ancestral home. As honest freedom-loving men, let them overthrow all signs of slavery and domination and follow the ancestral ways of devotion and national life'.[34] As Manu S. Pillai acidly observes, 'In other words, there is nothing a quiet *ghar wapsi* [reconversion to Hinduism] cannot solve when it comes to the building of a good dharmocracy.'[35]

The RSS's official understanding of Hindutva embraces this idea of Golwalkar's even today. In their reply to the tribunal constituted under the Unlawful Activities (Prevention) Act 1967 to hear a case on the RSS in 1993, the RSS made an official statement as follows:

> The term Hindu in the conviction as well as in the constitution of the RSS is a cultural and civilisational concept and not a political or religious term. The term as a cultural concept will include and did always include all including Sikhs, Buddhists, and Jains. The cultural nationality of India, in the conviction of the RSS, is Hindu and it was inclusive of all who are born and who have adopted Bharat as their Motherland, including Muslims, Christians and Parsis. The answer-

ing association submit that it is not just a matter of RSS conviction, but a fact borne out by history that the Muslims, Christians and Parsis too are Hindus by culture although as [adherents of different] religions they are not so.[36]

This statement, of course, elides the 'holy land' problem in Savarkar's famous tripartite formula: if you are a Muslim, Christian or Parsi, however 'Hindu' you may be culturally, India is not your holy land. Hindutva acolytes gloss over this contradiction by suggesting that the key lies in these minorities acknowledging their foundational Hindu-ness: if they see themselves as 'Muhammadan Hindus', 'Christian Hindus' and 'Parsi Hindus', India can accept them. Since few, if any, of the believers in those faiths are ready to see themselves in those terms, of course, it is logical to assume they remain unwelcome in Hindutva-led India.

It is striking how Hindutva's acolytes share so much formally with twentieth-century Muslim modernists in South Asia and the Middle East: their conception of the glorious past, their imagining of a fallen intermediary time (blamed on internal cultural failings and rapacious outsiders), their stilted conception of culture and cultural difference, their negative appraisal of 'Western' values and 'Westernisation', and their fervent desire for the political unity of a religious community as the essential requirement for the attainment or re-establishment of national glory. Golwalkar's views of nationalism continue to inspire his political followers nearly half a century after his death—except that, unlike when he expressed them, those who believe such things now hold power in India and are in a position to do something about them.

THE ADVENT OF THE BHARATIYA JANA SANGH
AND DEEN DAYAL UPADHYAYA

It took a while to happen. While Savarkar and Golwalkar had attracted a lot of attention with their ideas in the 1920s and 1930s, the only political party willing to take them seriously was the Akhil Bharatiya Hindu Mahasabha, a fringe movement of which Savarkar became president in 1937. The Hindu Mahasabha fancied itself as a sort of Hindu answer to the Muslim League, but never enjoyed even a fraction of its support; indeed, the overwhelming majority of Hindu voters backed the secular Indian National Congress Party, rather than the party that claimed to be acting in the name of India's Hindus. The Mahasabha, however, openly advocated both 'Hindutva' and 'Hindu Rashtra', even as the Muslim League's call for Partition was tearing the country apart on communal lines. The Mahasabha's best-known leader, Syama Prasad Mookerjee, its president in 1944, was conscious of the limitations of Hindu nationalism as a political platform in such circumstances, and called for the membership of Hindu Mahasabha to be thrown open to all communities. Not surprisingly—since this would have vitiated the communal logic of the Mahasabha itself—his own members spurned his call, prompting Mookerjee to resign and to form a new political party in collaboration with the RSS. This was the Bharatiya Jana Sangh.

Mookerjee's choice of name for his new party was instructive. 'Bharatiya' literally meant 'Indian', 'Jana' the people, and 'Sangh,' in a genuflection to the RSS, which liked to refer to itself as 'the Sangh', stood for 'organisation'. Thus the Bharatiya Jana Sangh was the Indian People's Organisation. The Jana Sangh was openly viewed as a political emanation of the RSS, which had been banned after Mahatma Gandhi's assassination in 1948 and only allowed to resume functioning as a purely social and cultural, rather than political, association. The RSS could continue to advocate Hindu Samaj (Hindu society) but not a Hindu Rashtra—that would be a political objective which only a political party could pursue. And so a political party was born. The Bharatiya Jana Sangh was linked to the RSS, it was said, by an umbilical cord; its establishment of the Bharatiya Jana Sangh gave the RSS a political arm that would pursue Hindu interests within a national, as opposed to communal, framework. Hence 'Bharatiya' rather than 'Hindu'—but since Mookerjee subscribed to the Savarkar idea that all Indians, strictly speaking, were Hindus, there was no great contradiction there. To Mookerjee and his followers, Hinduism was a national identity rather than a communal one and the Bharatiya Jana Sangh in effect claimed the national mantle for its Hindutva agenda.

In the two and a half decades of its existence, the Bharatiya Jana Sangh impressed itself upon the nation's consciousness as a well-organised and effective opposition party with some able leaders, but it never came remotely close to power. Its best electoral performance was in 1967, when it won 35 seats in a right-of-centre 'Grand Alliance' with the liberal, pro-free enterprise Swatantra Party, which claimed 44—a total dwarfed by the 283 of the ruling Congress Party. This was the time when the concept of Hindutva received its fullest flowering under the leadership of party president Deen Dayal Upadhyaya, whose ideas, in particular his philosophy of Integral Humanism, I discuss below in some detail.

* * *

Pandit Deen Dayal Upadhyaya is undoubtedly the most significant ideologue of the contemporary Hindutva movement. Despite having served only one year (1967–1968) as president of the Bharatiya Jana Sangh, the precursor party of today's ruling BJP, before his life was prematurely cut short, Pandit Deen Dayal Upadhyaya (1916–1968) is enjoying something of a renaissance these days. The Narendra Modi government ruling India since 2014 swears by his life and work, and there has been a proliferation of seminars and conferences discussing and dissecting his philosophy of Integral Humanism. Numerous institutions have been named after him, from the Pandit Deendayal Upadhyaya Shekhawati University in Sikar (Rajasthan) to the Deen Dayal Upadhyaya Hospital, Delhi and the Pandit Deendayal Petroleum University, Gandhinagar, Gujarat. Millions of pounds of government funds have been spent on various schemes (*yojanas*) to perpetuate his name.[37] There are medical colleges, hospitals, parks and a flyover (in Bengaluru) that bear his name, not to mention the Pt. Deen Dayal Upadhyaya National Academy of Social Security, Janakpuri, Delhi. The Antyodaya scheme of service to the poorest of the poor is said by the government to have been inspired by him. The 'Make in India' scheme is dedicated to him, or more precisely, 'laid at his feet'.[38] The Mughalserai railway station, where he died in mysterious circumstances at the age of fifty-two, has been renamed for him. The Deen Dayal

Research Institute is reportedly 'a hub of frenetic activity', drowning under a 'flood of queries from government departments' trying to learn about Upadhyaya's ideas, which are now expected to animate their work.[39]

Upadhyaya's writings and speeches on the principles and policies of the Bharatiya Jana Sangh, his philosophy of 'Integral Humanism' and his vision for the rise of modern India, constitute the most comprehensive articulation of what might be described as a BJP ideology. The reverence in which he is held by those in power today and the near-deification of the man give him an intellectual status within the Hindutva movement second to none.

Upadhyaya saw his own thinking as flowing from that of Guru Golwalkar, the Sarsanghchalak of the RSS with whom he worked most closely. Golwalkar, in turn, was inspired by Vinayak ('Veer') Savarkar's ideology of Hindutva. But whereas Golwalkar, with his desire to learn from Nazi practices, was judged too extreme for most mainstream opinion, Upadhyaya, who couched his ideas in moderate language, enjoyed broader acceptability. Unlike many ideologues, Pandit Deen Dayal Upadhyaya was not just a theorist, but the leader of a growing political party and also its principal organiser. This created a curious paradox. As a political leader, it was imperative for him to respond to the day-to-day problems facing the party, critique government policies, issue and direct party propaganda, lead agitations, evolve the party's electoral strategy and negotiate coalitions. His philosophy was thus the animating spirit of a life of practical action. Upadhyaya's political role and values thus emerged from his philosophy, and the latter justified the former.

At the same time, the Jana Sangh of Upadhyaya's day was not a realistic contender for power. Upadhyaya thus saw himself in the longer term as a thinker whose role was, as one admirer put it, to project genuine nationalistic thought in the political sphere, well beyond the limited and short-term aim of the attainment of political office. One might even argue that had the prospects of power been more imminent, the president of the party might have spent his energies on more immediately attainable objectives, rather than abstract philosophical reflections divorced from his day-to-day tasks. It is possible to argue that the philosophy of Upadhyaya is the credo of man who does not believe he can ever have an opportunity to implement it.

But such a situation is in many ways preferable, because it means that the philosopher in question is not tailoring his thoughts to the expediencies of the political moment. In keeping with his circumstances, Deen Dayal Upadhyaya could afford the luxury—unavailable, say, to any of his counterparts in the ruling party—to develop his theoretical ideas in their pure and unalloyed form. Thus it is said by his admirers that Upadhyaya saw his political party as merely a vehicle to build a nation. Much of his philosophical thinking, therefore, focused on what constituted the Indian nation, and why, in his view, it had failed to become strong and unified. Upadhyaya saw this failure in moral terms—political corruption, the general public's lack of any urge to make India strong and prosperous, a 'degeneration' of society and the fading away of the idealism that had inspired the struggle for freedom. Indians had misled themselves into equating freedom with the mere overthrow of foreign rule; this negative view overlooked the need for something far more positive, a genuine and patriotic love for the motherland.

Like Savarkar and Golwalkar, Upadhyaya too deplored the concept of territorial nationalism, which saw the Indian nation as being formed of all the peoples who reside in this land. In his view reducing the idea of India to a territory and to everyone living in that space elided fundamental questions that needed to be answered:

> Whose nation is this? What is freedom for?
> What kind of life do we want to develop here?
> What set of values are we going to accept?
> What does the concept of nationhood really signify?

What does the concept of nationhood really signify? A territory and its inhabitants, as Westernised Indians seemed to believe, would embrace Hindus, Muslims, Christians and others under a common nationhood to resist British rule. This was a fallacy, according to Upadhyaya. 'A nation is not a mere geographical unit. The primary need of nationalism is the feeling of boundless dedication in the hearts of the people for their land. Our feeling for the motherland has a basis: our long, continuous habitation in the same land creates, by association, a sense of "my-ness".'[40]

The disappearance of the foreign power, Upadhyaya believed, had left a vacuum before a people accustomed to the 'negative patriotism' of anti-colonialism. Nationalism had to consist of far more than the mere rejection of foreign rule. Upadhyaya spurned the Western idea that nationalism as a political force was a product of the French Revolution and the situation created by it; he abjured the notion that a nation is made up of various constituent elements that can be itemised, such as a common race, religion, land, traditions, shared experience of calamities, means of transport, common political administration and so on. Such ideas, he believed, missed the essential ethos of nationalism—love for the motherland.

Since love for the motherland had never been inculcated in its inhabitants, their lives in independent India were now centred on money and greed—*artha* and *kama* in the classic quartet of human aspirations enumerated in the *Purusharthas*, at the expense of *dharma* and *moksha*. This modern materialism Upadhyaya saw as a major societal flaw. As he wrote in his book, *Rashtra Jeevan Ki Disha*:[41]

> All our ailments in today's political life have their origin in our avarice. A race for rights has banished the noble idea of service. Undue emphasis on the economic aspect of life has generated a number of lapses... Instead of character, quality and merit, wealth has become the measuring rod of individual prestige. This is a morbid situation... It must be our general approach to look upon money only as a means towards the satisfaction of our everyday needs: not an end in itself...this transformation in our attitude can be brought about only on the basis of the ideals of Indian culture.[42]

Dazzled by the material advances made by the so-called developed countries, Upadhyaya argued, India too had taken to aping the foreigners under the rubric of 'Five-Year Plans' and development projects. India had written a Constitution imitative of the West, divorced from any real connection to our mode of life and from authentically Indian ideas about the relationship between the individual and society. (In this he was echoing Golwalkar, who had lamented that our 'cumbersome' Constitution[43] was all the more deficient for incorporating 'absolutely nothing' from the *Manusmriti*). Upadhyaya thus felt the need for a Hindu political philosophy befitting an ancient nation like Bharat. This would have to be based on a positive concept of patriotism and a comprehensive vision of the nation as a complete entity—its security, its unity, its growth and development, the welfare of its entire populace and the full development of every individual—based on its inherent character, culture, spiritual underpinnings and permanent values that have, as he saw them, stood the test of time.

For Upadhyaya, India had a special personality distinct from that of other nations; it had an ethos of its own. Only a national philosophy that reflected this could be successful; only an authentic Indian approach would ensure happiness for Indians. Upadhyaya was convinced that independent India could not rely upon Western concepts like individualism, democracy, socialism, communism or capitalism; it had to reject these formulae and find its own approach. Unfortunately, in his view, India's polity after Independence had been built upon these superficial and feeble Western foundations rather than authentic Hindu ones.

To Upadhyaya, Western thought was predicated on ideas of conflict: it presumed a conflict between individual and society, between ruler and ruled, between the power of clergy and temporal power, between haves and have-nots. Indian thinking, on the other hand, laid emphasis on cooperation and synthesis, not conflict. But Upadhyaya went further in his exegesis. To the Western mind, he argued, the main theme of this conflict was over rights: rights of the individual and the groups he represented. This was where Hinduism was different. To Upadhyaya, the Bharatiya ethos emphasised duties, not rights; it required coordination and understanding, not conflict and hatred. All India needed to do, Upadhyaya averred, was to 'turn the searchlight inwards' and base its thinking on 'self-revelation', just as the Hindu seeker looked within himself for self-realisation. India's polity had to be anchored in the traditions and ethos of India's own ancient Hindu culture.

As we have seen, Upadhyaya was clear that reducing the Indian national idea to a territory and the people on it was fallacious. It was this sort of thinking, he argued sternly, that had led the nationalist movement, from the Khilafat agitation onwards, to turn towards a policy of appeasement of the Muslim community, a policy in turn sought to be justified by the need to forge a united front against the British. The RSS's founder leader, Dr K. A. Hedgewar (whose Marathi biography Upadhyaya translated) had pointed to the 'ideological confusion' this approach created. Muslim communalism, in his and Upadhyaya's view, had become more prominent and aggressive, while Congress leaders bent over backwards more and more to accommodate them.

The Partition of 1947 was undoubtedly a defeat for those who had wanted to preserve a united India, but it was not a failure of India's unity as much as it was the defeat of misconceived utopian efforts to embrace non-Hindus made in the name of national unity. It was not that our objective was wrong, in Upadhyaya's view; rather the methods to preserve India's unity through minority appeasement were wrong and so we were defeated.

'Every nation,' Upadhyaya said, 'wants to live a happy and prosperous life according to its own nature and that is the motive behind its intense desire for freedom. The nation that tries to follow a path of thought and action discordant with its own nature, meets with disaster. This is why our nation has been caught up in a whirlpool of difficulties.' India could and should contribute to the world 'in consonance with our culture and traditions.'[44]

That culture was, of course, Hindu. In India, 'there exists only one culture... There are no separate cultures here for Muslims and Christians.' Every community, therefore, including Muslims and Christians, 'must identify themselves with the age-long national cultural stream that was Hindu culture in this country.' His logic was that 'unless all people become part of the same cultural stream, national unity or integration is impossible. If we want to preserve Indian nationalism, this is the only way.' To him, 'the national cultural stream would continue to remain one and those who cannot identify themselves with it would not be considered nationals.'

To Upadhyaya, the national culture to which he was referring had to be Hindu; it explicitly could not be Muslim. 'Mecca, Medina, Hassan and Hussain, Sohrab and Rustom and Bulbul may be very significant in their own ways but they do not form a part of Indian national life and stream of Indian culture. How can those who are emotionally associated with these and look upon [the] Rama and Krishna tradition as alien be described as nationals? We see that the moment anybody embraces Islam, an effort is made to cut him off from the entire tradition of this country and connect him to the alien tradition.'[45]

Muslims, said Upadhyaya, even related differently to India's past: 'Some events involve triumph, some our humiliation. The memories of our glorious deeds make us proud; ignominies make us hang our heads in shame.'[46] But Hindus saw such historical events differently from Muslims.

> 'Aggressions by Mohammed Ghori or Mahmood Ghazni naturally fill us with agony. We develop a feeling of attachment to Prithviraj and other patriots. If instead, any person feels pride for the aggressors and no love for the Motherland, he can lay no claim to patriotism. The memory of Rana Pratap, Chhatrapati Shivaji or Guru Gobind Singh makes us bow down our heads with respect and devotion. On the other hand, the names of Aurangzeb, Alauddin, Clive or Dalhousie, fill us with anger that is natural towards foreign aggressors.'[47]

Only Hindu society, Upadhyaya underscored, felt this way about its heroes, supporting Rana Pratap over Akbar; therefore there was really no ground for doubt that Indian nationalism is Hindu nationalism.

Upadhyaya's conclusion was blunt: Muslims sought 'to destroy the values of Indian culture, its ideals, national heroes, traditions, places of devotion and worship', and therefore 'can never become an indivisible part of this country.' In Upadhayaya's vision, the inherent consciousness of unity, identical ties of history and tradition, relations of affinity between the land and the people and shared aspirations and hopes, made Hindustan a nation of Hindus. 'We shall have to concede that our nationality is none other than Hindu nationality. If any outsider comes into this country he shall have to move in step and adjust himself with Hindu nationality.'

But Upadhyaya did not adopt his mentor Golwalkar's ideas about dealing with India's Muslims as Hitler had dealt with the Jews. 'No sensible man will say that six crores of Muslims should be eradicated or thrown out of India,' he admitted in an article titled 'Akhand Bharat: Objectives and Means'.[48] '[B]ut then they will have to identify themselves completely with Indian life.' Muslims had to be accommodated within the Indian reality, but on what basis? 'This unity...can be established only among homogeneous cultures, not among the contrary ones. A preparation of various cereals and pulses mixed together can be prepared: but if sand particles find their way into it, the whole food is spoilt', he explained.[49] The way to eliminate these 'sand particles' was to 'purify' or 'nationalise Muslims'—to 'make Muslims proper Indians'. The Congress had wrongly tried to forge Hindu-Muslim unity against the British, but 'unless all people become part of the same cultural stream, national unity or integration is impossible... A situation will have to be created in which political aspirations of Islam in India will be rooted out. Then and then alone can a longing for cultural unity take root.'[50]

In demanding of Muslims and other minorities this subordination to, and total identification with, a Hindu Rashtra, Upadhyaya—while his reasons differed in both premise and approach—arrived at the same place as Savarkar and Golwalkar. But Upadhyaya went a few steps beyond them in developing more fully the concept of what a Hindu Rashtra might consist of.

In building his case for a Hindu Rashtra, Upadhyaya specifically disavowed the existing Constitution of India (which makes all the more curious the enthusiastic zeal with which his devotees today, from Prime Minister Modi on down, swear by it and celebrate every milestone in its adoption). As Upadhyaya put it in *Rashtra Jeevan Ki Disha*: 'We became free in 1947. The English quit India. We felt what was considered to be the greatest obstacle in the path of our effort of nation building was removed and were all of a sudden faced with the problem as to what the significance of this hard-earned independence was.'

Indian leaders tried to resolve this problem in the drafting of a Constitution. But in Upadhyaya's view, their failure to conceive properly of the nation led them into error. 'We aped the foreigners to such an extent that we failed to see that our inherent national ideals and traditions should be reflected in our Constitution. We satisfied ourselves with making a patchwork of theories and principles enunciated by foreign countries... The result was that our national culture and traditions were never reflected in these ideologies borrowed from elsewhere and so they utterly failed to touch the chords of our national being.'

Having rejected its premise, Upadhyaya was scathing about the Constitution's drafting and adoption: a nation, he argued, 'is not like a club which can be started or dissolved. A nation is not created by some crores of people passing a resolution and defining a common code of behaviour binding on all its members. A certain mass of people emerges with an inherent motivation. It is,' he added, using a Hindu analogy, 'like the soul adopting the medium of the body.'[51]

In the classic Hindu formula, a king must function according to his *raj dharma*, or code of governance, which is not defined by him, but is laid down for him by selfless unattached *rishis*. In contemporary language, Upadhyaya saw a Hindu king almost as one might a chief executive receiving his authority from the shareholders (in this case, the people), mediated through the vision of the board (in this case, the wisdom of the sages). Observing that the Constitution requires that any person holding a position of power has to take a pledge of loyalty to that Constitution, Upadhyaya asks three questions: were the people who framed the Constitution endowed with qualities of selflessness, an intense desire for public service and a deep knowledge of the rules of *dharma* as the rishis were? Or did they formulate this *Smriti* of a free India under the influence of the unsteady circumstances prevailing at the time? Did these people possess originality of thought or did they have a tendency to primarily imitate others?

Upadhyaya's implicit answers to these questions were in the negative: the Constitution-makers were not figures imbued with selflessness and *dharma*, they were overly in thrall to the turbulent politics of that era, and their minds had been colonised by Western ideas. The founding fathers of the Republic of India were largely Anglophile Indians schooled in Western systems of thought; their work revealed no Indianness, no *Bharatiyata*. The Constitution, therefore, was to him a flawed document, one incapable of guiding India towards the path of *raj dharma*. In fact it condemned Hindus to slavery: 'Self-rule and independence are considered to be synonyms. A deeper thinking will bring home to us the fact that even in a free country, the nation can remain in slavery.' The Hindu nation had been enslaved by inappropriate Westernisation.

Even the language in which the Constitution had been drafted betrayed this reality: 'If the original draft of the Constitution had been in Hindi or in any other Indian language', he felt, the 'un-Indian element' would not have been as dominant. But his concerns, of course, went well beyond language. The Constitution's core conception of the nation, in his view, was fundamentally not Indian at all: 'in the constitution, as it is now, it is the sentiments of the English that have found better expression than those of the Indians,' observed Upadhyaya. 'Thus, our constitution, like an English child born in India, has become Anglo-Indian in character, instead of purely Indian.'[52]

Upadhyaya thus questioned the very legitimacy of the Constitution and not just the process by which it was created. For Upadhyaya, the absence of the Hindu Rashtra idea in the Constitution was unacceptable. For him *dharma* had to be the central idea behind governance and nation-building. He categorically repudiated the secularists' view that *dharma* is an entirely personal matter, that it had nothing to do with society or nation. On the contrary, Upadhyaya argued that there is undoubtedly a supreme purpose to life, which transcended all differences and peculiarities of caste, sect, or language. This purpose is not a worldly one—it does not consist of seeking to erect a huge political empire or to dominate the world militarily. Indeed, militarism and temporal power, Upadhyaya wrote, were not a Hindu preoccupation. Hindus had never shed the blood of other peoples or perpetrated atrocities on other countries as Alexander, Genghis Khan, Mahmud of Ghazni—non-Hindu conquerors all—had done. Hindus had, instead, always given a warm welcome and shelter to refugee groups like the

Parsis and the Jews, who had become the victims of aggression and atrocities elsewhere and had fled to India.

In keeping with his distaste for foreign concepts and terms, Upadhyaya explicated his beliefs through the use of Sanskrit terms to which he ascribed specific contemporary meanings. A favourite word of Upadhyaya's is '*chiti*', which he labels the 'soul power' of a nation. He describes this soul power through a homely analogy: a barber told his customer that his razor was sixty years old, and had been used by his father. Upon further scrutiny, the customer noticed that over the years the handle and blade had been replaced many times, but the barber still claimed that the razor was the same as used by his father. It was a point of pride and prestige for him: the essence of the razor was unchanged even if its physical trappings had been altered over the years. Every nation also had such an identity that did not change with circumstances and temporal alterations. Sadly, modern India—the democratic republic that had emerged under the Constitution—had no sense of its *chiti*.

One example of this was in the country's constitutional structure. Upadhyaya saw the seeds of division, for instance, even in the Constitution's decision to rename the provinces as 'states' as the Americans did; this reduced India to a federation of states, a dangerously divisive concept in his view. Upadhyaya acknowledged that, unlike the United States, every Indian state did not have its own constitution and that there was only one citizenship for the entire country, but he felt the formulation envisaged in the Constitution diluted the sacred idea of a unified Bharatvarsha (Indian sub-continent). The Constitution should have spoken of a unitary state rather than a union of states; the soul of Bharat was missing. He seemed unconscious of the argument that it was precisely because of these states and their linguistic basis that unity was achieved, for India was able to accommodate all its diversities and give them political expression without losing the bigger cause of united nationhood. Surely this was a way of preserving, not diluting, Bharat's *chiti*? Accompanying *chiti* is another force that Upadhyaya called '*virat shakti*', literally immense strength or power, but more precisely 'a scientific term,' in his words, 'with a definite connotation. So long as the *chiti* is throbbing and pure, the Nation continues to prosper.' It is the spirit of *chiti* that creates *virat shakti*, the organised and unified fighting strength that protects the nation from aggression and dissension. While *chiti* is the soul of a nation, *virat shakti* is its life force. Of course, neither idea is even implicitly present in India's Constitution, underscoring, for Upadhyaya, its deeply flawed nature.

Upadhyaya worried that India's constitutional system had been created in negation of its true inherent national spirit and that if the modern Indian nation continued in this way, Hindu civilisation would perish. This is what had happened, after all, to Greece and Egypt, whose modern incarnations bore no relationship to the ancient civilisations from which they claimed descent. The same stock of people might be living in those countries, but they bore no resemblance to their glorious past civilisations or forebears. Indeed, the essence of their society, its identity, had changed. This was the fate that Upadhyaya feared would befall India if it continued down the secular Westernised path charted for it in its Constitution: it would lose its core identity (which lay in the form of its *chiti*) and in effect become something other than the continuing Bharatiya civilisation that could trace its origins back to the mists of time.

Deen Dayal Upadhyaya, contra Savarkar and Golwalkar, accepted that the India of which he was writing had to accommodate its Muslims and Christians too. He rejected the notion that the Hindu Rashtra would have to mean 'a theocratic State propagating the Hindu religion'. Upadhyaya was conscious that his critics associated the very establishment of such a Hindu state with a revival of the ritualism associated with the Hindu religion, notions of casteism and inflexible social hierarchy, and the return of discrimination and social inequality. No, he insisted: his Hindu Rashtra was not based on hatred against any community, nor was it reactionary. Rather, his Hinduism would be inclusive.

As a Hindu, Upadhyaya averred that he was not opposed to the Muslim and Christian modes of worship; indeed he never criticised the Prophets of either faith. He believed that how to worship God, and which God to worship, was each person's personal choice; the state had no role in such considerations. His quarrel, he explained, was not with any sect or mode of worship: it was purely political.

Upadhyaya said that he respected other religions, while arguing that the problem of Muslims and Christians was not religious. Gandhiji had tried religious syncretism, singing bhajans to the effect that Ishwar and Allah were the same, but political unity between the two communities had not followed. The issue therefore was one of political commitment to the country and its values, not with the practice of religious faith or with the goodness of any individual.

Every society, after all, has good and bad people. Upadhyaya reminded his listeners that Muslim generals had fought in the armies of Shivaji and the Peshwas. He had high praise for Muslim patriots among his contemporaries, singling out as examples Mohammed Currim Chagla, the highly cosmopolitan, secular jurist and diplomat, Hamid Dalwai, a crusader for reform within the Muslim community and the revolutionary Ashfaqulla Khan. But these men, Upadhyaya said, were individuals; their personal behaviour did not warrant any conclusions about the mind and attitudes of the Muslim masses. If all the people in the Muslim community were like Chagla, Upadhyaya once opined, then 'there would be no problem whatsoever'. But they were not, and quoting a few rare examples of good persons would not solve the problem.

This distinction between 'a few good Muslims' and a problematic 'Muslim community' was central to Upadhyaya's misconception of Muslims in India. He assumed a monolithic 'Muslim community' when in fact Muslim practices across the country were also hugely diverse and a pan-Indian Muslim identity of the kind he suggests did not exist. Still, in making these points, however tokenistically, Upadhyaya was undoubtedly going beyond the exclusively Hindu Rashtra advocated by the earlier Hindutva ideologues. He was willing to acknowledge that 'the inhabitants of this country included Hindus, Muslims, Christians, Parsis and others'. But he saw communal unrest in terms of the aspirations of various communities to establish their political domination in particular geographical areas, just as Jinnah had led the Muslims to the creation of a separate state hostile to India and venomous in its denial of India's historical nationalism. To fulfil these aspirations, Upadhyaya argued, each community sought an increase in its numerical strength to strengthen its hands. This is why these communities behaved as they did—Muslims rejected family planning and monogamy, while Christians, supported by foreign agencies and news media, carried on systematic conversion campaigns. Christian missionaries had undoubtedly, Upadhyaya wrote, made a determined effort, under the patronage of the British imperialist government, to wean away Hindus from their traditional culture, but their attempts at conversion were not as fanatical or violent as those of the Muslims. Still, such practices had to stop.

These problems could be contained if a Hindu Rashtra were established.

The critics of Hindu Rashtra, Upadhyaya argued, found that the term was inexpedient for them in the country's competitive politics: they were afraid of losing millions of Christian and Muslim voters. Their misconception was that the use of the term 'Hindu Rashtra' excluded Muslim and Christian communities. If both these communities became one with the national cultural mainstream—without any change in their modes of worship—they would be welcome in the new India. All they had to do was to own up to the ancient traditions of India, to look upon Hindu national heroes as their national heroes, and to develop devotion for Bharat Mata. Then they would be fully accepted as nationals of the Hindu Rashtra.

In affirming this view of India's political identity, Upadhyaya was in effect returning to the Savarkar-Golwalkar home base: his political inclusiveness was illusory, for the terms in which it was formulated, despite the seeming openness to other forms of religious worship, left no room for anything but submission to Hindu dominance. However, to be fair, in other aspects of his political philosophy, especially in relation to the economic needs of the underclasses, Upadhyaya demonstrated a more substantive inclusiveness.

Rather like Gandhi, Upadhyaya believed in *swaraj* ('self-governance'), visualising for India a decentralised polity and self-reliant economy centered on its villages. But there was a more profound consequence of this approach. He eschewed the label of socialism, but expelled seven of the nine MLAs his Jan Sangh party had in Rajasthan for opposing the Zamindari (big landowner) Abolition Act piloted by the Congress to cut large landholdings down to size in the name of socialism. Individual freedom in a democratic system, he argued, enabled the rich to monopolise production, gain economic power and influence government machinery. Upadhyaya deplored the fact that Indian villagers had lost their jobs to large factories. Socialism, he said, was an understandable response to the exploitation of the masses in the industrial age.

Still, he considered himself a political opponent of the socialists. Both socialism and capitalism, Upadhyaya argued, concentrated their attention on man's material aspirations and on the fulfilment of his gross desires. Both had implicit faith in modern science and techno-logical progress. To Upadhyaya, the nature of production had come to be determined not by the needs or the welfare of human beings but by the nature and demands of machines. He wanted modern technology to be adapted to suit Indian requirements. In a centralised system of production, whether capitalist or socialist, whether under individual or state control, man's individuality is lost and he becomes a mere cog in the machine. Instead of bringing about human development by striking a balance between the material and spiritual needs, both systems have only created conflict. The answer lay in focusing on the human person-ality as a whole, and in creating a system that balanced competition with cooperation and harmonised material progress with spiritual advancement. This Upadhyaya dubbed 'Integral Humanism' (in con-trast, it is suggested, with the former communist leader M. N. Roy's theory of 'Radical Humanism', but also, I imagine, borrowing from Sri Aurobindo's 'Integral Yoga').

The philosophy of Integral Humanism advocated the simultaneous and integrated functioning of the body, mind, intellect and soul of each human being. The philosophy of Integral Humanism was a syn-thesis of the material and the spiritual, the individual and the collec-tive. It answered what Upadhyaya saw as the urgent need in India for a 'fresh breeze'.

He adumbrated this philosophy to some 500 party workers in 1964, developed it into an expanded version at the Jana Sangh party's plenary session in 1965, and expounded it finally and fully in the form of four lectures in Bombay, titled 'Integral Humanism'. The impact was strong, and lasting: Upadhyaya's Integral Humanism was adopted by the Jana Sangh as its official doctrine and has subsequently been inherited by the BJP, whose leaders treat it with the reverence a Lutheran accords to those famous theses nailed to the cathedral door.

Upadhyaya believed that humanity, in all its infinite diversity, had a common ethos or soul, which the ancient Hindu texts defined as *atman*. The apparent diversity is superficial; the essential unity is profound. This is the idea of Ekatmata or the unifying soul that pervades the world.

Man is a conglomerate of body, mind, intellect and soul: all four had to develop and thrive for society to progress. While material development was necessary, spiritual development was also indispensable. This was why Bharatiya culture had placed four objectives, *Purusharthas*, before every individual, which each of us was to pursue. The fulfilment of these goals occurred in society, since Ekatmata ensured that individual and society are mutually complementary. The desire for the welfare of humanity comes from that consciousness of unity. When an individual acts in the awareness that he and society are one *atman*, his actions will be conducive to the common good.

Systems that regard an individual as self-centered are defective, he argued, because they fail to take this into account. The ideal man, to Upadhyaya, views life through the four *Purusharthas* and works for their fulfilment; if everyone did so, in keeping with Bharatiya Advaita philosophy, whereby the good of the individual would coincide with the good of society, internal contradictions to achieve these ideals would be replaced by cooperation and compatibility. (This conviction required a leap of faith: the idea that the individual pursuing *artha* (material prosperity), for instance, would always do so selflessly in ways that would serve society collectively, did not seem grounded in practical experience.) Upadhyaya dissected what he saw as the failings of other prevailing systems before affirming the integral humanism of Bharatiya culture, which provided a unified view of the universe. The balanced pursuit of the *Purusharthas* would ensure that happiness was pursued across all four—man would not just gratify his senses but also seek mental, intellectual and spiritual happiness. Upadhyaya laid the greatest emphasis on the happiness of the soul: all other kinds of happiness, he believed, are derived from union with the soul.

Thus Upadhyaya took a stern view of those who saw *artha* as an end in itself. An excessive attachment to affluence, he felt, reduces man to a Mammon-worshipper who loses all sense of duty to his society, country and *dharma*. Similarly *kama* cannot be reduced to carnal pleasures at the expense of other priorities. *Dharma* is key since it ensures the maintenance and development of the people in harmony with the progress of society. *Dharma* went beyond the literal concept of religion and was not merely for Hindus: indeed, all places of worship, whether temples, churches, or mosques, should instil in the populace the practice of *dharma*.

All four Purusharthas are co-dependent, and together form a path to *moksha*. If a man is properly assembled as a function of the four Purusharthas, so will society be successfully constructed. When an individual starts on the path of fulfilling his *Purusharthas*, he comes into contact with a larger group of people, develops the willingness to work for others, and experiences shared joy and mutual understanding. Families, communities and nations are born of this. But the excessive individual freedom of the capitalist West and the collectivisation of the communist East had eroded this consciousness, which was now under threat in India.

For Upadhyaya, the Western theory of the social contract had to be rejected, for society is not a club that individuals can seek membership in. 'Society,' Upadhyaya writes (in terms similar to his conception of a nation), 'is not a institution created by individuals coming together. A society is born.... [T]he relation of a society to its individuals is the same as that of an organism and its limbs, or that of a tree and its branches, leaves and flowers. The question of who is more important of the two, society or individual, is not worth considering.'[53] In Bharatiya culture, we can neither ignore the individual nor lose sight of society's interests.

Society is a living organism, and has its own mind, intellect, and soul. Thus, it must have its own *Purusharthas*. The Samashti Dharma (*dharma* of society) embraces all that helps sustain the individual and the society. When applied to Bharat, it involves guarding the bonds of affinity to the motherland—an amalgam of common history, culture, clothing, and creed. The Artha Purushartha of society should be against *prabhav*, social bifurcations through granting high social status to the rich, as well as against *abhav*, or dependence on other nations (thus self-reliance and egalitarianism are vital). The Kama Purushartha of society embodies the nation's desires, such as the restoration of an undivided Bharat, or the expulsion of China from Indian territory, and the protection and spread of Indian culture. The Moksha Purushartha of society would imply freedom from foreign domination, through cultural, economic and political freedom. This would make India a well-organised, powerful, and wealthy Hindu nation, based on Hindu values of non-violence, literature, and culture.

The Purusharthas are not just objectives, but constitute bonds between the individual and society, which are connected by education, work, enjoyment and *yajna* or sacrifice. A man's *yajna* requires that the work should not be done for himself, but for society; thus a farmer grows corn not just for himself but for society, and work done with a sense of duty and sacrifice becomes beneficial to society.

Society has obligations to the individual too. If society fails to provide an individual with a good education, and he or she is unable to get an adequate job to sustain himself, society has failed him. However, if after receiving a good education, the individual does not work for society, he would have neglected Samashti Dharma, the *dharma* of society, and been morally degraded. Society and the individual are therefore complementary, and stand together by following *dharma*. When this does not happen and the underlying unity is lost, conflicts arise between privileged castes and Untouchables, industrialists and workers and so on.

The greatest blunder our politicians make, Upadhyaya argued, is their assumption of the existence of inherently and basically different classes—social, political, linguistic—with different interests. The truth is Bharat is one country; its subjects are one and have to live as one people. *Antodaya*, service of the poorest and least fortunate in society, was a Hindu obligation. Minority appeasement (and for that matter class distinctions) has no place in such a vision.

Nor did Upadhyaya shy away from facing the challenge of Varna Vyavastha, which he translates not as the caste system but as the class system. Upadhyaya opposed both those who believed that Varna Vyavastha is God-made—that people are born into castes on the basis of their past lives—and those who pretend to use ideological opposition to caste to garner political power. Upadhyaya asserted that Varna Vyavastha was introduced to fulfil the needs of society, by requiring each individual to do what he can do best. In the past, the valiant came forward for defence, the studious for advanced knowledge and to teach: there was no superiority and inferiority in the system, merely capability. Varna Vyavastha was based on the view that a society is an organic whole; its purpose was to bring physical and spiritual happiness within everybody's reach.

Upadhyaya's philosophy did not stop there, but extended from Samashti to Parameshthi (society to God). Bharatiya culture, after all, does not end with humanity, but includes all naturally occurring things in creation—flora, fauna, air, water, sunlight, animals, rivers, planets. The Bharatiya Advaita philosophy begins at the family, encompassing humanity, the animal world, plant life, the inanimate world, and stops at nothing short of the Universe. Thus the philosophy of Integral Humanism envisages, in the words of an admirer, 'an ennobling expanse of human consciousness'.

Unlike Western social and political theories, Upadhyaya stressed, Integral Humanism did not emerge as a reaction to any particular circumstance and was based on 'positive' thinking. 'If by nature man is such that he does not mind fighting with others to enrich himself at the cost of others, then it is impossible to teach him to love others and live for them'.[54] But, in the Indian context of Bharatiya Advaita, it was clear that Integral Humanism was the only way forward. Upadhyaya advocated national reconstruction on the basis of this philosophy. However, the duty of Indians was not only to protect their culture, but to make it dynamic and efficient. 'If we march ahead,' Upadhyaya concluded, 'we will be able to place before the world ideals like nationalism, democracy, equality and world-amity in a balanced and integral form, along with permanent values in Bharatiya culture.'

When Deen Dayal Upadhyaya was expounding his political philosophy, he could not have foreseen the day that a political party claiming
to be working in his name would govern with a crushing parliamentary
majority. To what extent can they be said to have put his beliefs into
practice?

The proliferation of Deen Dayal Upadhyaya institutions and schemes
is misleading. The prophet of the BJP has so far been honoured in lip-
service rather than literally.

In some senses, today's BJP leaders seem closer in spirit and conviction to the Hindu Rashtra of Savarkar and Golwalkar than to that of
Upadhyaya. Not for them the partial generosity of acknowledging the
place and role of the Muslims and Christians in the country; these are
less tolerant men and women (one of the latter, after all, a Minister in
the Modi government, divided the nation into Ramzaade, believers in
Rama, and Haramzaade, bastards).[55] Where Deen Dayal harked back to
ancient India's generosity in offering asylum to Parsis and Jews,[56]
today's BJP government announces its determination to expel
Rohingya Muslim asylum-seekers[57] because they happen to be Muslim,
and therefore ipso facto are assumed to constitute a threat to India's
security. Where Upadhyaya denounced materialism and embodied the
virtues of a simple village life, preached the abolition of large landholdings and spoke up for the humble peasant, his followers in power swear
by GDP growth and fiscal balance, subsidise the multi-billion pound
ventures of capitalist cronies, sport imported designer sunglasses,
wield Mont Blanc pens and wear the highest-quality tailored linens.
Their slogans are not about the poor in India's villages, nor about the
soul-force that animates this ancient civilisation, but about 'ease of
doing business' and 'start-up India'. Where Upadhyaya deplored materialism and extolled self-reliance, the men ruling in his name exalt
figures of GDP growth and clamour for Foreign Direct Investment; his
injunctions against an excessive attachment to affluence and *prabhav* (or
socio-economic distinctions) are ignored by rulers who crave the support of billionaires.

Upadhyaya believed that after Independence India lost its idealism,
because by failing to create a Hindu Rashtra, it never recognised one

grand uniting force to hold Indians together. It could be argued that for all its claims of supplying this force, Hindutva actually works by replacing hatred for the British with hatred for a minority—a formula that will result in division and destruction, not unity. I have often argued that we are all minorities in India, given our divisions of language, region, caste and cultural practices. Recognising and managing that diversity is a far better way of promoting unity than imposing one view on the rest—a method that will lead not back to a golden age but to certain disaster.

THE BJP AND HINDUTVA

Following Upadhyaya's death and its rout in the elections of 1971, the Bharatiya Jana Sangh merged in 1977 into the Janata Party, which was born from the resistance of all Opposition parties to Prime Minister Indira Gandhi's Emergency. But when the Janata Party won the national elections which followed, its internal contradictions soon surfaced. Foremost among these was the 'dual membership' issue, with many Janata Party members objecting to the continued involvement with the RSS of the former Bharatiya Jana Sangh politicians. The Janata Party split over RSS influence on its Sanghi elements, and the Bharatiya Jana Sangh members reconstituted themselves as the Bharatiya Janata Party (BJP) in 1980, vowing allegiance to 'Gandhian socialism' in an attempt to make themselves more appealing to the mainstream.

The experiment with moderate political messaging failed: the BJP won just two seats in India's 545-member Lok Sabha in 1984. Disillusioned with this unsuccessful attempt at seeking political respectability by tempering its core beliefs, the BJP remade itself into an explicitly Hindu party, stirring up Hindu sentiment.

The 1980s were a time of great ferment in Indian politics, with the Sikh separatist Khalistan movement at its peak, Assamese students rising in protest against Bangladeshi illegal immigrants who were transforming the demography of their state, Tamil separatism in neighbouring Sri Lanka drawing India into the maelstrom and a youthful but Westernised prime minister, Rajiv Gandhi, seemingly running the country from a great height, like the airline pilot he had once been. The BJP sensed an opportunity to carve out a distinctive space for itself as a defender of Hindu interests. In a resolution adopted officially at Palampur in 1989, it declared Hindutva as its ideology—while claiming that Hindutva represents 'cultural nationalism' and embodies 'Indian nationhood,' rather than a religious or theological concept. In the years following, the BJP established a distinctive Hindutva agenda in national politics, advocating 'Hindu' causes—some which manifestly went beyond religion, like the rights of Kashmiri Pandits brutalised by Islamist terrorists and driven from their homes in the Kashmir Valley to become refugees in their own land, and some which directly challenged other religions, such as the advocacy of a Uniform Civil Code to replace the personal laws of religious minorities.

The 'Muslim threat' presented itself in multiple ways—Muslim illegal migrants in Assam, reactionary Muslim conservatives opposing a liberal Supreme Court judgment in the Shah Bano Case (in which the court's award of alimony to a Muslim widow was then overturned by the government passing a law obliging her to seek support from the Waqf Board), and angry Muslim politicians denouncing Salman Rushdie's 'blasphemy' in his novel, *The Satanic Verses*. To those repelled by such developments, the BJP offered not just negative condemnation but a positive alternative cause dear to many Hindu hearts—a campaign to resurrect a legendary ancient temple to the birthplace of Lord Rama (the Ram Janmabhoomi) which had reputedly stood on the site of a disused sixteenth-century mosque, the Babri Masjid, in the north Indian holy town of Ayodhya.

The evidence for this claim is contested, though there is little doubt that some temple had indeed stood there, since in 1975, well before the mosque's destruction, the Archaeological Survey of India (ASI) unearthed fourteen pillar bases of kasauti stone with Hindu motifs in the foundations. Yet, very few details are available about the temple or whether it had indeed been destroyed to construct the masjid. But there is no doubt it is deeply entrenched in popular Hindu belief that this precisely was where Rama was born and where he must be worshipped. If this can be achieved without inflicting pain on Indian

Muslims, and while finding some way to make up for the barbarous destruction of the Babri Masjid, the nation will heave a sigh of relief, but a quarter-century after the demolition of the masjid, the case pends in the Supreme Court, and the temple remains unbuilt, its absence a potent symbol for the Hindutva movement and a perennial vote-winner for its acolytes.

The Ram Janmabhoomi campaign was incendiary politics, given the inflammatory potency of calls to replace a mosque with a temple; but for the BJP, it worked. The party's leader, L. K. Advani, rode across the Hindi heartland in a converted truck decorated to look like the chariot of an ancient Hindu warrior, making fiery speeches all the way. Hindu groups were exhorted to fire and consecrate bricks in every village in a Ram Shila Pujan (prayer ritual) and proceed with them to Ayodhya for use in the temple that would one day be built there. Pilgrimages were organised to Ayodhya to look at the spot where Hindus had to swallow the mortal insult of a holy site being occupied by a mosque. As emotions reached fever pitch, a howling, frenzied mob broke the 470-year old mosque apart in December 1992, levelling it to rubble while the police stood idly by.[58] The BJP had made its mark.

But while these two incidents tower above the others in the hall of infamy, the forces unleashed by Hindutva have led to numerous acts of violence in its name—and not only against non-Hindus. From the assassination of Mahatma Gandhi by Nathuram Godse in January 1948 for being too sympathetic to Muslims, to the murder of journalist Gauri Lankesh in September 2017 for her excoriating attacks on the Sangh Parivar, moderates, liberals and rationalists of Hindu background have also been targeted. It is distressing that there are BJP MPs who have publicly called for Gandhi's statues to be supplanted by those of Godse to commemorate his killing.

The catalogue of communal violence and riots, incited mainly by Hindutva organisations, is long and dismaying. Several erupted in 1964, 1965 and 1967, in places where Hindu refugees from the former East Pakistan were settled, notably Rourkela, Jamshedpur and Ranchi, where Hindu organisations exploited the refugees' tales of suffering to ignite communal passions and incite violence. The Bharatiya Jana

Sangh's resolution on the 'Indianisation of Indian Muslims' played a role in the Ahmedabad riots in 1969 while the Shiv Sena's ('Army of Shiva', a Mumbai-based Hindu right wing organisation supported by Marathi-speakers) communal agenda helped spark those in Bhivandi-Jalgaon in 1970. The 1980s saw thousands of Muslims being killed in riots, starting with Moradabad in 1980 and carrying on through the horrors of Biharsharif, Meerut, Bhiwandi and Baroda to the massacre at Nellie in Assam and a slew of riots around the 'Ram Shila Pujan' agitations to consecrate bricks in towns across northern India to rebuild the Ram Janmabhoomi. The 1990s, following the demolition of the Babri Masjid, witnessed what many have described as the worst riots of post-independence India—in Mumbai, Surat, Ahmedabad, Kanpur, Delhi and elsewhere. (And of course, unrelated to Hindutva, India also suffered the grotesque anti-Sikh riots of 1984, when mobs egged on by some leaders affiliated with the ruling Congress, and claiming to be revenging the assassination of Indira Gandhi by her Sikh bodyguards murdered 2,800 innocent Sikh civilians across India, including 2,100 in Delhi.)

Since the ascent of the BJP to power, the forces unleashed by the dominance of Hindutva have resulted in many incidents of violence. In one grim reckoning, more than fifty individuals have been killed in anti-minority acts of violence since mid-2014, and dozens of others stripped, beaten and humiliated. Particularly haunting is the story of fifteen-year-old Junaid Khan, returning home on a crowded train after buying new clothes for Id, who was stabbed repeatedly because he was Muslim and thrown off the train to bleed to death on the tracks. (Specific cases related to 'cow vigilantism' are discussed later.) Headlines have spoken continually of riots and killing, Hindu against Muslim, of men being slaughtered because of the mark on a forehead or the absence of a foreskin.

THE POLITICS OF DIVISION

There are essentially two kinds of politics in India: the politics of division and the politics of unity. The latter has increasingly been taken for granted and so the former has by far the greater momentum, as politicians seek to slice and dice the electorate into ever-smaller configurations of caste, language and religion, the better to appeal to such particularist identities in the quest for votes. But this resort to violence is a new low in our political life. The attacks on Muslim and (earlier) Christian families, the vandalism of their places of worship, the destruction of homes and livelihoods, and the horrific rapes, mutilations and burnings alive that have occurred, have nothing to do with religious beliefs—neither those of the victims nor of their attackers. They are instead part of a contemptible political project whose closest equivalent can in fact be found in the Islamist terrorism the Hindutva supporters claim to despise: the bomb blasts in Mumbai in January 1993 and the 'Indian Mujahideen' terrorist attacks in Delhi, Jaipur, and Ahmedabad, in which bombs were set to go off in hospitals, marketplaces and playgrounds.[59] The actions of both Hindu and Muslim terrorists are anti-national; both aim to divide the country by polarising people along their religious identities; and both hope to profit politically from such polarisation.

India must not let either set of terrorists prevail.

* * *

By 1996 the BJP had emerged as the largest single party in national elections, though the unwillingness of the 'secular' parties to ally with it had led to the collapse in thirteen days of its first attempt at forming a government. Two years later it was back, with an amiable conciliator, Prime Minister Atal Behari Vajpayee, heading a coalition government in 1998; though one more election intervened, this government lasted six years. The BJP, despite merely heading a coalition government, left no doubt about its ideological moorings, installing a plaque to honour Savarkar at the Andaman central jail where he had been imprisoned, while avoiding all mention of the obsequious letter of apology to the British that had won him his release. Describing himself as a 'prodigal son' longing to return to the 'parental doors of the government', despite the failure of his earlier letter of clemency in 1911 to obtain him a pardon, Savarkar wrote again on 14 November 1913:

'[If] the government in their manifold beneficence and mercy release me, I for one cannot but be the staunchest advocate of constitutional progress and loyalty to the English government which is the foremost condition of that progress. As long as we are in jails, there cannot be real happiness and joy in hundreds and thousands of homes of His Majesty's subjects in India, for blood is thicker than water; but if we are released, the people will raise a shout of joy and gratitude to the government, who knows how to forgive and correct, more than how to chastise and avenge.'[60]

Savarkar went on to add:

'Moreover, my conversion to the constitutional line would bring back all those misled young men in India and abroad who were once looking up to me as their guide. I am ready to serve the government in any capacity they like, for as my conversion is conscientious so I hope my future conduct would be. By keeping me in jail, nothing can be got in comparison to what would be otherwise. The Mighty alone can afford to be merciful and, therefore, where else can the prodigal son return but to the parental doors of the government.'

The parental doors of the BJP government were certainly thrown open to Savarkar; his behaviour towards the British rulers was airbrushed from official accounts of his life, a hagiographic biopic was released in 2001, and his portrait was even hung in Parliament's Central Hall, deliberately positioned to face that of Mahatma Gandhi.

During BJP rule at the head of a coalition government in Delhi, a purely BJP government, headed by a fiery and articulate ideologue, Chief Minister Narendra Modi, ruled Gujarat. It was on this government's watch that 1,000 to 2,000 people, mainly Muslims, were massacred in 2002, in a pogrom against that community that blighted the state's normally tranquil capital, Ahmedabad, and other places in Gandhi's homeland. The chief minister was accused of condoning the killings—or at the very least not taking prompt action to stop them—which ceased only after the Army was called in three days after they began. It was reported that Prime Minister Vajpayee wanted to dismiss him for his failure to prevent the massacre, but was dissuaded by the

Hindutva hardliners in his administration.[61] (Senior BJP leader Venkaiah Naidu confirmed this story on the record as an example of his party's democratic decision-making—according to Naidu, Prime Minister Vajpayee wanted Modi to resign as Gujarat chief minister after the 2002 riots, but had to give in to the party's 'collective decision' against the idea.) Be that as it may, the Gujarati public rallied behind him; Modi was re-elected as chief minister of Gujarat in elections later that year, 2002, and returned to office again with ever-larger majorities in 2007 and 2012. While his campaign rhetoric vehemently expressed Hindutva ideas, he also claimed to be governing effectively and promoting robust economic development, a message that resonated well beyond his state and gave him a credible national reputation for decisive and impactful leadership. This in turn propelled him to the position of the BJP's candidate for prime minister in 2014, and to a resounding victory in the general elections held across India that year.

Under Prime Minister Modi, the BJP has a sizeable parliamentary majority on its own that it had never enjoyed before; it is, therefore, not obliged to dilute its agenda to accommodate less Hindutva-minded coalition partners, since it does not need any of them to make up its majority. The BJP became the first governing party in the history of independent India to come to power without a single elected Muslim member of the Lok Sabha; the three Muslims who have served in its council of ministers are all appointees to the Rajya Sabha. Also, for the first time, Indian democracy finds itself facing the reality of its top three constitutional positions—president, vice president and prime minister—all being held by RSS members of the same ideological disposition.

It is difficult to escape the conclusion that this marks a significant step towards the Hindutva project of transforming India into a Hindu state, or at least a state with a distinctively Hindu identity. Many Hindutva ideologues have long deplored the fact that love for Hinduism had been, in India, a love that could not be acknowledged; officially promoted secularism, they argued, had made India a country where a Muslim could be proud to be Muslim, a Christian proud to be Christian, a Sikh proud to be Sikh, while a Hindu was proud to be...

secular. The groundswell of rage that anchors this perception takes in a host of factors: the uncritical acceptance by the Indian establishment of regressive practices among the Muslim community while demanding progressive behaviour from Hindus, the support for minority education while denying such aid to Hindus, the promotion of 'family planning' among Hindus but not among Muslims, the cultivation of 'vote banks' led by conservative Muslim leaders but the disparagement of their Hindu equivalents, and so on. The result is a widespread denunciation of the 'appeasement' of Muslims, which seems bizarre when one looks at the statistical evidence of Muslim socio-economic backwardness and the prevalence of discrimination in such areas as housing and employment. Muslims are under-represented in the nation's police forces and over-represented in its prisons. Yet Hindutva leaders have successfully stoked a perception that government benefits are skewed towards minorities, and thus justified their campaign for Hindu self-assertiveness. The unapologetic assertion of Hindutva, and its unabashed capture of the political pinnacle of authority in the land, thus represented a dramatic shift in India's political culture, whose implications are yet to be fully parsed.

Many Indian social scientists have described the Hindutva movement as fascist in the classical sense of the term. Marxist social scientist Prabhat Patnaik, for instance, is a prominent advocate of the argument that the Hindutva movement is 'classically fascist in class support, methods and programme'.[62] Patnaik and others find the following elements of classical fascism present in Hindutva: its attempt to create a unified homogeneous majority defined as 'the Hindus'; its sense of grievance against past injustice, especially by Muslim rulers; its sense of cultural superiority and affirmation of the timeless truths embodied in Hinduism; its interpretation of history in the light of its grievances against past oppressors and its faith in the superiority of its own tenets; its rejection of all arguments against such an interpretation of history; and its appeal to a religious and cultural Hindu majority articulated in terms of race and masculinity. (He could have added the frequent and easy resort to majoritarian mob violence against helpless members of minority faiths, occurring with increasingly troubling frequency in recent years.) Well before Modi became prime minister, the sociologist Ashis Nandy had described him as an archetypal fascist ('a classic, clinical case of a fascist').[63]

However, it must be said that Modi has not conducted himself in office in the manner Nandy's analysis would have suggested. He has repeatedly spoken of being a prime minister for all Indians; arguably his most effective slogan has been '*sab ka saath, sab ka vikas*'—'together with everyone, development for all'.

Nor can it be denied that the ascent of Hindutva supporters to the pinnacle of political power in India has occurred, significantly, under India's secular constitution, and through entirely democratic and legal means. The great question before us today is, therefore: Will constitutionalism tame Hindutva, or will Hindutva transform the workings of the constitution?

On 11 December 1995, a three-judge bench of the Supreme Court, headed by a famously liberal Chief Justice, J. S. Verma, declared that Hindutva was a 'way of life and not a religion'. The court explained: 'Ordinarily, Hindutva is understood as a way of life or a state of mind and is not to be equated with or understood as religious Hindu fundamentalism...it is a fallacy and an error of law to proceed on the assumption...that the use of words "Hindutva" or "Hinduism" per se depicts an attitude hostile to all persons practising any religion other than the Hindu religion... It may well be that these words are used in a speech to promote secularism or to emphasise the way of life of the Indian people and the Indian culture or ethos, or to criticise the policy of any political party as discriminatory or intolerant.'[64]

Unsurprisingly, this Supreme Court judgment found its way into the campaign manifesto of the BJP in the general elections of the following year, 1996. The party claimed the Supreme Court had 'endorsed the true meaning and content of Hindutva as being consistent with the true meaning and definition of secularism'. This could be said to mark the beginning of the constitutional acceptability of the concept of Hindutva—something that arguably is no longer in question, since on 2 January 2017, the Supreme Court of India declined to reconsider its 1995 judgment.

So the Constitution and its custodians have made their peace with Hindutva. But can Hindutva wholeheartedly accept the Constitution?

The more conformist of the two BJP prime ministers India has had, Atal Behari Vajpayee (in office from 1998 to 2004), took a moderate approach to constitutional change, arguing that 'even in the mightiest fort one has to repair the parapet from time to time' (while V. P. Singh cautioned that the 'tenants' should not go for 'rebuilding in the name of repairs').[65] His rule saw no dramatic change in India's constitutional arrangements, though his government did conduct a constitutional review that produced a 1,979-page report, universally unread. There has so far been no dramatic challenge to the Constitution under the second BJP prime minister, Narendra Modi, either, but here it is far less certain that the present approach will endure.

Deen Dayal Upadhyaya, who rejected the Constitution of India in conception, form and substance, would be astonished to find his supposed acolytes extolling its every line and holding special commemorations in Parliament with grandiloquent speeches to mark the anniversary not just of its adoption—which, after all, is Republic Day—but even of its passage by the Constituent Assembly in a newly anointed 'Constitution Day'. What would Upadhyaya have made, I wonder, of a prime minister, who swears by him, saying that this Constitution—the very document that Upadhyaya found fallacious, Westernised and devoid of *chiti* and *virat shakti*—is his 'holy book'?

It is, of course, difficult to know whether we should take the Hindutvavadis' claims to be admirers of the present secular, liberal, Western-influenced Constitution of India to be as sincere as their professions of devotion to Upadhyaya. Will Modi and his tribe, after consolidating their hold on both the Lok Sabha and the Rajya Sabha, and after taking over most of the state governments, feel emboldened to tear up the very Constitution to which they have so far so enthusiastically pledged allegiance?

There are already hints that the Constitution in its present form cannot long survive unscathed. Hindutva ideologue K. N. Govindacharya has declared that the Constitution must be transformed: 'Amendment is a short-term goal while rewriting is a long-term objective,' he stated.[66] His fundamental critique, expressed in interviews to leading Indian newspapers in 2017, is not far from Upadhyaya's of half a century earlier:

> 'Our Constitution is based upon the idea of individualism. It promotes individualism, which is against the Indian value system… while Indian civilisation is based upon family system, collectiveness. Other important components of our society such as caste system, panchayat system are not mirrored in the Constitution. Individualism is a western idea. It cannot be the basis of the Indian Constitution. A new Constitution should be written which would talk in favour of *Sarva* (all), not an individual.'

Aside from giving caste an honoured place in the Hindutva political system, 'We believe that Indian society and its cultural reality should be included in the Constitution.' For instance, 'in 'Bharatiya' society, family is the basic brick of society, and as in the Cuban Constitution, it is not the individual but family values that are crucial.'

Cuba as a model for India is a nice touch from a supposedly rightwing movement. But as in many communist systems, Parliament as we know it would cease to exist. 'The new Constitution would be based on the principles of collectiveness. In political terminology, you can call it a Guild System. Representatives of the different castes, professions, communities would be included in National Guild. Instead of the Upper House (Rajya Sabha) and Lower House (Lok Sabha) of Parliament, there would be only one National Guild in which 1,000 representatives from all over the country will discuss the problems of India. In the National Guild, 500 representatives would come through territorial representation, while 500 would come through functional representation.'

Human rights are another example of the Westernisation of the Indian constitutional system, according to Govindacharya: 'There cannot be any rights without checks and balances. If the Constitution gives us fundamental rights, it mentions fundamental duties too. But no one cares about that. Rights and duties should be seen in relation to each other. To exercise your rights, you should follow your duties. No one can exercise absolute freedom.' As Deen Dayal Upadhyaya had argued,

'fundamental duties, not just rights, must also be incorporated.'
Secularism, like human rights, will have to go: it 'implies opposition of
Hindus and appeasement of Muslims or other minorities. We should
get rid of this word as soon as possible. It is completely irrelevant in
the Indian context.'

Deen Dayal Upadhyaya's inspiration crops up again in the Hindutva
rejection of the Western word 'socialism' in the Preamble of the
Constitution. 'We have a better word—of Indian tradition—to express
the spirit of socialism. It is [Upadhyaya's coinage] antodaya. Antodaya
means antim aadmi (the last man).' Similarly democracy is a troubling
term because it implies political contention. 'Instead of competitive-
ness, consensus and collectiveness should be the spirit of the democracy', says Govindacharya.[67] Shades of Cuba again!

The process of incorporating such Hindu concepts seems to have
begun: 'We are doing it very silently. Discussions and debates have been
taking place for some time. What I told you above are the initial outcomes of the debate', Govindacharya confirms. 'There may be many
gaps which need deliberations, and a cool, calm, dispassionate discussion needs the right atmosphere and a mechanism. However, this is just
not possible in the media glare.' Would a Hindutva-inspired revision of
the Constitution, for example, move the issue of cow slaughter from
the Directive Principles of the Constitution, where it is linked specifically to the preservation of milch-cattle and scientific principles of
animal husbandry, to somewhere more binding, and anchored more
explicitly to religious sanction? Govindacharya is clear: a Hindutva-
drafted Constitution would provide for:

> 'eco-centric not anthropocentric development. I mean not just rights
> of the cow, but a holistic view of *zamin, jal, janwar, jungle* [land, water,
> animal, jungle]; for only in this protection lies the well-being of man.
> All the five must have sacred rights, and this should not just be rights-
> based but duty-based, and not just be components of state power. The
> cow is part of our civilisational past and it reflects those values, it
> should be a civilisational continuity in the preamble. The cow, envi-
> ronmental protection, all this requires constitutional protection. It is
> part of Hindu ethos, culture—like Bishnois who embrace death by

hugging those trees, this is all 'Bharatiya' culture. Instead of assuming man is conqueror of nature, it is the duty of humans to protect nature, and all this must be incorporated in the Constitution.'

Environmentalists may well approve, but the key question remains whether a Hindutva-modified Constitution, assuming that it ever comes to pass, will retain the core principle of independent India, that all adult Indians are deemed equal, irrespective of religion. Or would it consciously embrace the central theme of Hindutva, which would discriminate against non-Hindus? If it did so, it would be true to Hindutva as expounded by Savarkar, Golwalkar and Upadhyaya, but not to the Hinduism of Swami Vivekananda or Mahatma Gandhi, who did not define citizenship or Indianness in terms of the gods one worshipped, what one ate, the way one dressed or where one went for pilgrimage. But if it did not do so, it would betray a century's worth of political philosophising in the name of Hindutva, surrendering its tenets to the dominant nationalist stream it had long derided as 'pseudo-secular'.

This will be a crucial dilemma for the Hindutva ideologues. Do they take the opportunity given to them by their crushing political majority—which might not endure if they wait too long—to remake the Constitution as their principal thinkers had advocated? Or do they accept that the reality of ruling a multi-ethnic, multi-lingual and multi-religious polity makes the goal of 'Hindu, Hindi, Hindutva' unattainable?

Another litmus test would lie in whether a revised Hindutva Constitution would mandate a Uniform Civil Code for all the citizens of India. Leaders subscribing to Hindutva have long argued that differential laws based on religion—essentially the personal laws governing marriage, inheritance and divorce for Muslims, and also for other religious minorities—violate Article 44 of the Indian Constitution and have sowed the seeds of divisiveness between different communities; if we are all Hindus (albeit 'Hindu Muhammadans', 'Hindu Christians' and so on) why should we not all be subject to one civil code? Secular Congress leaders from Jawaharlal Nehru onwards have argued that while a Uniform Civil Code might be a desirable objective, it could only be adopted with the consent of the affected communities. This could not be obtained by pressure or by legal coercion; it required persuasion. Since minority leaders, especially Muslims, showed no inclination to be persuaded, seeing a uniform civil code as the imposition of majoritarian Hindu sensibilities, the idea needed to be deferred indefinitely, until the time was ripe. Hindutva leaders have long mocked this approach as caving in to minority prejudices; accepting Sharia law, they argue, violates the human rights principles of gender equality by discriminating against Muslim women and allows unelected and in some cases self-appointed religious personalities to interpret religious dictates and so 'lay down the law'. Could they now concede the permissibility of religious personal laws without losing credibility?

And would a Hindutva Constitution preserve the anomaly of Article 370, which grants a special status to the state of Jammu and Kashmir, to the extent that no law passed by the Parliament of India can apply to that state without being also passed by the Assembly of Jammu and Kashmir? Would the advocates of Hindutva allow the state to continue to restrict land-holding to 'state subjects', a status a woman would lose if she married a man from outside the state?

India's constitutionalists have long argued that it is a living document, susceptible to amendment in keeping with the evolving demands of time, subject of course to judicial interpretation, which has decreed that its 'basic structure' cannot be tampered with. Would transforming an egalitarian and secular Constitution into a document infused with the principles of Hindutva not violate its basic structure? And yet, can the advocates of Hindutva—the intellectual legatees of Savarkar, Golwakar and Upadhyaya—afford not to try?

A TRAVESTY OF HINDUISM

While not everything in the philosophy I have sought to summarise is objectionable—and there is much to admire, for instance, in Upadhyaya's humanistic thinking—there is much that is troubling too. By rejecting the territorial idea of the nation in favour of an abstract ethos of patriotism, it excludes many who belong on the territory of modern India and are loyal citizens but feel differently about Bharat

Mata (Mother India). In its emphasis on cultural authenticity and allegiance to ancient Indian traditions and beliefs, it risks alienating those who do not share these assumptions. While extolling the virtues of harmony and cooperation, it sows the seeds of further division by setting those who subscribe to these values against those who—for reasons of religion, politics or intellectual conviction—do not. And in dismissing minority appeasement but requiring minorities to accept Hindu ways of being as their own, it offers no real solution to the undeniable reality that 20 per cent of India's population are not Hindus and cannot be expected to conform to Hindu ideas of how they should live and what they should believe.

It also ignores, in its desire to portray a Hindu vision, the diversity within Hinduism itself. The faith is practised differently by people in different parts of the country, or worshipping different manifestations of the Divine, or adhering to different castes or sects. Even the Brahmins, who are spread throughout the country and are associated everywhere with learning, priestly functions and religious erudition, manifest diversity in their social practices: while the Malayali Brahmins grow their tuft of hair at the front, most orthodox Tamil Brahmins wear it at the back; where Iyengar Brahmin women regard white as the colour of widowhood, the Namboothiri Brahmin bride wears white at her wedding. As we have seen, Hinduism is not a totalising faith. Each Hindu may have a different conception of her own *dharma*. Integral Humanism undoubtedly emerges from a close and sustainable reading of Advaita philosophy, but Upadhyaya's is not the only way of being Hindu, and other sages and *rishis* may offer alternative approaches to the same conundrums. Upadhyaya's philosophy suffers the demerit of its own certitudes; it is unable to accommodate dissent.

Some have seen in his approach a reaction to Islam's assertiveness. In response to the suggestion that Hindus are behaving like Islamists, the one-time journalist and former BJP minister Arun Shourie commented tartly:

'In a word, three things are teaching the Hindus to become Islamic:
the double-standards of the secularists and the State, the demonstrated

success of the Muslims in bending both the State and the secularists by intimidation, and the fact that both the State and the secularists pay attention to the sentiments of Hindus only when the Hindus become a little Islamic... [My] forecast: the more the secularists insist on double-standards, the more Islamic will the Hindus become.'

What does this 'Islamicised Hinduism' of the 'Sangh Parivar' consist of? The ideological foundations laid by Savarkar, Golwalkar and Upadhyaya have given members of the RSS a fairly coherent doctrine. It rests on the atavistic belief that India has been the land of the Hindus since ancient times, and that their identity and its identity are intertwined. Since time immemorial, Hindutva advocates argue, Hindu culture and civilisation have constituted the essence of Indian life; Indian nationalism is therefore Hindu nationalism. The history of India is the story of the struggle of the Hindus, the owners and custodians of this ancient land, to protect and preserve their religion and culture against the onslaught of hostile alien invaders. It is true that the territory of India also hosts non-Hindus, but these are invaders (Muslims, Christians) or guests (Jews, Parsis); they can be tolerated, depending on their loyalty to the land, but cannot be treated as equal to the Hindus unless they acknowledge the superiority of Hindus in India and adopt Hindu traditions and culture. Non-Hindus must acknowledge their Hindu parentage, or, better still, convert to Hinduism in a return to their true cultural roots.

Those political forces in India who are opposed to the Sangh's ideology are mistaken, the doctrine goes on, since they make the cardinal error of confusing 'national unity' with the unity of all those who happen to be living in the territory of India, irrespective of religion or national origin. Such people are in fact anti-national, because their real motivation is the selfish desire to win minority votes in elections rather than care for the interests of the majority of the nation. The unity and consolidation of the Hindus is therefore essential. Since the Hindu people are surrounded by enemies, a polarisation must take place that pits Hindus against all others. To achieve this, though, Hindus must be unified; the lack of unity is the root cause of all the evils besetting the

Hindus. The Sangh Parivar's principal mission is to bring about that unity and lead it to the greater glory of the Hindu nation.

The problem with this doctrine, coherent and clear though it is, is its denial of the reality of what Hinduism is all about. What Swami Vivekananda would have seen as the strength of Hinduism—its extraordinary eclecticism and diversity, its acceptance of a wide range of beliefs and practices, its refusal to confine itself to the dogmas of a single holy book, its fluidity, the impossibility to define it down to a homogenous 'Semitic' creed—is precisely what the RSS ideologues see as its weakness.

The Sanghivadi quest for polarisation and unity is also a yearning to make Hinduism what it is not—to 'Semitise' it so that it looks like the faiths of the 'invaders': codified and doctrinaire, with an identifiable God (preferably Rama), a principal holy book (the Gita), a manageable ecclesiastic hierarchy, and of course a unified race and a people to profess it. This is not the lived Hinduism of most Hindus. And so the obvious question arises: must every believing Hindu automatically be assumed to subscribe to the Hindutva project? And since manifestly most do not, does the viability of the project require a continued drive to force the dissenters into the Hindutva straitjacket?

Whereas Hinduism is an inward-directed faith, focusing on Self-Realisation above all and the union of the soul with the Absolute, Hindutva is an outward-directed concept, aimed at creating social and cultural distinctions for a political purpose. Hindutva, therefore, is disconnected from the central assumptions and tenets of my Hinduism. Yet it piggy-backs on the faith, claiming to represent Hinduism, though it does so not as a set of doctrines or precepts but as a cultural marker. Hindutva adopts the Hindu religion not as a way of seeking the Divine but as a badge of worldly political identity. This has little to do with the Hinduism of Vivekananda, or of Adi Shankara; it is a twentieth-century idea, born of twentieth-century forms of political thinking that were already beginning to be dangerously out of date elsewhere in the world when they were propounded in India. Parties professing to speak for an entire people or 'volk' were discredited as well as destroyed in Europe in 1945; seven decades later, the idea flourishes in India, in the name of Hindutva.

Speaking for myself, any attempt to reduce my Hinduism—which sits comfortably with the Nehruvian notion of Indianness—to a sectarian notion of Hindutva is a travesty of what Hinduism really is. I too, as a Hindu, can say, when people tell me '*Garv se kaho ki tum Hindu ho*', that I am proud to be a Hindu, but in what is it that we are to take pride? I take pride in the openness, the diversity, the range, the lofty metaphysical aspirations of the Vedanta; of the various ways in which Hinduism is practised, eclectically, and of its extraordinary acceptance of differences.

Unfortunately, as I have noted, the votaries of Hindutva seem to take pride in Hinduism the way in which one might support a football team as a badge of identity, rather than as a set of values, principles and beliefs, and so Hinduism becomes reduced in their retelling to little more than a label on a T-shirt, a badge of allegiance rather than a way of relating to the cosmos.

My notion of Indianness and Hinduness is very much caught up in what Dr Radhakrishnan so memorably spoke of as a view of life. That view of life has very little room for intolerance, for dogma, for attacks on others because of what they do or do not believe. I am a Hindu, and I am a nationalist, but I am not a Hindu nationalist. My nationalism is unquestioningly, all-embracingly, Indian. The Sangh does not speak for Hindus like me.

6

BEYOND HOLY COWS

THE USES AND ABUSES OF HINDU CULTURE AND HISTORY

My own faith in religious pluralism is a legacy of my upbringing in 'secular' India. Secularism in India did not mean irreligiousness, which even avowedly atheist parties like the communists or the southern DMK, Dravida Munnetra Kazhagam (Dravidian Progress Federation) party found unpopular amongst their voters; indeed, in Calcutta's annual Durga Puja, the communist parties compete with each other to put up the most lavish *Puja pandals* (Hindu religious displays). Rather, secularism meant, in the Indian tradition, a profusion of religions, none of which was privileged by the state. I remember how, in the Calcutta neighbourhood where I lived during my high school years, the wail of the muezzin calling the Islamic faithful to prayer blended with the chant of the mantras and the tinkling of bells at the nearby Shiva temple and the crackling loudspeakers outside the Sikh gurudwara reciting verses from the Guru Granth Sahib. And just around the corner was St Paul's Cathedral.

As we have seen, the irony is that India's secular coexistence was paradoxically made possible by the fact that the overwhelming majority of Indians are Hindus. That acceptance of difference, which I have explored in this book and elsewhere, characterised the Hinduism propagated by Vivekananda and other visionary Hindu seers. This meant that it came naturally to Hindus to coexist with practitioners of other faiths. In a plural society, religious pluralism was merely one more kind of difference everyone accepted, just as we knew that around us were people who spoke different languages, ate different foods, dressed differently and had different shades of skin colour from ours.

SECULARISM AND SYNCRETISM

Secularism in India, therefore, did not mean separation of religion from state. Instead, secularism in India means a state that was equally indulgent of all religious groups, and favoured none.

Nor did it mean secularity in the French sense, or *laïcité*. The French concept keeps religion out of governmental institutions like schools and government out of religious institutions in turn, whereas Indian secularism cheerfully embraces financial support to religious schools and the persistence of 'personal law' for different religious communities. The Indian system has created incentives for various religious denominations to start and operate 'minority schools' and colleges with substantial government funding, impart religious education, and be exempt from various regulations and stipulations the Indian government imposes on non-minority institutions. (Critics, especially of the Hindutva variety, do not hesitate to point out that while government schools and colleges may not impart religious instruction, religious sects and charities affiliated to minority communities may open their own schools and receive state financial assistance even as they impart religious indoctrination.)

Under the Indian version of secularism, the government's financial largesse is extended to the Muslim Wakf Boards, Buddhist monasteries, and certain Christian religious institutions; and under a 1951 Religious and Charitable Endowment Law, state governments are empowered to take over, own and operate Hindu temples, collect revenue from offerings and redistribute that revenue to such purposes as it deems fit, including any non-temple-related ones. This may well be worth reexamination. Still, it came as a shock when, in 2016, the BJP government invited a Jain monk to address the Haryana state assembly, seating him in an exalted position above the Speaker of the House. Many Hindus saw this as a grave mistake. Religiosity is hardly unknown in our politics—there are several saffron-robed *sadhus* who have been elected to Parliament and one, Yogi Adityanath, serves as the chief minister of India's biggest state, Uttar Pradesh—but giving an *unelected* religious figure a position of prominence in an elected, representative democratic legislative body was fundamentally wrong, and crossed a line that had hitherto never been breached.

While the Haryana government's actions might have been unconscionable, there is no getting away from the fact that India is not secular in the commonly understood sense of the word. What it is, is pluralist: an overwhelmingly Hindu-majority country running political and governmental institutions that promote the survival, success and perpetuation of religious minorities. It is the idea that rather than distancing itself from religion (the idea of *dharma-nirpekshata* condemned by the critics of secularism), the state can embrace *all* religions.

My generation grew up in an India where our sense of nationhood lay in the slogan, 'unity in diversity'. We were brought up to take pluralism for granted, and to reject the communalism that had partitioned the nation when the British left. In rejecting the case for Pakistan, Indian nationalism also rejected the very idea that religion should be a determinant of nationhood. We never fell into the insidious trap of agreeing that, since Partition had established a state for Muslims, what remained was a state for Hindus. To accept the idea of India you had to spurn the logic that had divided the country.

In some ways, this kind of Indian secularism has ancient roots in our history. Admired monarchs from Ashoka, in the third century BCE, to Harsha, in the sixth century CE, gave their recognition and patronage to different religions. Ashoka's Rock Edict XII forbade people from honouring their own sects at the expense of others, and condemning the beliefs of others. Citizenship and political status in his state were never linked to one's religion. The coexistence of religions is evident from the fact that the Ellora Cave temples, some Jain, some Hindu and some Buddhist, were carved next to each other between the fifth and tenth centuries. While this traditional approach to secular or pluralist practice was not that of the Islamic kingdoms that established themselves from the twelfth century onwards, even Muslim rulers bound to uphold the less welcoming tenets of their faith had to reconcile themselves to ruling an overwhelmingly non-Muslim populace and accommodating prominent Hindus in government and the military. One monarch, the Mughal Emperor Akbar, went so far as to create his own syncretic religion, Din-e-Ilahi, to meld the best features of Islam, Hinduism and the other faiths of which he knew into a new 'national faith'. It did not outlast his reign, but the attempt was extraordinary.

The concept of *sarva dharma sambhava*—accepting the equality of all religions—was propounded by great Hindu sages like Ramakrishna and Vivekananda, as we have seen, and upheld by Mahatma Gandhi and the Indian nationalist movement. While it was an axiomatic tenet of the post-Independence India in which I grew up, *sarva dharma sambhava* has been increasingly rejected by some proponents of Hindutva who spurn the notion of religious universalism in favour of a more robust assertion of Hindu cultural identity and Hindus' political rights. The Hindutva ideologue David Frawley (Pandit Vamadeva Shastri), for instance, warns against *sarva dharma sambhava*, arguing that only Hindus are asked to practise this belief, which simply leads to confusion and 'does not convince the opponents but deludes the Hindus themselves'. Frawley asks: 'When have Christians or Muslims in India ever been criticised for violating Sarva Dharma Samabhava?... Under the guise of religious tolerance this idea of equality of religions is used to prevent scrutiny of [others'] religious dogmas'.[1]

Yet the lived reality of Indian syncretism is difficult to deny. Hindus who made the arduous uphill trek to the cave temple of Amarnath in northern Kashmir, where an ice lingam, a naturally-formed stalactite, is worshipped, would have known that a third of their offerings went to the family of Adam Malik, a Muslim shepherd who, it was said, found the cave four centuries ago and led a Hindu *sadhu* to see the astonishing sight. In my novel, *Riot*, I wrote of Syed Salar Masud Ghazi, popularly known as Ghazi Miyan, a Muslim warrior who is worshipped as a saint by Hindus in the Bahraich area of Uttar Pradesh. A number of

Muslim religious figures such as Nizamuddin Auliya, Moinuddin Chishti, Shah Madar and Shaikh Nasiruddin (alias Chiragh-i-Dilli) are also worshipped by Hindu devotees to this day. Even the richest Hindu temple, at Tirupati, has a Muslim connection. One legend has it that Lord Balaji's second wife is Muslim, Bibi Nanchira, the daughter of a sultan who was enamoured of the Lord, much to her father's dismay, until Balaji appeared in the Sultan's dreams and informed him that He wished to marry his daughter. The Sultan, overwhelmed, acquiesced and today Balaji's second wife is said to live in the town below, at His feet, while His first wife Padmavati resides on Tirumala hill, at the temple, in His heart.

Such stories are not uncommon in India. A Muslim goddess, Bonbibi, is worshipped in idol form as the protector of the mangrove forests adjoining the Bay of Bengal. The Nawabs of Oudh celebrated the annual Ram Leela and Krishna Leela; Nawab Wajid Ali Shah, who was to be deposed by the British, personally directed a Krishna Leela performance in which he asked his Begums to dance the parts of the gopis. The Nawabs of Oudh both established and patronised the Hanuman festival in Lucknow known as Bada Mangal. In Bengal, Muslim Patua painters specialised in painting the Hindu epics on long pieces of craft paper. And as I have mentioned earlier, Hindus are regular worshippers at Christian shrines like the Basilica of Our Lady of Good Health in Velankanni or Mount Mary Church in Mumbai; and in Kerala's Ambalappuzha, an image of St Thomas used to be carried in procession to the Krishna temple on festive occasions, alongside those of Krishna and associated Hindu divinities.

Stories abound of different communities habitually working together in pre-colonial times on issues that benefited principally one: for instance, Hindus helping Muslims to rebuild a shrine, or Muslims doing the same when a Hindu temple had to be reconstructed. Devout Hindus were sometimes given Muslim names and were often fluent scholars in Persian; Muslims served in the army of the Maratha (Hindu) warrior king Shivaji, as did Hindu Rajputs in the forces of the fiercely Islamist Aurangzeb. The Vijayanagara army included Muslim horseback contingents. At the village level, many historians argue that Hindus and

Muslims shared a wide spectrum of customs and beliefs, at times even jointly worshipping the same saint or holy spot. In Kerala's famous pilgrimage site of Sabarimala, after an arduous struggle up to the hill-top shrine of Lord Ayyappa, the devotee first encounters a shrine to his Muslim disciple, Vavar Swami. In keeping with Muslim practice, there is no idol therein, merely a symbolic stone slab, a sword (Vavar was a warrior) and a green cloth, the colour of Islam. Muslim divines manage the shrine. (In another astonishing example, astonishing since it is both anachronistic and syncretistic, a temple in South Arcot, Tamil Nadu, hosts a deity of Muttaal Raavuttan, a Muslim chieftain—complete with beard, kumkum and toddy pot—who protects Draupadi in the *Mahabharata*. Note, of course, that Islam did not exist when the *Mahabharata* was composed, but in post-Islamic retellings, a Muslim chieftain has entered the plot!)

Indians of all religious communities had long lived intertwined lives, and even religious practices were rarely exclusionary: thus Muslim musicians played and sang Hindu devotional songs, Hindus thronged Sufi shrines and worshipped Muslim saints there, and Muslim artisans in Benares made the traditional masks for the Hindu Ram-Leela per-formances. Northern India celebrated what was called a 'Ganga-Jamuni tehzeeb', a syncretic culture that melded the cultural practices of both faiths. The renowned scholar Romila Thapar has recounted how deeply devotional poetry was written by some poets who were born Muslim but worshipped Hindu deities, notably Sayyad Ibrahim, popularly known as Raskhan, whose *dohas* (couplets) and *bhajans* (hymns) dedi-cated to Lord Krishna were widely recited in the sixteenth century. The Mughal court, she points out, became the most impressive patron of the translation of many Sanskrit religious texts into Persian, including the epic *Mahabharata* (translated as the *Razmnamah*) and the *Bhagavad Gita*, with Brahmin priests collaborating on the translations with Persian scholars.

To Gyanendra Pandey, such tales, as well as parables of Hindu generals in Mughal courts, or of Hindu and Muslim ministers in the Sikh ruler Ranjit Singh's entourage, suggests there was 'fuzziness' about self-conscious identities and a lack of self-definition on the basis of religion (or even of caste), within both the Hindu and Muslim populations. These stories do not suggest mutually incompatible or hostile ideologies.

The reality of syncretism runs deep into social practice. Muslim artisans create the masks for the major Hindu festival of Dussehra in the holy city of Varanasi; the Ram Leela could not be performed without their work. Muslim Patachitra painters sing and paint *pats* (scrolls) about Hindu divinities. And among the most famous exponents of Hindu devotional music are the Muslim Dagar brothers—not to mention the Baul singers, a legacy of the Bhakti tradition, who sing Sufi-inspired folk songs in praise of a universal God. Muslim sociologists and anthropologists have argued that Islam in rural India is more Indian than Islamic, in the sense that the faith as practised by the ordinary Muslim villagers reflects the considerable degree of cultural assimilation that has occurred between Hindus and Muslims in their daily lives. The late Muslim reformist scholar Asghar Ali Engineer once wrote that 'rural Islam... [is] almost indistinguishable from Hinduism except in the form of worship.... The degree may vary from one area to another; but cultural integration between the Hindus and Muslims is a fact which no one, except victims of misinformation, can deny.'

One of the most striking images of India that went around the internet in recent years was a photograph of a Muslim couple on Janmashtami day setting out on their scooter, the man with a beard and skullcap, the woman in all-encompassing burqa, taking their child to act in a school performance—and this Muslim boy was dressed as Krishna, complete with kiritam, peacock feather, blue-hued skin and flute.

Sadly, some Hindu chauvinists have distorted the basic tenets of their own religion—as described in the preceding chapters—to propagate a version of the faith in opposition to other religions, especially Islam and Christianity. Worse, this violent, extremist brand of Hinduism, which has no sanction in Hindu scriptures, theology or practice, appears to be gaining ground in recent times, with the covert or active assistance of many Hindutva-inclined politicians, religious leaders and groups. The two worst examples of these affronts to the spirit of Hinduism in modern times are undoubtedly, as I have mentioned, the demolition of the Babri Masjid in December 1991 by a howling, chanting mob of fanatics, and the massacre of innocents, mainly Muslims, in Gujarat in 2002.

What have we come to, that a land that has been a haven of tolerance for religious minorities throughout its history should have sunk so low? India's is a civilisation that, over millennia, has offered refuge and, more importantly, religious and cultural freedom, to Jews, Parsis, Muslims and several varieties of Christians. Christianity arrived on Indian soil, or so legend has it, with St Thomas the Apostle ('Doubting Thomas'), who is said to have come to the Kerala coast some time before 52 CE and was welcomed on shore by a flute-playing Jewish girl. He made many converts, so there are Indians today whose ancestors were Christian well before any European discovered Christianity (and before the forebears of many of today's Hindu chauvinists were even conscious of themselves as Hindus). One of the oldest mosques in the world outside the Arabian peninsula is also in Kerala, in Kodungalloor. The India where the muezzin's prayer and the pujari's mantra co-exist is an India of which we can all be proud.

But, as we know, there is also the India in which murderous mobs in Odisha sought to kill Christians and destroy their places of worship and homes, pulled down the Babri Masjid, conducted the pogrom in Gujarat and lynched Mohammed Akhlaq and Pehlu Khan more recently.

Tragically, the cycle of violence goes on, spawning new hostages to history, ensuring that future generations will be taught new wrongs to set right. We live, Octavio Paz once wrote, between oblivion and memory. Memory and oblivion: how one leads to the other, and back again, has been the concern of much of my writing. Today we are facing people who wish to wipe out memory, and supplant it with new 'memories' of their own invention. As I pointed out in the last words of my novel *Riot*, history is not a web woven with innocent hands.

But as this book is about Hinduism, what sticks in my craw is the claim of the perpetrators of such violence that they are acting in defence of my faith. Hinduism believes that there are various ways of reaching the ultimate truth. To me, the fact that adherents of this faith, in a particular perversion of its tenets, have chosen to take human life and destroy somebody else's sacred place in its name, to kill others because of the absence of a foreskin or lack of a mark on the forehead, this ultimately makes me, as a Hindu, deeply sorrowful and, in a very fundamental way, ashamed.

As I have shown throughout this book, how, after all, can such a religion lend itself to 'fundamentalism'? That devotees of this supremely tolerant faith have assaulted Muslims and Christians in its name is particularly galling. As we have seen, Hinduism has survived the Aryans, the Mughals, the British; it has taken from each—language, art, food, learning—and outlasted them all. Muslim invaders destroyed Hindu temples, putting mosques in their place, but this did not make India a Muslim land, nor did Hinduism suffer a fatal blow. Survival is the best revenge, rather than reprisal; undoing the wrongs of a different era through new wrongs in a different context only compounds the original sin ('an eye for an eye,' as Mahatma Gandhi famously said, 'makes the whole world blind'). Large, eclectic, agglomerative, the Hinduism that I know understands that faith is a matter of hearts and minds, not bricks and stone. 'Build Ram in your hearts' is what Hinduism has always enjoined: if Ram is in your heart, it would matter very little where else He is, or is not. How does it matter, then, what bricks or stones Ram can also be found in?

Living with people of various kinds of faith, Hindus developed their tradition of acceptance of difference, but also understood that in both principle and practice, religion and politics should be divorced. Our founding fathers, the majority of whom were Hindus, decided that India was not a Hindu Pakistan—and the vast majority of Indians took pride in that assertion. Where Pakistan reserved its top constitutional positions only for Muslims, and stamped 'non-Muslim' on the passports of its minority citizens in confirmation of their second-class status, Indians revelled in the prominence enjoyed by its various minorities in public life. Neither politics nor governance—and certainly not culture, sport or entertainment—was based on religious principles, and success in no field required a litmus test of faith.

Throughout the decades after Independence, the political culture of the country reflected these 'secular' assumptions and attitudes.

Though the Indian population was 80 per cent Hindu and the country had been partitioned as a result of a demand for a separate Muslim homeland, three of India's eleven presidents were Muslims; so were innumerable governors, cabinet ministers, chief ministers of states, ambassadors, generals, and Supreme Court justices. During the war with Pakistan in 1971, when the Pakistani leadership was foolish enough to proclaim a jihad against the Hindu 'unbelievers', the Indian Air Force in the northern sector was commanded by a Muslim (Air Marshal, later Air Chief Marshal, I. H. Latif); the army commander was a Parsi (General, later Field Marshal, S. H. F. J. Manekshaw), the general officer commanding the forces that marched into Bangladesh was a Sikh (General J. S. Aurora), and the general flown in to negotiate the surrender of the Pakistani forces in East Bengal was Jewish (Major-General J. F. R. Jacob). They led the armed forces of an overwhelmingly Hindu country.

That is India.

HINDU NATIONALISM

So the idea of India is of one land embracing many. As I have written before, it is the idea that a nation may endure differences of caste, creed, colour, culture, cuisine, conviction, costume and custom, and still rally around a consensus. That consensus is around the simple principle that in a diverse democracy you don't really need to agree—except on the ground rules of how you will disagree. The reason India has survived all the stresses and strains that have beset it for seventy years, and that led so many to predict its imminent disintegration, is that it maintained consensus on how to manage without consensus.

But the twentieth-century politics of deprivation has eroded Indian culture's confidence. As we have seen, Hindu chauvinism has emerged from the competition for resources in a contentious democracy. Politicians of all faiths across India seek to mobilise voters by appealing to narrow identities; by courting votes in the name of religion, caste and region, they have urged voters to define themselves on these lines. As religion, caste and region have come to dominate public discourse, to some it has become more important to be a Muslim, a Bodo or a Yadav than to be an Indian.

For Hindutva thinkers, the principles of tolerance and acceptance are emasculating. 'It is no longer enough for Hindus to be apostles of tolerance with no clear principles or doctrines with which to sustain it', argues Frawley. 'They must stand for the truth, which cannot always be popular, and not simply seek to placate everyone'.[2] But their truth is built on the denial of the truths that Hindus have lived by for millennia.

This is why the development of what has been called 'Hindu fundamentalism' and the resultant change in the public discourse about Indianness is so dangerous. The suggestion that only a Hindu, and only a certain kind of Hindu, can be an authentic Indian, is an affront to the very premise of Indian nationalism. An India that denies itself to some of us could end up being denied to all of us.

The reduction of non-Hindus to second-class status in their homeland is unthinkable. It would be a second Partition: and a partition in the Indian soul would be as bad as a partition in the Indian soil. But the roots of such thinking run deep in the ideology of Hindutva, and that is a cause for alarm for all concerned Hindus.

* * *

Hindutva (or as some would prefer to call it, *Sanghivad*—the beliefs and philosophy of the Sangh—to strip it of its religious connotations) is in many ways a distraction from the real issues facing the country: poverty and economic development, oppression and injustice, the evolution of our still-imperfect democracy. Identity politics becomes a diversion from the bread-and-butter (or dal-and-roti) issues that actually affect most Hindus. As discussed in Chapter Five, the Hindutva project involves an attempt to create an overarching political ideology that would subsume all the adherents of a highly differentiated and eclectic religious faith. Accordingly, the idea of Hindu nationalism conflates ideas of religion and culture with those of nation and state.

Nationalism is by definition indivisible, whereas religion and culture take on multiple manifestations. Culture, of course, contributes to national identity, yet culture alone cannot mould the nationalism of a country, let alone that of a plural land like India. In India during colonial rule, the reassertion of Indian culture was a nationalist project, which witnessed the revival of dance forms like Bharata Natyam and traditional classical music as well as modern literature in Indian languages, modern art (from Raja Ravi Varma to the Bengal School and painters like Husain who derived inspiration from the Indian epics) and what evolved into the gaudy cinema of Bollywood.

But an India confident in its own cultural diversity could celebrate multiple expressions of its culture. Hindutva sees culture differently; as Golwalkar wrote, culture 'is but a product of our all-comprehensive religion, a part of its body and not distinguishable from it'. For Hindutva's devotees, India's national culture is Hindu religious culture, and cultural nationalism cloaks plural India in a mantle of Hindu identity. Since Hindutva's conception of nationalism is rooted in the primacy of culture over politics, the historian K. N. Panikkar has pointed out, the Hindutva effort is to create an idea of the Indian nation in which the Hindu religious identity coincides with the cultural.

As David Frawley explains, after being ruled by Westernised Hindus for many decades after Independence, today, Hindus are rediscovering their roots. 'This movement is not simply a regressive return to medieval Hindu values, but a rediscovery of the validity and importance of Hindu culture and spirituality for both the future as well as the past. It includes discovering the importance of Hindu Yoga, Vedanta, Ayurveda, Vedic astrology, classical Indian art and culture, and the Hindu view of society and government'.[3]

What he calls 'the Bharatiya spiritual urge', he says, after extolling Yoga and meditation, 'did not arise from the suppression of other human urges but from a full flowering of human nature in all aspects, including the arts and the sciences. This we see lavishly embodied in Indian music and dance, mathematics and medicine'. This sounds reasonable enough, except when he adds that 'Hindus must learn to project a united front and reclaim the greater field of Hindu Dharma that covers all aspects of life and culture'.[4] This call for unity replaces variety with uniformity and dissent with dogma; a notion of Hindu *dharma* that is all-encompassing and covers 'all aspects of life and culture' has no room for difference or for heterodoxy, let alone for deviance.

But the Hindu religious identity exalted by Hindutva ideologues is defined in narrow terms. The inclusive Hinduism propagated by the thinkers whose views I explored in the first four chapters of this book is not the Hinduism of the Sangh Parivar. Vivekananda, Dayanand Saraswati, Aurobindo and Mahatma Gandhi are ostensibly revered, but their paeans to inclusivity are glossed over or ignored. The Hindutva premise, in Panikkar's words, is 'that national regeneration and resurgence would require the recreation of an authentic culture by reclaiming the indigenous and purging the exogenous. Hindutva's cultural project, encoded in the slogan "nationalise and spiritualise", therefore, is twofold: First, to retrieve and disseminate the cultural traditions of the "golden" Hindu past; and second, to eliminate all accretions that had become part of the heritage.'[5]

The former project, of digging up ancient glories of the past, is well under way; the latter is proceeding somewhat fitfully and episodically. We will examine both processes below, starting with the battles being fought over history.

One of the amusing, but nonetheless important, sidelights of the development of Hindutva theory has been the controversy about the origins of the Aryans. The Hindutva approach inevitably had implications for the commonly accepted narratives about India, including the idea that the Indo-Aryan people had migrated to northern India from the Central Asian steppes some time around 1500 BCE and authored the foundational texts of Hinduism, the Vedas. Golwalkar believed that was impossible; Hinduism, he was convinced, was an indigenous faith that grew from rather than put down roots in Indian soil, and so the Indo-Aryans could not possibly have come from elsewhere. His and Savarkar's idea of India being the *punyabhumi* of the Hindus required the Aryans to be indigenous to India, in contrast to India's Muslims, whose faith clearly originated in the Arabian peninsula. A veritable cottage industry was born of RSS-inclined historians debunking the Aryan migration theory, insisting that the Aryans, as the founders of Hinduism, belonged all along to India.

Some less-ideological scholars point out that the *Rig Veda* does not speak of any other land but northern India or Aryavarta. In her *Sacred*

Plants of India, Dr Nanditha Krishna shows how every plant and animal mentioned in the *Rig Veda* originates from this area. This leads some to the conclusion that the Aryans could not have come from anywhere else. But the same textual and vegetal evidence could also suggest that while the Aryans came from elsewhere, they only composed the Vedas after having created a settled civilisation in the Indo-Gangetic plains, which is why their allusions are all to India.

Unfortunately for the Hindutva ideologues, who seemed to be winning the historical battle, recent genetic research—published in a paper (in a peer-reviewed journal called *BMC Evolutionary Biology*) by Professor Martin P. Richards and fifteen other scientists, titled 'A Genetic Chronology for the Indian Subcontinent Points to Heavily Sex-biased Dispersals'—has confirmed that there were indeed significant migrations from the Central Asian steppes into the Indian subcontinent, starting from around 2000 BCE–1500 BCE.[6]

DNA studies show that the Indo-Aryan ethno-linguistic group has a higher signature of Central Asian genes than the corresponding Dravidian speakers; and given that Indo-Aryan languages have close affinities with the larger Indo-European linguistic family, it appears beyond dispute that a common proto-language was involved. The implications for the Savarkar-Golwalkar theory, though, are subversive, since they suggest that Hinduism or the Vedic religion may itself have originated with invaders from outside India, making it as 'un-Indian' in its origins as Islam or Christianity. The conclusions are sufficiently tentative to fall short of conclusive; one critical analysis concludes that 'it is difficult to deduce the direction of haplogroup R1a migration either into India or out of India, although the genetic data certainly show that there was migration between the regions'.[7] The advocates of Hindutva continue to insist the Indo-Aryans and their faith are indigenous to India, but DNA evidence may prove impossible to refute. Much of the dispute seems to centre not around whether there were infusions from abroad but as to whether they occurred 12,000 years ago or 4,000–3,500 years ago. If the first hypothesis is right, the resulting population was indigenous well before they composed the Vedas; the latter suggests a shorter gap between their arrival in India and the emergence of Hinduism.

To me this seems a distinction without a difference, but then I am much more comfortable with the idea that migrations into the subcontinent have been a permanent feature of Indian history than the Hindutva brigade is. In fact the Hindu Pallava kingdom even imported a monarch from Southeast Asia, when King Parameshwaravarman died without an heir in c. 731 CE.[8] A Pallava princess had been given in marriage to the Cham dynasty generations earlier and it was presumed one of her descendants could carry on the royal lineage. Accordingly, a delegation of nobles was sent to the Cambodia–Vietnam region and returned with a fourteen-year-old boy, who ruled for sixty-four years as King Nandivarman II (reigned c. 731–795 CE) and built a number of magnificent temples, including the famous Vaikuntha Perumal in Kanchipuram. Hinduism has been strengthened by its imports too.

HINDUISM AND SCIENCE

Similar battles are being waged over other kinds of intellectual terrain, with Hindu nationalists insisting upon recognising the glories of ancient Indian thought and long-neglected ancestral accomplishments, notably in science. There is definitely a case for enhancing the Indian public's awareness of the genuinely impressive accomplishments of their forebears (of which more below), rather than remaining schooled in a colonial-era Westernised view of the world. But the uncritical, indeed fantasy-laden, manner in which its Hindutva aficionados have advocated the cause has only discredited it.

The dominance of the BJP at the centre and in the states has propelled a number of true believers of Hindutva into positions of unprecedented influence, including in such forums[9] as the Indian Council for Historical Research, the University Grants Commission, and, it turned out, the programme committee of the Indian Science Congress, which scheduled a talk on 'Vedic Aviation Technology' in 2015 that elicited howls of protest from many delegates.

It has also given a licence to unqualified voices who gain in authority from their proximity to power. The 2018 statement by India's junior education Minister, Satyapal Singh, that Darwin's theory of evolution was "unscientific"—on the grounds that "no one has ever seen an ape turn into a man"—drew attention to the latest challenge posed to modern India by its current government. Earlier, another BJP stalwart, Rajasthan's education minister Vasudev Devnani, had dealt science another body blow by claiming that the cow is something of an obsession for the BJP, whose followers have assaulted human beings in the name of cow protection, but this was a step too far even for many of its sympathisers among the educated public.

The two Ministers are educated men: Satyapal Singh is a chemistry graduate, and Vasudev Devnani is a trained engineer. Whether their statements reveal the quality of science education in India, or merely confirm that Hindutva ideology trumps both scientific fact and common sense, neither learning nor governmental office appears to insulate either man from ignorance.

No greater proof of this can be found than the Prime Minister himself. Narendra Modi likes to be portrayed as a technology-friendly 21st century leader, but on 25 October 2014, Modi startled the world at the inauguration of a Mumbai hospital with the claim that the elephant-headed Hindu god Ganesh was proof of ancient India's knowledge of plastic surgery. He went on to cite the ancient epic, the Mahabharata, as confirming that "people then were aware of genetic science."

That the smallest imaginable elephant head cannot possibly fit into the largest available human neck does not appear to have occurred to the Prime Minister, whose fatuous claim discredited ancient India's genuine scientific accomplishments. Such ideas, because they are patently absurd, except in the realm of metaphor, have embarrassed those who advance them as well as those who cite them in support of broader, but equally unsubstantiated, claims to past scientific advances from genetic science to cloning and interstellar travel and the use of nuclear devices (by the philosopher-sage Kanada in the first century BCE). Petty chauvinism is always ugly but never more so than in the field of science, where knowledge must be uncontaminated by ideology, superstition or irrational pride.

India was indeed the world pioneer in plastic surgery; it produced the world's first known surgeon, Susruta, and archaeologists have found the world's oldest surgical instruments (dating from the 1st century) in India. There is evidence for rhinoplasty operations in the ancient texts. But the moment these historical facts were subsumed in a narrative about mythological transplated elephant heads, the actual facts were discredited.

This was not the Prime Minister's only offence. Before heading off for the Paris climate change negotiations, Modi told schoolchildren on Teachers' Day in 2014 that climate change was a myth because it was actually human beings whose capacity to cope with heat and cold has changed, rather than the environment. Global warming, he explained on national television, "is just a state of mind." What made it worse was that this came as an answer to a schoolchild's question about climate change. "That's because as you grow older you are less able to withstand heat and cold. The climate isn't changing." he said, "we are."

The disease is catching. On 31 May 2017, Justice Mahesh Chandra Sharma of the Rajasthan High Court, reportedly a science graduate himself, suggested to the Union of India that the cow be declared the national animal and that cow slaughter be punished with life imprisonment. In an interview to a television channel, Justice Sharma later told the nation that India's national bird, the peacock, "is a lifelong celibate" who "does not indulge in sex" but impregnates the peahen by shedding a tear. He cited Lord Krishna's use of a peacock feather as proof of its celibacy.

The idea of a peacock reproducing through tears may seem laughable, but there is nothing lachrymose about the ruling dispensation's dominant Hindutva ideology, which has helped propagate an astonishing amount of pseudoscience across the country. The gaggle of gurus who have made religion into a hugely successful business in India have inevitably joined the party. Modi associates like the yoga teacher and Ayurveda entrepreneur Baba Ramdev are regular offenders. Ramdev pronounces his pseudo-spiritual wisdom to the world, seeking, for instance, to sell medicines to "cure homosexuality".

Others assert, with some level of official encouragement, that the ancients had already discovered or invented every scientific accomplishment in the Vedic age, including jet aircraft (pushpak viman) and atomic weaponry. The underlying message is that ancient India had all the answers, and that traditional and indigenous practices and ways of life are vastly better than imported modern scientific ideas.

But the controversy also discredits the modern rationalists who, in their contempt for such exaggerated and ludicrous claims, also dismissed the more reasonable propositions pointing to genuine Indian accomplishments by the ancients. It is not necessary to debunk the genuine accomplishments of ancient Indian science in order to mock the laughable assertions of the Hindutva brigade. Separating the reasonable from the absurd is a necessary condition of well-founded criticism.

A BJP government choosing to assert its pride in yoga and Ayurveda, and seeking to promote them internationally, is, to my mind, perfectly acceptable. Not only are these extraordinary accomplishments of our civilisation, but they have always been, and should remain, beyond partisan politics. It is only if the BJP promoted them in place of fulfilling its responsibility to provide conventional healthcare and life-saving modern allopathic medicines to the Indian people, that we need object on policy grounds. But when the national manifesto of the BJP for the 2009 General Election claimed that in ancient times, rice yields in India stood at 20 tonnes per hectare—twice what farmers can produce today using intensive agriculture in the most fertile and propitious conditions imaginable—all one can do is to throw one's hands up in despair.

On the other hand, in asserting (in his own speech to the Indian Science Congress) that ancient Indians anticipated Pythagoras, Science and Technology Minister Dr Harsh Vardhan was not incorrect and should not have been ridiculed. In fact he could have added Newton, Copernicus, Kepler and Galileo as well, every single one of whom had been beaten to their famous 'discoveries' by an unknown and unsung Indian centuries earlier.

The *Rig Veda* asserted that gravitation held the universe together twenty-four centuries before the apple fell on Newton's head. Scholars working in Sanskrit anticipated his discoveries of calculus by at least 250 years. The Siddhantas are amongst the world's earliest texts on astronomy and mathematics; the *Surya Siddhanta*, written about 400 CE, includes a method for finding the times of planetary ascensions and eclipses. The notion of gravitation, or *gurutvakarshan*, features in these early texts. *Lost Discoveries*, by the American writer Dick Teresi, a comprehensive study of the ancient non-Western foundations of modern science, spells it out clearly: 'Two hundred years before Pythagoras,' writes Teresi, 'philosophers in northern India had understood that gravitation held the solar system together, and that therefore the sun, the most massive object, had to be at its centre.'[10]

Aryabhata was the first human being to explain, in 499 CE, that the daily rotation of the earth on its axis is what accounted for the daily rising and setting of the sun. (His ideas were so far in advance of his time that many later editors of his awe-inspiring *Aryabhatiya* altered the text to save his reputation from what they thought were serious errors.) Aryabhata conceived of the elliptical orbits of the planets a thousand years before Kepler, in the West, came to the same conclusion (having assumed, like all Europeans, that planetary orbits were circular rather than elliptical). He even estimated the value of the year at 365 days, six hours, 12 minutes and 30 seconds; in this he was only a few minutes off (the correct figure is just under 365 days and six hours). The translation of the *Aryabhatiya* into Latin in the thirteenth century taught Europeans a great deal; it also revealed to them that an Indian had known things that Europe would only learn of a millennium later.

The Vedic civilisation subscribed to the idea of a spherical earth at a time when everyone else, even the Greeks, assumed the earth was flat. By the fifth century CE Indians had calculated that the age of the earth was 4.3 billion years; as late as the nineteenth century, English scientists believed the earth was a hundred million years old, and it is only in the late twentieth century that Western scientists have come to estimate the earth to be about 4.6 billion years old.

India invented modern numerals (known to the world as 'Arabic' numerals because the West got them from the Arabs, who first encountered them in India). It was an Indian who first conceived of the zero, *shunya*; the concept of nothingness, *shunyata*, integral to Hindu and Buddhist thinking, simply did not exist in the West. Modern mathematics would have been impossible without the zero and the decimal system; just read a string of Roman numbers, which had no zeros, to understand their limitations.

Indian mathematicians invented negative numbers as well. The concept of infinite sets of rational numbers was understood by Jain thinkers in the sixth century BCE. Our forefathers can take credit for geometry, trigonometry, and calculus; the 'Bakhshali manuscript', seventy leaves of bark dating back to the early centuries of the Christian era, reveals fractions, simultaneous equations, quadratic equations, geometric progressions and even calculations of profit and loss, with interest.

The *Sulba Sutras*, composed between 800 and 500 BCE, demonstrate that India had Pythagoras's theorem before the great Greek was born, and a way of getting the square root of 2 correct to five decimal places. (Vedic Indians solved square roots in order to build sacrificial altars of the proper size.) The Kerala mathematician Nilakantha wrote sophisticated explanations of the irrationality of 'pi' before the West had heard of the concept. The *Vedanga Jyotisha*, written around 500 BCE, declares: 'Like the crest of a peacock, like the gem on the head of a snake, so is mathematics at the head of all knowledge.' India's mathematicians were poets too!

Hindus also invented the *Katapayadi* system (also known as Parralperru in Malayalam). In an age without paper and climatic conditions that tended to destroy records, this was a method where numbers could be transcribed as words or even verses. The idea that mathematical formulas could be written down as meaningful sentences helped preserve and perpetuate mathematical expertise in the country.

Indian numbers probably arrived in the Arab world in 773 CE with the diplomatic mission sent by the Hindu ruler of Sind to the court of the Caliph al-Mansur. This gave rise to the famous arithmetical text of al-Khwarizmi, written around 820 CE, which contains a detailed exposition of Indian mathematics, in particular the usefulness of the zero. It was al-Khwarizmi who is credited with the invention of algebra, though he properly credits Indians for it.

But the point is that, alas, India let this knowledge lapse. The reverence for the past that is integral to the ruling ideology is also reflective of a fear of rejecting the past, since the promotion of a faith-based communal identity is central to the Hindutva project, and faith is seen as emerging from the timeless wisdom of the past. Traditionalism benefits those who want to uphold the social order, ensure discipline and conformity, and prevent radical change. Science and rationality threaten such conformism.

This is why the ruling dispensation's political project of transforming secular India into a Hindu state requires the supremacy of religion over science. Religion is no longer just a question of your personal beliefs, a form of stretching out your hands to the divine; it is part of the assertion of a politics of identity built around faith. This requires an assault on science, since science challenges the established verities as religion does not.

When an Education Minister questions Darwin or asserts the miraculous powers of the cow, he is not merely offering a choice between a scientific theory and a faith-based one, he is reminding the public of their allegiance to a total worldview. That worldview embraces a larger political project that prescribes a set of beliefs and behaviours incompatible with science, skepticism and inquiry.

We had a glorious past; wallowing in it and debating it now will only saddle us with a contentious and unproductive present. Indians should take pride in what our forefathers did but resolve to be inspired by them rather than rest on their laurels. We need to use the past as a springboard, not as a battlefield. Only then can we rise above it to create for ourselves a future worthy of our remarkable past.

The BJP is still bent on creating a Hindu state in India. Sadly, this would not be the kind of Hindu state that has made India the scientific superpower of the ancient age, but one plunged in obscurantism and atavistic complacency. It is enough to make one shed a tear. One can only hope that there are no peahens around.

HINDUTVA AND HISTORY

Unsurprisingly, a later period of Indian history, following the Muslim conquests of north India, has become 'ground zero' in the battle of narratives between team Hindutva and the pluralists. When, with the publication of my 2016 book *Inglorious Empire: What the British Did to India*, I spoke of 200 years of foreign rule, I found it interesting that at the same time the Hindutva brigade, led by Prime Minister Modi himself, was speaking of 1,200 years of foreign rule. To them, the Muslim rulers of India, whether the Delhi Sultans, the Deccani Sultans or the Mughals (or the hundreds of other Muslims who occupied thrones of greater or lesser importance for several hundred years across the country) were all foreigners. I responded that while the founder of a Muslim dynasty may have well have come to India from abroad, he and his descendants stayed and assimilated in this country, married Hindu women, and immersed themselves in the fortunes of this land; each Mughal Emperor after Babar had less and less connection of blood or allegiance to a foreign country. If they looted or exploited India and Indians, they spent the proceeds of their loot in India, and did not send it off to enrich a foreign land as the British did. The Mughals received travellers from the Ferghana Valley politely, enquired about the well-being of the people there and perhaps even gave some money for the upkeep of the graves of their Chingizid ancestors, but they stopped seeing their original homeland as home. By the second generation, let alone the fifth or sixth, they were as 'Indian' as any Hindu.

This challenge of authenticity, however, cuts across a wide intellectual terrain. It emerges from those Hindus who share V. S. Naipaul's view of theirs as a 'wounded civilisation', a pristine Hindu land that was subjected to repeated defeats and conquests over the centuries at the hands of rapacious Muslim invaders and was enfeebled and subjugated in the process. To such people, independence is not merely
British rule but an opportunity to restore the glory of their culture and religion, wounded by Muslim conquerors. Historians like Audrey Truschke, author of a sympathetic biography of the Mughal emperor Aurangzeb,[11] have argued that this account of Muslims despoiling the Hindu homeland is neither a continuous historical memory nor based on accurate records of the past. (For instance, it was a pious Hindu, Raja Jai Singh of Jaipur, who led Aurangzeb's armies against the Hindu warrior-hero Shivaji, just as the Hindu General Man Singh had led Akbar's forces against the Hindu hero Rana Pratap, whose principal lieutenant was a Muslim, Hakim Khan Sur.) But there is no gainsaying the emotional content of the Hindutva view of the past: it is for them a matter of faith that India is a Hindu nation, which Muslim rulers attacked,

looted and sought to destroy, and documented historical facts that refute this view are at best an inconvenience, at worst an irrelevance.

Indeed, Truschke has disputed the widespread belief in India that Aurangzeb was a Muslim fanatic who destroyed thousands of Hindu temples, forced millions of Indians to convert to Islam, and enacted a genocide of Hindus. Though there is little doubt that he was indeed, in Jawaharlal Nehru's words, 'a bigot and an austere puritan'—he ended royal patronage of music, prohibited rituals of Hindu origin in his court, imposed the bigoted *jizya* tax on his non-Muslim subjects, withdrew land grants given to Hindus and introduced policies that favoured Muslims alone—none of the other propositions, she demonstrates in her work, was true, least of all the claim (made by many of those who fought successfully to remove his name from a prominent road in Delhi) that his ultimate aim was to eradicate Hindus and Hinduism. Historical evidence suggests that Aurangzeb did not destroy thousands of Hindu temples as is claimed and that the ones he did destroy were largely for political reasons; that he did little to promote conversions, as evidenced by the relatively modest number of Hindus who adopted Islam during Aurangzeb's rule; that he increased the proportion of Hindus in the Mughal nobility by co-opting a number of Maratha aristocrats from the Deccan; that he gave patronage to Hindu and Jain temples and liberally donated land to Brahmins; and that millions of Hindus thrived unmolested in his empire. History is a complex affair: Aurangzeb was undoubtedly an illiberal Muslim ruler, unlike his ancestors or the brother he decapitated on his ascent to the throne, Dara Shikoh, but he was not the genocidal mass-murderer and iconoclast many Hindus depict him as having been.

For Truschke, who concedes that Aurangzeb demolished a 'few dozen' temples, a 'historically legitimate view of Aurangzeb must explain why he protected Hindu temples more often than he demolished them'. Critics find this an insufficient excuse for his intolerance. One, Girish Shahane, no Hindutva apologist himself, retorts:

> 'Should we not criticise sportspersons who take money to fix matches unless they do so in most games they play? Should we

defend sexual predators on the grounds that the vast majority of their interactions with women are respectful? Should we object to a serial killer being called a psychopath because we can't be sure why he targeted particular victims but not hundreds of other people he met? It is important to push back against the Hindutvavadi idea of Muslim rulers as genocidal maniacs who destroyed shrines indiscriminately. But it is imperative we do it without explaining away Muslim religious prejudice where it exists.'[12]

A fairer assessment, in other words, might be to say that like many rulers of his time, whether Muslim or Hindu, Aurangzeb both protected and attacked Hindus and Muslims alike, though his religious bigotry was, of course, directed only at the former. But such nuanced accounts of Aurangzeb enjoy little traction amongst those who prefer their history in unambiguous shades of black and white. To quote Truschke once more, 'Aurangzeb is controversial not so much because of India's past but rather because of India's present... The narrative of Aurangzeb the Bigot, which crops up largely in polarising debates about Indian national identity, has more to do with modern politics than premodern history and is a byproduct and catalyst of growing intolerance in India.'

In this Hindutva-centred view, history is made of religion-based binaries, in which all Muslim rulers are evil and all Hindus are valiant resisters, embodiments of incipient Hindu nationalism. The Hindu nationalists believe, in Truschke's words, 'that India was subjected to repeated defeats over the centuries, including by generations of Muslim conquerors that enfeebled the people and their land...many in India feel injured by the Indo-Muslim past, and their sentiments [are] often undergirded by modern anti-Muslim sentiments.'[13] As K. N. Panikkar has pointed out, liberal and tolerant rulers such as Ashoka, Akbar, Jai Singh, Shahu Maharaj and Wajid Ali Shah do not figure in Hindutva's list of national heroes. (Indeed, where many nationalist historians extolled Akbar as the liberal, tolerant counterpart to the Islamist Aurangzeb, the Hindutva lobby has begun to attack him too, principally because he was Muslim, and like most medieval monarchs, killed princes who stood in his way, many of whom happened to be Hindu.)

Communal history continues past the era of Islamic rule. Among those Indians who revolted against the British, Bahadur Shah, Zinat Mahal, Maulavi Ahmadullah and General Bakht Khan, all Muslims, are conspicuous by their absence from Hindutva histories. And of course syncretic traditions such as the Bhakti movement, and universalist religious reformers like Rammohan Roy and Keshub Chandra Sen, do not receive much attention from the Hindutva orthodoxy. What does is the uncritical veneration of 'Hindu heroes' like Rana Pratap (portrayed now in Rajasthani textbooks as the victor of the Battle of Haldi Ghati against Akbar, which begs the question why Akbar and not he ruled the country for the following three decades) and of course Chhatrapati Shivaji, the intrepid Maratha warrior whose battles against the Mughals have now replaced accounts of Mughal kings in Maharashtra's textbooks. The Maharashtra Education Board's newly-revised class VII history book of 2017 has eliminated all mention of the pre-Mughal Muslim rulers of India as well, including Razia Sultan, the first woman queen of Delhi, Sher Shah Suri and Muhammad bin Tughlaq, who notoriously and disastrously moved India's capital south from Delhi to Daulatabad. (The educational system is the chosen battlefield for Hindutva's warriors, and curriculum revision their preferred weapon.)

THE STRUGGLE FOR FREEDOM

The debates over history are not confined to the distant past alone. Prime Minister Modi chose the anniversary of the Quit India movement in 1942 to launch a campaign called '*70 Saal Azadi: Zara Yaad Karo Qurbani*' ('Seventy years of freedom: remember the sacrifices'). The BJP which, led by the PM, has sought to drape itself in the mantle of nationalism, is now seeking to appropriate the freedom struggle for its cause. Ironically the Quit India movement is an occasion the BJP could well have chosen to criticise rather than celebrate, since it resulted in the jailing by the British of all the leaders and thousands of workers of the nationalist movement, giving the Muslim League the freedom it needed to build up a support base it had lacked in the elections of 1937, and thus, strengthened the hands of those who wanted Partition.

But the Modi government has no intention of repudiating Quit India as a Congress folly. It wants to make heroes of freedom fighters, by implication placing them on its own side in a contemporary retelling of history pegged to the seventieth anniversary of our independence. The complication is that the Sanghivadi political cause to which the BJP is heir—embodied in the Jana Sangh, the RSS, and the Hindutva movement—had no prominent freedom fighter of its own during the nationalist struggle for *azadi* (freedom). The BJP traces its origin to leaders who were not particularly active during the nationalist movement. The lack of inspiration for the people in the parent body of the BJP means they have to look for role models elsewhere.

The process had already begun, lest we forget, when then Chief Minister Modi moved aggressively to lay claim to the legacy of one of India's most respected founding fathers, Sardar Vallabhbhai Patel, before the 2014 election. In his quest to garb himself in a more distinguished lineage than his party can ordinarily lay claim to, Modi called on farmers across India to donate iron from their ploughs to construct a giant 550-foot statue of the Iron Man in his state, which would be by far the largest statue in the world, dwarfing the Statue of Liberty. But it will be less of a monument to the modest Gandhian it ostensibly honours than an embodiment of the overweening ambitions of its builder.

Modi's motives are easy to divine. His own image had been tarnished by the communal massacre in Gujarat when he was chief minister in 2002. Identifying himself with Patel—who is portrayed as the leader who stood up for the nation's Hindus during the horrors of Partition, stood up to Nehru in ordering the rebuilding of the ruined Somnath temple and was firm on issues like Kashmir—is an attempt at character-building by association: Modi himself as an embodiment of the tough, decisive man of action that Patel was, rather than the destructive bigot his enemies decry.

It helps that Patel is widely admired for his extraordinary role in forging India that gave him an unchallenged standing as 'the Iron Man'. Patel has both the national appeal and Gujarati origin that appeal to Modi. The Modi-as-latter-day-Patel message has been resonating well with many Gujaratis, who are proud to be reminded of a native son the nation looks up to, and with many of India's urban middle-class, who see in Modi a strong leader to cut through the confusion and indecision of India's messy democracy.

But Patel's conduct during the violence that accompanied Partition stands in stark contrast to Modi's in 2002. Both Patel and Modi were faced with the serious breakdown of law and order in their respective domains, involving violence and rioting against the Muslims. In Delhi in 1947, Patel immediately and effectively moved to ensure the protection of Muslims, herding 10,000 in the most vulnerable areas to the security of Delhi's Red Fort. Because Patel was afraid that local security forces might have been affected by the virus of communal passions, he moved army troops from Madras and Pune to Delhi to ensure law and order. Patel made it a point to send a reassuring signal to the Muslim community by attending prayers at the famous Nizamuddin Dargah to convey a clear message that Muslims and their faith belonged unquestionably on the soil of India. Patel also went to the border town of Amritsar, where there were attacks on Muslims fleeing to the new Islamic state of Pakistan, and pleaded with Hindu and Sikh mobs to stop victimising Muslim refugees. In each of these cases, Patel succeeded, and there are literally tens of thousands of people who are alive today because of his interventions.

The contrast with what happened in Gujarat in 2002 is painful. Whether or not one ascribes direct blame to Modi for the pogrom that year, he can certainly claim no credit for acting in the way Patel did in Delhi. In Gujarat, there was no direct and immediate action by Modi, as the state's chief executive, to protect Muslims. Nor did Modi express any public condemnation of the attacks, let alone undertake any symbolic action of going to a masjid or visiting a Muslim neighbourhood to convey reassurance.

One cannot imagine Patel saying to an interviewer, as Modi did, when asked how he felt about the killings of Muslims in Gujarat: "[if] someone else is driving a car and we're sitting behind, even then if a puppy comes under the wheel, will it be painful or not?"[14] There is a particular irony to a self-proclaimed 'Hindu nationalist' like Modi, whose speeches have often dripped with contempt for Muslims, laying claim to the legacy of a Gandhian leader who would never have qualified his Indian nationalism with a religious label.

Sardar Patel believed in equal rights for all irrespective of their religion or caste. It is true that at the time of Partition Patel was inclined to believe, unlike Nehru, that an entire community had seceded. In my biography *Nehru: The Invention of India* (2003) I have given some examples of Nehru and Patel clashing on this issue. But there are an equal number of examples where Patel, if he had to choose between what was the right thing for many Hindus and what was the right thing morally, invariably plumped for the moral Gandhian approach.

An example, so often distorted by the Sangh Parivar apologists, was his opposition to Nehru's pact with Liaquat Ali Khan, the prime minister of Pakistan, on the question of violence in East Pakistan against the Hindu minority. The Nehru-Liaquat pact was indeed criticised by Patel and he disagreed quite ferociously with Nehru on the matter. But when Nehru insisted on his position, it was Patel who gave in, and his reasoning was entirely Gandhian: that violence in West Bengal against Muslims essentially took away Indians' moral right to condemn violence against Hindus in East Pakistan. That was not a Hindu nationalist position but a classically Gandhian approach as an *Indian* nationalist.

History has often been contested terrain in India, but its revival in the context of twenty-first century politics is a sobering sign that the past continues to have a hold over the Hindutva movement in the present. While the Mughals will be demonised as a way of delegitimising Indian Muslims (who are stigmatised as 'Babur ke aulad', the sons of Babur rather than of the Indian soil), the arguments over Patel confirm that he and other heroes of the freedom struggle will be hijacked to the present ruling party's attempts to appropriate a halo of nationalism that none of its forebears has done anything to earn.

HINDUTVA AND CULTURE

If the rewriting of the historical past is a vital first objective of the Hindutva project, the second is the removal of what they see as the various accretions to the Hindu idea that had arisen over the years.

These accretions, to the more rabid of the Hindutva brigades, include the acceptance of difference that Vivekananda and Radhakrishnan had celebrated. Indeed, the distinctive difference between what one might call the Nehruvian version of Indian nationalism and the Hindutva version of it is the latter's active rejection of different interpretations and the diversity of representations for which the Indian cultural tradition had become known, and which other Hindus portrayed as the strength of their culture.

One aspect of this is the relentless campaign being waged against heterodox interpretations of Hinduism itself—and this in the name of a faith which proudly includes no concept of heresy. Thus Hindutva mobs attacked and vandalised the invaluable Bhandarkar Oriental Research Institute's library in Pune to protest its co-operation with the research work of the historian James Laine, whose book allegedly cast aspersions on the parentage of Shivaji. The courts offer a less dramatic form of censorship, since Hindutva activists can invoke Section 295(a) of the Indian Penal Code, which criminalises insults to religious sentiments, though the intent was only to outlaw inflammatory writings published with deliberate and malicious intent. Under this provision, serious scholars like Wendy Doniger, who has authored several learned and brilliant studies of Hinduism, have been sued, and publishers, intimidated by the forces arrayed against them and reluctant to spend what it would take to defend their authors' freedoms, have usually caved in. One of Doniger's books on Hinduism was not only withdrawn from the marketplace by its publishers, but all existing copies pulped in order not to give offence to the Hindutva lobby.

The destruction and pulping of books, and the burning of libraries, is possible because the colonial-era law criminalises even accurate statements about Indian religion and history if these offend the sentiments of any community in India. Still, to see such actions being carried out in the name of the Hindu faith is profoundly disquieting. In the Hindu culture that I grew up with, books are revered. If I so much as accidentally touched a fallen book or even a magazine or newspaper with my foot, I was brought up to bend down, touch it again with my fingertips in apology and apply my fingers to my eyes and forehead to beg forgiveness from the Goddess Saraswati for my transgression, a practice I still perform in my seventh decade. This respect for the printed word can be found among Hindus of every part of the country. How can people who claim to be Hindu not just disrespect but actually destroy books?

The destruction of some people's books is inevitably accompanied by the promotion of other books. Foreign Minister Sushma Swaraj, not known to be an RSS sympathiser but aggressive in her cultural nationalism, proposed the adoption of the Bhagavad Gita as the 'Rashtriya Granth', or national holy book. There are four problems with Sushma Swaraj's advocacy of the Bhagavad Gita as our 'national holy book', of which the first is that, to cite no less a source than Prime Minister Modi himself, we already have a national holy book: it's called the Constitution of India.

The second is that we are a land of multiple faiths, each of which has its own holy books; on what basis would we pick any one of them in the capacity of a national holy book? Which Sikh would put the Gita ahead of the Guru Granth Sahib, for instance?

And if the answer to that question is, as Smt. Swaraj suggests, that it is the holiest book of the overwhelming Hindu majority of our population, the proposition is contestable, like most things in Hindu philosophy. As a practising (and reasonably widely-read) Hindu myself, I find many ideas in the *Upanishads* and the *Puranas* that are not in the *Gita*. I see Hinduism as a pluralistic faith of many holy books and many ways of worshipping the Divine. You don't have to agree with those Hindu scholars who argue that the *Gita*, being part of an *itihasa*, a subset of *smriti* (that which is heard and remembered, orally), ranks lower in the hierarchy of Hindu sacred texts than the Vedas and the *Upanishads*, which are *sruti* (seen, heard and recorded divine revelation). But such arguments apart, there is no doubt that there are many views of the relative merits of several Indian holy books.

Smt. Swaraj (like many before her, including Vivekananda and Gandhiji) may be inspired by the *Gita*, but other, equally devout, Hindus might have other preferences. As Dayanand might have asked: Why not the *RigVeda*, for instance, the primordial revelatory text of the

Hindu faith? Why not the *smriti* text known as the Srimad Bhagavatam, or Bhagavata Purana, which is recited for an entire week (*saptaham*) every year in many Hindu temples and homes? The quest to anoint a national holy book will not just divide Indians—it will divide Hindus as well.

But it's the fourth problem that's most relevant to a political discussion of the issue. For a government minister to raise the idea of a national holy book serves to ignite not just controversy, but fears—fears of a majoritarian project that will slowly but surely erode India's pluralist (officially secular) identity and replace it with an overtly Hindu one.

Signs of such inclinations have been accumulating since the BJP rode to power in May 2014. There has been the overt declaration by RSS leader Mohan Bhagwat that all Indians are Hindus,[15] and by implication that those who do not consider themselves Hindus aren't actually Indian, and don't belong here. There's the statement by a minister, Giriraj Singh, that those who don't vote for Modi should move to Pakistan,[16] and the one by another minister, Sadhvi Niranjana Jyoti, that people are either followers of Rama or bastards (*Ramzaade ya Haramzaade*). Neither of these offenders has been required to pay for their statements by relinquishing their seats on Prime Minister Modi's Council of Ministers.

There was the Shiv Sena MP, a member of the ruling coalition, shoving food down the throat of a fasting Muslim during Ramzan, and getting away without the slightest censure from the ruling party.[17] There have been numerous incidents of communal violence, instigated for political purposes no doubt, but instilling fear in the targeted minorities. And there was the faintly ridiculous episode of the mass conversion of fifty-seven bewildered Bengali Muslims in Agra, through a mix of intimidation and inducement, under the Sangh Parivar's long-dormant '*ghar wapsi*' scheme.[18] (Many of them, it seems, were illegal immigrants from Bangladesh, who thought that signing up would be an excellent dodge to regularise their status in India.)

The resultant uproar put '*ghar wapsi*' on the back burner, but the 'reconversion' to the parent faith of those Indians who are not Hindu remains a cherished Hindutva project. As Manmohan Vaidya of the RSS has explained: 'Ghar wapsi is a natural urge to connect to our roots.'

So Smt. Swaraj's declaration joins a long list of statements and actions by our Hindutva-inspired rulers that cumulatively have stirred disquiet across the country.

Is this wise? It is ironic that Prime Minister Modi keeps on empha-sising the message of development and economic transformation, while his aides persist in raising bogeys that their leader has been attempting to lay to rest. There is little doubt that after the BJP rode to power on a mantra of inclusive development 'sab ka saath, sab ka vikas' its Hindutva core has begun to take advantage of its proximity to govern-ment to assertively push a sectarian agenda. As has been noted, Hindutva acolytes are being appointed to research professorships and vice-chancellorships; the Indian Council of Historical Research was headed for three years by a true believer whose Hindutva credentials reportedly outshine his historical ones, textbooks in BJP-ruled states like Maharashtra and Rajasthan are being rewritten to privilege ancient Hindu glories, and Sanskrit is being promoted. Some of this, one might argue, is inevitable in any democracy after a transfer of power from one ruling dispensation to another. But some, at least, distracts from the Prime Minister's central (and oft-repeated) message that economic growth is his faith, the Constitution is his holy book and Parliament is his temple.

Just as investors tend not to come to war zones—which is why peace on our borders is in our national interest—so too do investors prefer to risk their capital in harmonious societies that are focused on the future rather than divided by the past. The BJP and its Government should heed one simple dictum: leave religion to the personal space and preference of every Indian. Let us have no national holy book, just as our constitution forbids us from having a national religion. Our country was once divided over religion; let us not now promote a partition in the Indian soul that will be as bad as the partition we have already endured on Indian soil. Let us not awake demons that seven decades of secular Indian democracy have put to rest after the tragic horrors of 1947.

It is time to let sleeping dogmas lie.

NARROW-MINDED BIGOTRY

Hindutva takes a dully static view of India's cultural tradition, ignoring its capacity to react to and absorb foreign influences, and negating its inherent dynamism. In the name of this limited and narrow view of Hindu culture, and in addition to its threats to books, Hindutva activists have assaulted a film-maker for allegedly planning to shoot a love-scene between a Rajput princess and a Muslim conqueror (of which more later); vandalised exhibitions of M. F. Husain's paintings because he had depicted Hindu goddesses in the nude; disrupted the shooting of the Indo-Canadian Deepa Mehta's film on Benares widows for insulting an age-old Hindu practice; denigrated the Malayalam writer Kamala Das for her conversion to Islam as Kamala Suraiya; banned A. K. Ramanujam's classic text on the hundreds of versions of the *Ramayana* from the syllabus of Delhi University; and trashed a SAHMAT exhibition on the Ayodhya dispute. The politicisation of culture is truly complete under India's Hindutva government.

Of these, the assault on M. F. Husain and his works was typical of Hindutva intolerance. In 1996 a mob destroyed several paintings of the artist at an exhibition in Ahmedabad, outraged that a Muslim artist had portrayed Hindu goddesses in the nude. Husain had long been known to use Hindu iconography—goddesses and *apsaras* were among his favourite themes, and he had depicted Indira Gandhi as Durga, and the actress Madhuri Dixit as the *apsara* Menaka, to telling effect in the past, infusing his work with energetic reimaginings of the tales and legends of Hindu tradition. But rather than feeling flattered that a Muslim artist should draw so liberally from the Hindu ethos, the self-appointed custodians of Hindu culture were outraged that he had done so. An irate Hindutva cadre declared that no Muslim had the right to portray Hindu deities 'any way he wishes', going on to demand that Husain's paintings should all be immersed in the Ganga, so they might be simultaneously cleansed and destroyed.

At one time one could have said that this was not Hindu behaviour, and indeed the paintings objected to had been displayed for twenty years previously without any Hindu objecting to them. But this was not about Hinduism, it was about Hindutva politics: the Bajrang Dal and its ilk were practising a basic form of political me-too-ism. Having seen successive governments pandering to the offended sentiments of minority communities, they wanted to show they could be offended too, and thereby bend society to their will.

After the vandalism came the legal harassment of the nonagenarian artist by malicious lawsuits seeking his prosecution for allegedly having offended the petitioners' notions of morality by the use of nudity in his art, particularly in paintings of Hindu goddesses and in the depiction of the contours of India in the shape of a semi-nude female figure. The piling up of a number of cases motivated essentially by anti-Muslim bigotry drove Husain into self-imposed exile in Dubai and London and deprived India of a national treasure. So many abusive cases were filed against him that a court even went so far as to attach his home and his property—a decision later reversed by the Supreme Court. But Husain feared the harassment would not end there; the moment he set foot in Delhi or Mumbai, he said, he was sure to be dragged off to the lock-up, tormented by legal proceedings. He was nearly ninety-one when he fled the country, at an age when he should have been living as a beloved and honoured eminence in his native land. But he did not want to spend his last years battling the persecution of the petty hypocrites who had turned on him. So he stayed away, and passed away in exile.

Delhi High Court Justice Sanjay Kishan Kaul (later elevated to the Supreme Court) authored a magisterial judgment in 2007 disposing of several of these cases in a learned, closely-argued and meticulously-footnoted ruling that bears detailed reading and extensive citation.[19] Recalling the richness of India's 5,000-year-old culture, the judge noted:

> 'Ancient Indian art has been never been devoid of eroticism where sex worship and graphical representation of the union between man and woman has been a recurring feature. The sculpture on the earliest temples of (the) Mithuna image or the erotic couples in Bhubaneshwar, Konark and Puri in Orissa (150–1250 CE); Khajuraho in Madhya Pradesh (900–1050 CE); Limbojimata temple at Delmel, Mehsana (tenth century CE); Kupgallu Hill, Bellary,

Madras; and Nilkantha temple at Sunak near Baroda [are fine examples of this]... Even the very concept of (the) "lingam" of the God
Shiva resting in the centre of the yoni, is in a way representation of
the act of creation, the union of Prakriti and Purusha. The ultimate
essence of a work of ancient Indian erotic art has been religious in
character and can be enunciated as a state of heightened delight or
ananda, the kind of bliss that can be experienced only by the spirit.'

But Husain's tormentors seemed to know nothing of these ancient
Hindu traditions; instead, they professed to be defending their idea of
the Hindu faith and the nation's cultural integrity. (In objecting to his
use of nudity, they were in fact being far more Puritan, in the Christian
sense of the term, than Hindu.) Instead of applauding the decision of a
Muslim artist to derive inspiration from the ancient legends of his
homeland, they accused him of desecrating a faith that was not his.
Instead of honouring an artist who had revived worldwide appreciation
of the richness and diversity of the sources of Indian culture, they
attacked him for insulting Indian culture, reducing Indianness to the
narrow bigotry of their own blinkers.

It is a disgrace that India allowed the most intolerant elements of its
society to derail the life and work of such a great artist. These so-called
Hindus had clearly never seen the inside of any of our ancient temples,
had never marvelled at Khajuraho or seen a sunset at Konark. Theirs is
a notion of 'Bharatiya Sanskriti' that is profoundly inauthentic, because
it can be traced back no further than the Puritanism that accompanied
the Muslim conquests.

The elderly artist had sought the dismissal of various cases filed
against him for allegedly offending public decency and morality by his
'obscene' use of nudity in his paintings, particularly those of Hindu
goddesses and of 'Bharat Mata'. While Justice Kaul's ruling took care
of the legal aspects of the cases against Husain, his larger observations
on the issue deserve the attention of every thinking Indian.

The most important of these, I believe, is the judge's rejection of the
tendency of thin-skinned (or maliciously motivated) people across the
country to claim to be offended by artistic and literary works. If you're

easily offended, he argues, don't read the book, look at the painting or open the website that offends you, but don't prevent the artist or writer from enjoying his constitutionally protected freedom of expression. What is vital, according to Justice Kaul, is to look at the work of art from the artist's point of view—his or her intent rather than the hyper-sensitive viewer's reaction. Lest he be promptly denounced by the Hindutva brigade as a deracinated pseudo-secularist, the judge wisely cites Swami Vivekananda's words in defence of his approach: 'We tend to reduce everyone else to the limits of our own mental universe and begin privileging our own ethics, morality, sense of duty and even our sense of utility. All religious conflicts arose from this propensity to judge others. If we indeed must judge at all, then it must be "according to his own ideal, and not by that of anyone else". It is important, therefore, to learn to look at the duty of others through their own eyes and never judge the customs and observances of others through the prism of our own standards.'

But Justice Kaul goes even further in extending the boundaries of the permissible in India. Nudity and sex, he argues, have an honoured place in art and literature: 'In the land of the Kama Sutra, we shy away from its very name?' he asks in surprise. 'Beauty lies in the eyes of the beholder and so does obscenity... [In Hindu tradition], sex was embraced as an integral part of a full and complete life. It is most unfortunate that India's new "puritanism" is being carried out in the name of cultural purity and a host of ignorant people are vandalising art and pushing us towards a pre-Renaissance era.'

I am not disrespecting those of my Hindu readers who, while fully respecting Husain as an artist, and without expressing any of the communal bigotry that I found particularly distasteful about this affair, nonetheless expressed anguish at seeing representations of goddesses in the nude. They wrote to me at the time of their hurt that images they worshipped should have been so depicted; many asked why Husain has not depicted figures of other faiths, including his own, undressed. (He had once painted the Prophet's wife as a fully clad woman in a sari which even covered her head.) Several added that this was because Hindus are a pushover; other faiths are more robust in their self-defence, whereas Hindus like me are all too willing to accept being insulted.

There's a lot to be said about all this that go beyond the scope of this book. But some points must be made. First: I don't feel insulted by the paintings because (unlike the Danish cartoonists who caricatured the Prophet Muhammad) no insult was intended. Husain was, after all, a major artist, with a long record of being inspired by Hindu mythology as a vital source of inspiration for his work. His paintings of goddesses were consistent with fifty years of his paintings of other iconic Hindu images, clad and unclad. Husain, who grew up in Pandharpur, a major pilgrim centre, and spent all his formative years interacting with devout Hindus, watching Hindu festivals, and drawing nourishment from these influences, was fascinated by Hindu gods. More than the Prophet or any Muslim imagery, what fired his imagination was Hindu India, in which he was reared and which he sought to celebrate. I saw the paintings in that context; his critics saw them out of context (and judging by some emails I received, grossly exaggerated what the paintings depicted). Husain saw his paintings as being within a millennial Indian tradition in which nudity has been widely used in art, including on temple walls. So did I; in Thiruvananthapuram's annual Attukal Bhagavathy festival, the goddess is routinely portrayed topless in posters throughout the city.

Husain as an artist had long used form to suggest ideas beyond form; images in his works are both less and more than realistic depictions of what they portray. His paintings are full of metaphors and allusions; the body, he often said, is a representation of something formless, illusory (a form of *maya*). As a Hindu, I did not see his goddesses as literal depictions of the images I worship. I believe in the Upanishadic view that the Divine is essentially unknowable, and that all worship consists of human beings stretching out their hands to that which they cannot touch. But since we humans, with our limited minds, need something more specific to aid our imaginations, we visualise God in forms that we find more easily recognisable. Hinduism, in accepting that need, also gives its adherents an infinite variety of choices about how to imagine God. That's why there are 333,000 (or million) names and depictions of the Divine in Hinduism; each Hindu may pick the ones he wishes to venerate, and the form in which he wishes to venerate them. There's nothing more 'authentic' about a Raja Ravi Varma image of Saraswati than that of a calendar artist; each is imagining the goddess according to his own sensibility. As a Hindu, I had no difficulty in according Husain the same right.

The question of why Husain doesn't paint Muslim figures in the nude is a red herring. The Islamic tradition is a different one from either the Hindu or the Western. Islam, after all, prohibits any visual depiction of the Prophet, whereas visualising our gods and goddesses is central to the practice of Hinduism.

It is time all Indians, but especially Hindus, woke up to what is being done to our heritage in our name. To reduce the soaring majesty of an inclusive, free-ranging, eclectic and humane faith to the petit-bourgeois morality of narrow-minded bigots is a far greater betrayal of our culture than anything an artist can paint.

For where, in the Hindutva brigade's definition of '*Bharatiya sanskriti*', do the erotic sculptures of Khajuraho belong? Should their explicitly detailed couplings not be pulled down, as Fashion TV's cable signals were during the last BJP government? What about the *Kama Sutra*, the tradition of the devadasis, the eros of the Krishna Leela—are they all un-Indian now?

When the late, great Nobel Prize-winning Mexican poet Octavio Paz wrote his final ode to our civilisation, *In Light of India*, he devoted an entire section to Sanskrit erotic poetry, basing himself, among other things, on the Buddhist monk Vidyakara's immortal eleventh-century compilation of 1,728 *kavya* (poems), many of which are exquisitely profane. Are poets like Ladahachandra or Bhavakadevi, who a thousand years ago wrote verse after verse describing and praising the female breast, to be expelled from the Hindutva canon of 'Bharatiya sanskriti'? Should we tell the Octavio Paz of the future seeking to appreciate the attainments of our culture that the televised *Mahabharata* is 'Bharatiya sanskriti', but a classical portrayal of the erotic longings of the *gopi*s for Krishna is not?

The televised *Mahabharata*, which broke a viewership record set by its predecessor the *Ramayana* series, has much to answer for. It would be unwise to underestimate the significant role of Ramananda Sagar's

Ramayana serial on Doordarshan in promoting Hindutva revival through a cardboard depiction of Rama as a Bollywood B-film hero, complete with crude special effects, melodramatic dialogue and theatrical acting. Encouraged by its success, B. R. Chopra offered similar treatment to the *Mahabharata*; both epics became the most widely-watched shows on television, attracting some 92 per cent of all television viewers to their weekly telecasts. A nation glued to its television sets in an era where there was only one channel, the public broadcaster Doordarshan, found itself alternately unified and exalted by seeing its collective national myths rendered simply and accessibly on the small screen. One of the many ironies of contemporary India is how a secular government and a materialistic Bollywood combined to produce the religious underpinnings for the rise of Hindu cultural nationalism in India.

(This has actually continued into the present day. There has been a proliferation of television channels, but several show hugely popular 'serials', the Indian version of soap operas, which embody and propagate conservative 'Hindu' values. Many Bollywood superstars are themselves Muslim, including five who sport the surname Khan, and they have all portrayed devout Hindu heroes and danced to devotional songs before Hindu idols. The portrayal of sympathetic Muslim characters in popular cinema, like the brave and patriotic Pathan in *Zanjeer* (1972) or the lovable Akbar in *Amar Akbar Anthony* (1977) has declined, subliminally reinforcing the notion of India as a land of Hindu ethos rather than pluralist culture.)

Hindutva hypocrisy is also much in evidence in relation to alcohol, deemed to be un-Hindu and officially banned in the prime minister's own home state of Gujarat (though, reportedly, widely available, at a price, under the table). Wide and frequent are the calls for Prohibition, and rare indeed the figure in Indian public life who would be willing to be photographed with a drink in his hand. And yet alcohol has a hoary history in Hindu literature. As I have mentioned earlier, Soma, or Som-Ras, was the favourite beverage of the Vedic deities and was offered in most of the sacrifices performed in honour of Rig Vedic gods like Indra, Agni, Varun, and others. The Vedic gods were no teetotallers, and drinking was an essential feature of these sacrifices: for instance, in one ritual (performed at the beginning of the Vajapeya sacrifice), the historian D. N. Jha describes a collective drinking ritual in which a sacrificer offered five cups to Indra as well as seventeen cups of soma and seventeen cups of sura to thirty-four gods.[20]

A large variety of some fifty intoxicating drinks are mentioned in ancient Hindu texts. Jha tells us that the use of alcohol by men was quite common, though sometimes discouraged among Brahmins, and instances of drinking among women were not rare. Sanskrit literature, including the plays of Kalidasa, and Buddhist Jataka texts, frequently mention alcoholic drinks. Ancient Hindus were far less puritanical than those who claim to be custodians of their legacy today. The prohibitionist instincts of Hindutva's shock troops find their sternest rebuke in the divine hedonism of their most ancient gods.

But the disapproval of alcohol as a sinful Western indulgence is of a piece with the assault on any cultural practice deemed to be insufficiently Hindu by the self-appointed guardians of Indian culture. The news from UP, telling us that Chief Minister Yogi Adityanath's anti-Romeo squads have questioned 21,37,520 people for being out with girls between 22 March and 15 December 2017, has offered a sobering reminder of how far moral policing has gone in today's India. Worse, it turns out that of those questioned, 9,33,099 have been officially "warned" and 1,706 FIRs issued against 3,003 persons. All this has happened in less than nine months.

So this is what a once-free society has been reduced to: multiple police squads, each consisting of a sub-inspector and two constables, patrolling Uttar Pradesh's university campuses, college yards, cinema theatres, parks and other public places, looking for "Romeos". The term seems to be loosely defined, entitling the cops to stop and question any young couple. While it may have once been intended to curb harassment by louts loafing in public places to "eve-tease" unwary women, the sheer numbers reported confirm that the harassment is now coming mainly from the authorities and not from their targets.

The term "anti-Romeo squad" is itself telling. It traces its origins to the "Roadside Romeos" of my own youth—raffish fellows in drainpipe pants, wavy locks and rakish moustaches, usually unemployed, who lounged about whistling at, or singing snatches of Bollywood film songs to, passing women. They were usually ignored, and mostly harmless. Today's UP police have a far broader target: a Romeo is any young man aspiring to woo his own Juliet. Shakespeare's Romeo, after all, defied convention and evaded his disapproving parents to pursue his love for a woman from the wrong family. That is precisely what Yogi Adityanath does not want Romeo's 21st century imitators to do.

The anti-Romeo squads are merely the latest sign of the continuing assault on any cultural practice deemed to be insufficiently Hindu by the self-appointed guardians of Indian culture. A new spurt of arrests is likely as the anti-Romeo squads double their vigilance for Valentine's Day. Until Yogi's victory, policing Valentine's Day lovers was a task undertaken by lumpen activists of assorted *senas* and *dals*; now, in a sort of reverse privatisation, it is a task that has been taken up by the BJP-run state.

And what of the freelance anti-romance troublemakers? After years of attacking couples holding hands on 14 February, trashing stores selling Valentine's Day greeting cards and shouting slogans outside cafes with canoodling couples, Hindutva activists changed tactics last year. The Hindu Mahasabha announced that it would send squads out to catch any unmarried couples out for a tryst on Valentine's Day and promptly cart them off to a temple to be married. (And, if the Hindutvavadi MP and Godse admirer Sakshi Maharaj has his way, they will be lectured on the virtues of producing between four and ten children forthwith, in order to give his fantasies a voting majority.)

The police-uniform-clad face of intolerance might be amusing if it weren't for the fact that all involved are deadly serious. The nativists argue that Valentine's Day is an imported celebration, which it is (but so is Christmas, or Id-ul-Nabi, or International Women's Day, for that matter, and they don't have the nerve to attack those). They also argue that it is un-Indian because it celebrates romantic love, and they're completely wrong. Historians tell us that there was a well-established Hindu tradition of adoration for Kamadeva, the lord of love, which was only abandoned after the Muslim invasions in medieval times. But then no one in the Hindu Mahasabha has any real idea of Hindu tradition—

their idea of Indian values is not just primitive and narrow-minded, it is also profoundly anti-historical.

In fact, what young people call 'PDA' or 'public display of affection' was widely prevalent in ancient India. As late as the eleventh century, Hindu sexual freedoms were commented on by shocked travellers from the Muslim world. Today's young celebrants of Valentine's Day are actually upholding India's ancient pre-Muslim culture, albeit in a much milder form than is on display, for instance, in Khajuraho. In a sense, 14 February is their attempt at observing *Kamadeva Divas*. How ironic that they should incur the disapproval of the self-appointed custodians of Hindu culture!

But let's face it: this is less about teenagers dating than about the ruling dispensation's political project of transforming secular India into their idea of a Hindu state. Tradition is sought to be upheld in the name of culture: Traditionalism benefits those who want to uphold the social order, ensure discipline and conformity, and prevent radical change. Love affairs, which may after all cross caste or religious lines, are to be disapproved of for threatening this social order. Worse still, they reflect the autonomy of the individual and her right to choose, which is anathema to those who would prefer to make faceless cow-worshippers of us all.[21] Would it have been better if the BJP government, with its fondness for rebaptising government schemes with new Sanskrit appellations, gave serious thought to just calling Valentine's Day *Kamadeva Divas*, to link it to ancient Hindu culture?

But it's in the 'self-appointed' part that the real problem lies. All this is being done in the name of a notion of Indian culture whose assertion is based on a denial of India's real rather than imagined past. India's culture has always been a capacious one, expanding to include new and varied influences, from the Greek invasions to the British. The central battle in contemporary Indian civilisation is that between those who, to borrow from Walt Whitman, acknowledge that as a result of our own historical experience, we are vast, we contain multitudes, and those who have presumptuously taken it upon themselves to define—in increasingly narrower terms—what is 'truly' Indian.

TARNISHING THE TAJ

The latest victim of this definitional exercise is India's most iconic monument, the Taj Mahal. In a country whose toxic politics has led to everything—from festival firecrackers to animal husbandry (the care and protection of cows, of which more anon)—taking on a 'communal', religious colouring, it shouldn't be too much of a surprise that its most famous monument hasn't been exempt.

The Taj Mahal is India's most magnificent piece of architecture. Built nearly four centuries ago by the Mughal Emperor Shah Jahan as a mausoleum for his beloved wife, who had borne him thirteen children and died in the process of producing the fourteenth, it attracts tens of millions of tourists and is by far the country's most-photographed building. The exquisite marble monument to love was hailed by India's only winner of the Nobel Prize for literature, Rabindranath Tagore, as 'a teardrop on the cheek of Time'.

But the Taj now has other reasons for tears. Its gleaming white surface is yellowing as a result of rampant air pollution from factories and small businesses around it, as well as the Mathura refinery not far way. Repairs are needed so frequently that scaffolding often obscures its famous minarets. There has been a 35 per cent drop in foreign tourists from the 743,000 who went there in 2012 to the 480,000 tourists who came in 2015.[22] The crowded and grimy town of Agra in Uttar Pradesh, which hosts the Taj, puts visitors off: American basketball player Kevin Durant sparked a row with his graphic descriptions of the awful conditions around the Taj Mahal after a visit there in the summer of 2017.

And worst of all, the new ruling party in Uttar Pradesh, the BJP, has decided that far from being proud of its most famous edifice, it wants as little to do with it as possible.

Yogi Adityanath, the chief minister, began the controversy by deploring the fact that his government used to give models of the Taj as gifts to visiting foreign dignitaries. Declaring that the monument did not 'reflect Indian culture', the Yogi announced the government would be handing out copies of the Hindu holy book, the Bhagavad Gita, instead.[23]

It got worse. The Uttar Pradesh Tourism Department issued a brochure listing the state's principal attractions—and omitted the Taj

Mahal altogether. The state's (and the country's) biggest tourism draw
was denied any cultural heritage funding in the allotments for the current fiscal year.

Domestic tourists have also decreased significantly. Indian tourists
reportedly prefer the attractions of the holy city of Varanasi in the same
state, Uttar Pradesh. This mirrors and reinforces the monument's
neglect by the state government in favour of Hindu religious tourism.

But the objection to the Taj is more basic. One extremist BJP legisla-
tor labelled the tomb 'a blot' on the fair name of his state, a relic that
had been 'built by traitors'. The Taj Mahal 'should have no place in
Indian history,' he said, demanding that India's history be 'changed' to
remove it. [24]

The ruling party's campaign against the Taj Mahal might seem
bizarre; after all, why would anyone undermine a universally admired
architectural marvel that is such a revenue generator? But those familiar
with the tortured prejudices of the ruling BJP would be less surprised.
The attacks on the Taj are part of their politics of hate towards anything
associated with the history of the centuries of Muslim rule in India.

As we have seen, to many in the BJP, this was a period of slavery
and discrimination against the Hindu population, conducted by foreign invaders who had despoiled a prosperous land, destroyed temples
and palaces, assaulted Hindu women and converted millions of
Hindus. In their telling, this sordid saga culminated in the vivisection
of the motherland in the 1947 Partition of India by the British, which
created Pakistan.

That this is an unduly simplistic black-and-white rendition of a complex history, in which there was far more assimilation and co-existence
than religious conflict, is irrelevant to Hindu chauvinists who constitute the bulk of the BJP's support base. To them, the Taj is an enduring
symbol not of love, but of conquest and humiliation.

Resentment that a monument built by a Muslim emperor is Hindu-
majority India's most recognisable monument was, in the past, a fringe
obsession of the 'loony' Hindu right. But the fringe is now in power in
Uttar Pradesh and its enablers rule the roost in Delhi.

Before becoming chief minister in a surprise appointment by his
party, Yogi Adityanath was best known for his incendiary, anti-Muslim

speeches, laden with toxic rhetoric, and for leading a volunteer squad of hoodlums who specialised in attacking Muslim targets. Adityanath spent eleven days in jail in 2007 for fomenting religious tension through hate speech, earned notoriety by calling India's most beloved film star (the Muslim Shah Rukh Khan) a terrorist,[25] and has urged his party's government in New Delhi to emulate Donald Trump's travel ban on Muslims.

But even he has been obliged by public and political opinion to surrender to national outrage over the latest controversy. After stoking it in the first place, the chief minister was forced to visit Agra officially to assure an anxious public that his government was committed to protecting the Taj. 'What is important,' he conceded grudgingly, 'is that it was built by the blood and sweat of India's farmers and labourers.'[26]

This acknowledgement is only partly reassuring. It opens the door to another divisive fringe view of the Taj, that of the chauvinist historian P. N. Oak, who argued that the monument was originally a Shiva temple named 'Tejo Mahalaya'. Some misguided Hindutva elements have already been caught trying to perform a Shiva puja in the mausoleum. The RSS, the parent body of the Hindu 'family' of organisations that includes the BJP, has called for Muslims to be prohibited from praying there as well.

To many Indians, in these circumstances, the BJP's newfound love for the Taj might be as alarming as its well-expressed hate for it. (Meanwhile, while the Yogi was busy criticising the Taj, it was the Kerala government far away in the south that brought out an ad 'saluting' the Taj for its role in helping tourists discover India!)

The Taj Mahal is merely the latest victim of a political campaign over Indian history that seeks to reinvent the idea of India itself. Whereas for seven decades after Independence, Indianness rested on faith in the country's pluralism, the ascent of the Hindu-chauvinist BJP has brought with it attempts to redefine the country as a Hindu nation long subjugated by foreigners. This 'cultural nationalism' by the Hindu right, stoking long-buried resentments and promoting hatred for the Muslim minority, is not just deeply divisive; it undermines the country's global soft power and fragments its domestic political and social discourse. As the author Nayantara Sahgal wrote: 'Vast slices of our multi-religious, multi-cultural heritage—which includes our literature, architecture, language, food, music, dance, dress and manners are being dishonoured and disowned, leaving us shrunk into a monoculture which is not only not Hinduism, but the antitheses of all that India has stood for, worked for, and safeguarded as a proud and cherished inheritance.'[27]

At almost the same time as the Taj controversy came one over a film on the Rajput queen Padmavati, who is said to have immolated herself, together with 16,000 other Rajput women, rather than be captured alive by the invading Delhi Sultan Alauddin Khilji. The historicity of the incident is somewhat in doubt: no contemporary account of Khilji's attack on Chittorgarh, including by historians accompanying his forces, mentions the queen. But Padmavati became legend more than two centuries later, when the Sufi mystic poet Malik Mohammed Jayasi devoted his lyrical epic *Padmavat* to her story. It has been suggested that Jayasi did not intend his tale to be taken literally, and that he had chosen Khilji's attack on Chittor because its name included the word 'chit' (consciousness); his poem is said to have been an allegory for the union of mind and soul, under attack from external forces, with the man-woman story a standard trope of the Persian mystic poetry tradition.

But literature, once published, acquires a life of its own. The tale was picked up and retold with enthusiasm—by Bengali bards, Rajasthani folk-tellers, and even the English Colonel Tod, who included Padmavati's tale in his compilation, *Annals and Antiquities of Rajputana*. In countless retellings, Padmavati was soon deified: she became the symbol of Rajput female honour and purity, nobly resisting the lustful Muslim, her self-immolation ('*jauhar*') the epitome of sacrificial Hindu womanhood. The reputed site of her suicide became a tourist attraction. The legend grew, with one colourful figure, the head of a Rajput organisation, the Karni Sena, claiming to be directly descended from her. (When confronted with the theory that she was fictional, he replied, 'I am 37th in her direct line of descent. Am I a ghost?')

The controversy confirmed once again that to some Hindus, the difference between historical fact and cultural myth matters not at all; what is remembered and believed is as important as what is verifiable.

228

No less an ardent secularist than India's first Prime Minister, Jawaharlal Nehru, had written seven decades earlier: 'Facts and fiction are so interwoven together as to be inseparable, and this amalgam becomes an imagined history, which may not tell us exactly what happened but does tell us something equally important—what people believed had taken place, what they thought their heroic ancestors were capable of, and what ideals inspired them... Thus, this imagined history, mixture of fact and fiction, or sometimes only fiction, becomes symbolically true and tells us of the minds and hearts and purposes of the people...'[28] This, in a nutshell, explained Rajput passions over the depiction of a cultural heroine who may or may not have existed.

With so much riding on Padmavati's image, the Bollywood film-maker who set out to make a film of her story found himself treading unwittingly on the newly-roused passions about the past. The Karni Sena trashed his film set, at Jaigarh Fort in Jaipur, and disrupted further shooting in a new (less 'authentic') location at Kolhapur, accusing him of filming a love scene between the Hindu queen and the Muslim invader. Though he denied this, the Rajput community then success-fully delayed the release of the film, claiming that it 'distorted his-tory'—the fact that they had not actually seen it before making this claim was apparently irrelevant to the protestors (as well as to four BJP chief ministers, who pre-emptively announced a ban on screening the yet-unreleased film in their states). When the film was eventually released on the orders of the Supreme Court, violent protests by hood-lums, including an attack on a school bus, successfully intimidated theatre owners, so that the film was not shown in several states even though they were free to screen it.

'Taking offence' is the name of the game these days; 'hurting the sentiments of a community' is the name of the crime. The old Hindu boasts of expansive tolerance are wearing thin. (But the film-maker should well have been warned by the experience of another film a decade ago, this time unconnected to any religious community. The threat of protests and possible prosecution had caused a Bollywood star and producer to retitle a film originally named *Billoo Barber* without the second word, because the hairdressers' community absurdly protested that the term 'barber' was an insult to their profession.)

It may not seem to matter very much what some lumpen elements think of a Bollywood film, or of Valentine's Day, for that matter. But it is precisely this kind of narrow-mindedness that also led to the notorious 'pulping' of Wendy Doniger's erudite study of Hinduism. If these intolerant bullies are allowed to get away with their lawless acts of intolerance and intimidation, we are allowing them to do violence to something profoundly vital to our survival as a civilisation.

Pluralist and democratic India must, by definition, tolerate plural expressions of its many identities. To allow the self-appointed arbiters of Bharatiya sanskriti to impose their hypocrisy and double standards on the rest of us is to permit them to define Indianness down until it ceases to be Indian.

But I am not optimistic about the prospects for any such development. My late father, Chandran Tharoor, used to tell me more than five decades ago that India is not just the world's largest democracy, it is also the world's largest hypocrisy. The wisdom and accuracy of his perception was again on display when my two attempts to introduce a Private Member's Bill to amend Section 377 of the Indian Penal Code (which criminalises homosexuality) were comprehensively defeated in the Lok Sabha by homophobic bigotry in the name of Hindutva.

Here was the spectacle of a parliamentary democracy refusing to entertain debate—the ruling party using its brute majority to defeat a motion without even a discussion. How can a deliberative legislature in what claims to be the temple of democracy dismiss an issue out of hand without even hearing the arguments in its favour or against it?

And to add to the hypocrisy, nowhere in over two thousand years of recorded Hindu texts is there any evidence that the Indian ethos was intolerant of sexual difference or gender orientation. Ours is a culture that embraces Shikhandi in the *Mahabharata*, the homoerotic sculptures (mixed in with the rest) in Khajuraho, and the very concept of the Ardhanarishwara, the half-man half-woman embodiment of divinity. No historical records reveal the persecution or prosecution of sexual deviancy in India. Now we have the spectacle of the party of Hindutva, the self-appointed guardians of Bharatiya Sanskriti, betraying a Hindu history of tolerance in order to uphold (without debate) an iniquitous law from the British colonial era. It is a new low in the annals of Indian democracy and a triumph for Indian hypocrisy.

In proposing to amend Section 377, I had explained that we shouldn't have a law on the books that can be used to oppress and harass innocent people conducting their personal lives in private. What two people do to express their love and desire for each other should be strictly between them. The government has no place in India's bedrooms.

But equally important, I had tried to explain (though alas, I was not allowed to do so in Parliament) that my Bill was not about sex but about freedom. Section 377 violates the constitutional rights of dignity, privacy, equality and non-discrimination (Articles 14, 15 and 21) guaranteed to all Indian citizens. It is a British relic, drafted in 1860 and based on outdated Victorian morals rather than authentically Indian values. It has no place in twenty-first century India.

To compound the ironies, within half an hour of the defeat of my amendment, I was rising in the same Lok Sabha to speak in favour of the Rights of Transgender Persons Bill, which had already been passed earlier in the Rajya Sabha. The passage of this progressive bill would have the indirect effect of nullifying the application of Section 377 to transgenders, while leaving it on the books to be used to harass and oppress homosexuals and straight people. How's that for both democracy and hypocrisy taken to their extreme?

Ironically, the one source of hope for a progressive outcome in keeping with the long-established Hindu tradition rests with a secular institution—the judiciary. The Supreme Court's willingness to conduct a curative review of Section 377, and their assertion in a separate case that Indians enjoy a right to privacy, may well signal a return to that tradition. It is ironic that where a Hindutva-inclined majority renders our elected legislature a bastion of illiberalism, it is the unelected judiciary that remains the last repository of hope for the timeless values of our civilisation.

THE COW BELT AND BEEF POLITICS

Indian politics, in all its manifestations, continues to both amaze and appal. The latest example of both lies in a uniquely Indian phenomenon, one which has begun to flourish under the current government—cow vigilantism.

Many orthodox Hindus, particularly in the northern Indian states irreverently dubbed 'the cow belt', not only do not eat beef, but worship the cow as Gaumata, the mother of all, a provider of nourishment and sustenance. Several Indian states have passed laws outlawing cow slaughter; some go farther and neither permit the possession nor the consumption of beef. These are, for the most part, barely enforced; the police have better things to do than to check people's kitchens.

But following the BJP's victory in the 2014 elections, a wave of Hindu triumphalism has swept India. In its wake have come new laws to protect cows and vociferous demands for their strict enforcement. Gaurakshak or cow protection societies have been revived, and many have taken it upon themselves to compel compliance. In the process, not only have they taken the law into their own hands, but they have perpetrated grave crimes, including murder, in the name of the cow. Seventy cases of cow-related violence have been reported in the last eight years, of which 97 per cent (68 out of 70) have occurred during the three years of BJP rule and a majority of these have occurred in BJP-ruled states. 136 people have been injured in these attacks and 28 killed: 86 per cent of the victims were, of course, Muslim.[29]

Many of the incidents are well known: the case of a dairy farmer, Pehlu Khan, transporting cattle legally with a licence, being beaten to death on 1 April 2017 while his tormentors filmed his pleas for mercy on their mobile phones, is particularly egregious. A cattle-herder in Haryana, Mustain Abbas, was murdered and mutilated a year earlier for doing his job, herding cattle. Truckers, cattle traders and alleged cow smugglers have also been killed by 'cow protection' groups. A sixteen-year-old Kashmiri Muslim boy was murdered for having hitched a ride on a truck that was transporting cattle.

In 2015, when a Muslim, Mohammed Akhlaq, father of a serving Indian Air Force serviceman, was lynched by a mob in Uttar Pradesh on suspicions of having killed a cow, the authorities launched a forensic investigation into whether the meat in his refrigerator was beef (it was not). The fact that the man had been killed and his son nearly beaten to death was equated with an unfounded allegation of beef consumption, as if the latter 'crime' could extenuate the former. Worse, when a man who was part of the lynch mob died of natural causes a few weeks later, his coffin was draped with the Indian flag and a serving union minister who attended his funeral hailed him—an unspeakable act, and coming from a high office-holder of the secular Indian state, an unacceptable one.

Muslims have not been the only targets of the cow vigilantes. In addition, the lynch-mobs have linked their cause to another staple of Indian society—violence against Dalits. Many Dalits still make a living performing tasks that other Hindus are unwilling to take on. Upper caste Hindus may worship the cow, but cows, alas, are not immortal, and when they die (ideally of natural causes), their carcasses need to be disposed of. This task has traditionally been left to Dalits, who for centuries and more have skinned the animal to sell its hide to tanners and leather-makers, disposed of its meat to Muslim butchers in the few states where it is legal, and buried or cremated the rest. It is a distasteful task to many caste Hindus, and most are happy to let willing Dalits do it. In turn, dead cows have become a source of livelihood for many Dalits and Muslims.

But several recent incidents have shaken the foundations of this arrangement. Four Dalit youths caught skinning a cow were stripped, tied and beaten with iron rods in the state of Gujarat by cow vigilantes who accused them of killing the animal (they had not).[30] Two Dalit women were assaulted in BJP-ruled Madhya Pradesh for carrying cow meat (which turned out, upon inspection, to be buffalo meat and therefore not illegal).[31]

Such incidents have heightened the sense of vulnerability felt by many who do not necessarily share the reverence the vigilantes feel for cows. Yet, for the first time, India has a central government that refuses to disapprove of cow vigilantism. The Minister for Social Justice, whose principal responsibility is to promote the welfare of India's Dalits, regretted not the vigilantes' violence but the fact that they had perpetrated it on the basis of ill-founded rumours.[32] In other words, their mission was so transcendently just that their misbehaviour could be condoned if their targets really had killed or eaten a cow.

The atmosphere of cow fundamentalism enforced by the vigilantes has caused immense economic complications. Many farmers look after their cows with respect, but once they are too old to produce milk, they find it unaffordable to maintain them and quietly sell their cows to butchers (or to those who could transport them across state lines to states where cows could legally be slaughtered). With this option now foreclosed in the present climate, many farmers are being driven into debt by the expense of maintaining unproductive and uneconomic cattle. And the country's population of cows is proving increasingly unsustainable.[33]

It is not a coincidence that 63 per cent of atrocities against Dalits because of cow vigilantism occur in just four states—U.P., Bihar, M.P. and Rajasthan, in order of magnitude. The rise of Hindu chauvinism, unchecked by government, has given rein to assorted petty bigotries.

There are signs of an incipient Dalit backlash against the injustice of being obliged to do unpleasant work to make a living and then being assaulted for doing it. After the Gujarat incident one group of Dalits in the state has flatly refused to continue with its traditional profession of disposing of dead cows. 'If the cow is your mother,' they asked upper-caste Hindus, 'why don't you bury her?'

The irony is that, as a commentator on the Dharmashastras points out, though the cow was sacred in Vedic times, it was this that allowed for beef to be consumed.[34] There are references in the *Rig Veda*, in the Dharmashastric literature, the *Taittiriya Brahmana* ('Verily, the cow is food') and the *Vajasaneyi Samhita* that support the contention of beef being eaten at the time.[35] The historian D. N. Jha has pointed out dozens of examples to prove that the *Rig Veda* is full of allusions to the slaughter and consumption of cows. Ancient lawgivers, Manu included, appear to grant sanction for the slaughter and consumption of cow meat. The great sage and law-giver Yajnavalkya (of the Upanishads) is quoted as saying, on the subject of whether beef should be eaten: 'I, for one, eat it, provided that it is tender'.[36]

Ambedkar theorised that the worship of the cow emerged from the struggle between Buddhism and Brahmanism; by making the cow a sacred animal and beef-eating a sacrilege, he argued, Brahmanism sought to establish its supremacy over Buddhism. Be that as it may, the ruling dispensation's relentless drive to promote its ideology of Hindutva has latched on to the cow as its current instrument of choice. Cow protection has become the façade for a broader agenda, and is being resisted precisely for that reason.

There is no doubt about the veneration of the cow across India, and the respect for it as a source of milk and nourishment for all and, after its death, of meat and nourishment for some. Calls during the Constituent Assembly deliberations to ban cow slaughter, opposed by a vocal minority, were finally reduced to a 'directive principle' anchored in economics and not religion: Article 48 of the Constitution says that 'the State shall endeavour to organise agriculture and animal husbandry on modern and scientific lines and shall, in particular, take steps for preserving and improving the breeds, and prohibiting the slaughter, of cows and calves and other milch and draught cattle.' So this 'endeavour' (stopping well short of a ban) was related specifically to the needs of agriculture and animal husbandry, not of worship.

Mahatma Gandhi himself said that though he did not eat meat and was personally opposed to cow slaughter, in a multi-religious country like India he could not justify imposing his Hindu views on the many who did not share his faith. Many Hindus feel the same way; I am vegetarian myself, and abhor the idea of consuming the corpses of animals, but I do not judge those who, for cultural or other personal reasons, do so. I only ask that animals be treated decently and without cruelty, and that even their slaughter, for purposes of consumption, be conducted humanely and with minimal pain and suffering for the poor creatures.

The furore that accompanied the new Prevention of Cruelty to Animals Act (Regulation of Livestock Markets) Rules, 2016, rolled out by the Ministry of Environmental Affairs in Delhi, polarised opinion across the country, especially in beef-eating states like Kerala. There it produced a strong reaction from an indignant chief minister, invited condemnation across the local political spectrum, forced the state to drag the centre to court, united warring student union factions to organise beef festivals across the state and even gave Twitizens a field day with #PoMoneModi (Go Away Modi), used last when the PM compared Kerala to the African nation of Somalia, resurfacing as a popular hashtag.[37]

Though the new rules do not directly impose a beef ban, they contrive to make cow slaughter all but impossible through the back door, by making it impossible to transport or sell cattle for slaughter. In the process, they have raised fundamental questions the government cannot escape, even as it tried to shift the focus to the misbehaviour of a few young men who misguidedly slaughtered a calf in public as a form of protest.

The first issue is constitutional—the decision to institute the full prohibition of cow slaughter is a prerogative of the states, not the government at the centre. Entry 15 of the State List of the Seventh Schedule of the Constitution provides for the 'Preservation, protection and improvement of stock and prevention of animal diseases, veterinary training and practice', empowering the state legislatures to legislate the prevention of slaughter and preservation of cattle. Different states have different approaches to cow welfare. Some states like Uttar Pradesh, Madhya Pradesh and Delhi have strict laws while others such as Kerala, Tamil Nadu, West Bengal, Manipur, Mizoram and Nagaland have milder rules or no rules governing the welfare of cows. The blanket new rule is clearly an infringement on the rights of the states, undermining the federal rights guaranteed by our Constitution.

The second objection is practical. The Constitution rightly speaks of milch and draught cattle. Cows produce milk for about eight years, at which point they are too old for either milch or draught purposes. But they go on to live another eight years. Farmers have to spend large sums of money on their food and fodder requirements and other maintenance costs of a cow, a fortune for agriculturalists who often live barely above subsistence level. This is why they sell non-lactating cows, normally for slaughter. Even our highest courts, despite their variety of views on the matter, have recognised that 'a total ban on [cattle slaughter] was not permissible if, under economic conditions, keeping useless bull or bullock be a burden on the society and therefore not in the public interest.'

India is already home to nearly 512 million cows, according to the 19th National Livestock Census 2012. Aside from maintaining them decently, India would also have to deal with deforestation and over-grazing, as well as the problems caused by abandoned cattle, who stray onto the streets and in many cases die of malnutrition in old age. The previous policy recognised that banning cow slaughter would impose an economic burden on farmers, who, given the paucity of resources at their disposal, would struggle to maintain these animals. As a result, India is or was the largest exporter of buffalo meat in the world—a multi-billion-dollar business. Since the sale and transfer of animals is integral to keep this going, the new rules are likely to severely cripple the meat export, dairy, leather and other allied businesses, which provide employment for over one million individuals within the country, mainly from minority communities. The state of Maharashtra's 2015 beef ban had already destroyed the livelihoods of a million Muslim butchers and truckers in that state; a nationwide ban would push more people into poverty who are currently leading economically productive lives.

Where beef was legally available, it was consumed not just by Muslims and other minorities, but also by a section of Hindus, as a vital source of protein for those who cannot afford other kinds of meat. Statistics suggest that just 2 per cent of the Hindu population consume beef, but this 2 per cent translates to 12.5 million individuals, making them the second largest consumers of beef in the country. And in reality many others do so who do not admit to the practice. Scheduled castes and tribes (SC/ST) comprise the overwhelming majority (more than 70 per cent) of the beef-eating Hindu population, while 21 per cent hail from the OBC community. The government decision is therefore socially discriminatory, since it specifically and disproportionately harms the poorer and less privileged sections of Indian society.

But the real concern about the government's rules is not just about beef or the welfare of the cow, but about freedom. For most of India's existence, the default approach has essentially been 'live and let live'—make your own choice about beef, and let others do the same. Like many Hindus, I have never considered it my business what others eat. Indians have generally felt free to be themselves, within our dynamic and diverse society. It is that freedom that the BJP's followers are challenging today.

The Hindutva lobby, emboldened by the BJP's absolute majority, seek to impose their particular view of what India should be, regardless of whom it hurts. This is why the reaction has been so visceral, even from non-beef eaters like myself. Our resistance is to the way India is being changed into something it never was—an intolerant majoritarian society.

THE QUESTION OF CONVERSION

An issue that erupted in the past, has been simmering for a while and is waiting to explode is the issue of conversions of Hindus to other faiths, notably Islam and Christianity. In the case of Islam, the issue has been complicated by allegations of 'love jihad', the alleged entrapment of unwary Hindu girls by Muslim men with the sole intent of conversion to their faith. In the case of Christianity, the existence of missionary societies with an avowed intent of harvesting souls for the Lord has created suspicion among Hindu groups. Some states have already outlawed conversions without the specific permission of the government; the use of inducements or threats to convert is already illegal across much of the country.

Hindu leaders known for their liberality have tended to be less accommodative on the question of conversions. Swami Vivekananda memorably told his American listeners a century and a quarter ago: 'Christian brethren of America, you are so fond of sending out missionaries to save the souls of heathens. I ask you: what have you done and are doing to save their bodies from starvation? In India, there are 300 million men and women living on an average of a little more than 50 cents a month. I have seen them living for years upon wild flowers. During the terrible famines, thousands died from hunger but the missionaries did nothing. They come and offer life but only on condition that the Hindus become Christians, abandoning the faith of their fathers and forefathers. Is it right? There are hundreds of asylums, but if the Muslims or the Hindus go there, they are kicked out. There are thousands of asylums erected by Hindus where anybody is received. There are hundreds of churches that have been erected with the assistance of the Hindus, but no Hindu temples for which a Christian has given a penny.'

To Vivekananda, it was a case of misplaced priorities. 'Brethren of America, you erect churches all through India, but the crying evil in the East is not religion', he declared. 'They have religion enough, but it is bread that the suffering millions of burning India cry out for with parched throats. What they want is bread, but they are given a stone. It is an insult to a starving people to offer them religion; it is an insult to a starving man to teach him metaphysics. Therefore, if you wish to illustrate the meaning of "brotherhood", treat the Hindus more kindly, even though they are Hindus and are faithful to their religion. Send missionaries to them to teach them how better to earn a piece of bread and not to teach them metaphysical nonsense.'

And he recalled the non-proselytising instincts of his own faith: 'Do I wish that the Christian would become Hindu? God forbid. Do I wish that the Hindu or Buddhist would become Christian? God forbid... The Christian is not to become a Hindu or a Buddhist, nor a Hindu or a Buddhist to become a Christian. But each must assimilate the spirit of the others and yet preserve their individuality and grow according to their own law of growth.'

Similarly, Mahatma Gandhi considered religious conversion harmful. He wrote, 'If I had power and could legislate, I should certainly stop all proselytising... In Hindu households the advent of a missionary has meant the disruption of the family coming in the wake of change of dress, manners, language, food and drink.'

At the same time, Hindus like me accept that every individual's spiritual needs are different, and if some wish to find salvation through another faith, that is surely their prerogative. Certainly, episodes of anti-missionary violence in Odisha and Gujarat some years ago do not speak well of those who perpetrate it: a self-confident faith like Hinduism, secure in its own broad-minded liberality, has no need of gangster-like violence in its defence. When, at the time of such violence, specifically the brutal murder in 1999 of Australian missionary Graham Staines, and his two sons in Odisha, I wrote a column passionately denouncing it, I was gratified by the large number of readers (including several describing themselves as believing Hindus) who were as outraged as I was at the anti-Christian thuggery that had been perpetrated in the name of Hinduism. Killers of children have no right to claim the mantle of Hinduism, even if they insist they are acting on behalf of their faith: it is as simple as that. Murder does not have a religion—even when it claims a religious excuse.

Of course, it is easy enough to condemn anti-Christian violence because it *is* violence, and because it represents a threat to law and order as well as to that nebulous idea we call India's 'image'. But an argument that several readers made needs to be faced squarely. In the words of one correspondent: could the violence 'be a reaction to provocations from those religions that believe that only their path is the right path and the rest of humanity are infidels?' He went on to critique 'the aggressive strategy being pursued by some interests in the US to get people in India converted en masse to Christianity, not necessarily by fair means.' In his view, 'aggressive evangelism directed against India by powerful church organisations in America enjoying enormous money power, has only one focused objective—to get India into the Christian fold, as they have succeeded, to a considerable extent, in South Korea and are now in the process of conquering Mongolia.' Arguing that 'mass conversions of illiterates and semi-literates—and they also happen to be poor, extremely poor' is exploitative, he concluded: 'powerful organisations from abroad with enormous money power indulging in mass conversion' are 'a destabilising factor provoking retaliation'.

Such concerns, which are widely shared, including by people in responsible positions in government, must be heeded; but at the same time I cannot accept any justification for the thugs' actions, nor am I prepared to see behind the violence an 'understandable' Hindu resistance to Christian zealotry. Put simply, no non-violent activity, however provocative, can ever legitimise violence. We must reject and denounce assaults and killings, whatever they may claim to be reacting to. Our democracy will not long survive if we condone people resorting to violence in pursuit of their ends, however genuine and heartfelt their grievances may be. The whole point about our system of governance is that it allows all Indians to resolve their concerns through legitimate means, including seeking legal redress or political change—but not violence.

Staines himself had devoted his life to the care of leprosy patients; his widow continued this work after his murder, and was awarded a Padma Shri, a major national honour, by the previous government of India. But let us assume, for the purposes of argument, that Christian missionaries are indeed using a variety of inducements (development assistance, healthcare, education, sanitation, even chicanery—though there is only anecdotal evidence of missionary 'trickery') to win converts for their faith. So what? If a citizen of India feels that his faith has not helped him to find peace of mind and material fulfilment, why should he not have the option of trying a different item on the spiritual menu? Surely freedom of belief is any Indian's fundamental right under our democratic constitution, however ill-founded his belief might be. And if Hindu zealots suspect that his conversion was fraudulently obtained, why do they not offer counter-inducements rather than violence? Instead of destroying churches, perhaps a Hindu-financed sewage system or *pathshala* (village school) might reopen the blinkered eyes of the credulous.

Freedom of conscience is not a negotiable right. An India where an individual is not free to change his or her faith would be inconceivable. Some have been citing Gandhi's criticism of conversions, but his view was based on an eclectic, all-embracing view of religiousness that is a far cry from the narrow bigotry of those who today quote him in opposing conversions. Gandhi's point was that there was no need to convert from one religion to any other because all religions essentially believed the same thing.

The fact is that many faiths do tend to see theirs as the only true path to salvation, and their religious leaders feel a duty to spread the light of a supposedly superior understanding of God to those less fortunate. As Gandhians or as rationalists we are free to decry their views, but the Indian Constitution gives each Indian the right to 'propagate' his religion—and to challenge that right would, in the most fundamental sense, be unconstitutional.

So let each religion do its thing, and let each Indian be free to choose. At the same time, let conversion be an issue of individual conscience and not mass delusion. I would have no difficulty in considering, in principle, the idea of a democratically-elected legislature deciding that the constitutionally-protected right to convert to another faith can only be exercised by an individual, rather than by an entire clan, tribe or village. An end to ceremonies of mass conversion (often suspected to be achieved by inducements) might not be a bad thing: let each individual who believes he or she has seen the light go through an individual act of conversion—one in which he or she must affirm that they know what they are giving up and what they are entering into.

Of course, the debate is not merely a religious one—it is profoundly political. The devotees of Hindutva let me know in no uncertain terms what they thought of me when I expressed such views in three columns in the *Times of India* in September and October 2008. But I reject their presumption that they speak for all or even most Hindus. Hinduism, we are repeatedly told, is a tolerant faith. The central tenet of tolerance is that the tolerant society accepts that which it does not understand and even that which it does not like, so long as it is not sought to be imposed upon the unwilling. Of course, it is true that, while Hinduism as a faith might privilege tolerance, this does not necessarily mean that all Hindus behave tolerantly. But one cannot simultaneously extol the tolerance of Hinduism and attack Christian homes and places of worship.

In one of those columns I argued that the premise behind much of the criticism of conversions is troubling because it seems to accord legitimacy to the argument that conversions are inherently anti-national. I made the point that India is founded on the rejection of the very idea that religion should be a determinant of nationhood, and cautioned that the distinction between Hindu nationalism and Indian nationalism could be all too easily blurred. Your Indianness has nothing to do with which God you choose to worship, or not.

In any case, as we have discussed, Hinduism teaches *ekam sat vipra bahudha vadanti* (The Truth is one thing though the sages call it by different names). Why, then, are any of my co-religionists unhappy about some tribal Hindus becoming Christian? If a Hindu decides he wishes to be a Christian, how does it matter that he has found a different way of stretching his hands out towards God? Truth is one, the Hindu believes, but there are many ways of attaining it.

As we have seen, Hinduism has never claimed a monopoly on spiritual wisdom; that is what has made it so attractive to seekers from around the world. Its eclecticism is its strength. So the rejection of other forms of worship, other ways of seeking the Truth, is profoundly un-Hindu, as well as being un-Indian. Worse, the version of Indianness propagated by the opponents of conversion—the presumption that to be Hindu is more authentically Indian, and that to lapse from Hinduism is to dilute one's identification with the motherland—resembles nothing so much as the arguments for the creation of Pakistan, of which the nationalism of Gandhi, Nehru and Azad is the fundamental repudiation. In many Muslim countries it is illegal for a Muslim to convert to any other faith; in some, such apostasy is even punishable by death. India has no room for such practices. There is no such thing as a Hindu heresy. Yet, ironically, it is the most chauvinist of the Hindutva brigade who seek to emulate this Muslim convention.

They are therefore being untrue both to Hinduism and to Indian nationalism. The nationalist movement rejected the belief that religion was the most important element in shaping political identity. In India, our system recognises the diversity of our people and guarantees that religious affiliation will be neither a handicap nor an advantage. By challenging that right, the advocates of Hindutva are undermining the very basis for Indian citizenship and the constitutional basis of the Indian state.

To say that conversions are somehow inherently wrong would accord legitimacy to the rhetoric of the Bajrang Dal and its cohorts— who declare openly that conversions from Hinduism to any other faith are anti-national. Implicit is the idea, as I've noted, that to be Hindu is somehow more natural, more authentically Indian, than to be anything else, and that to lapse from Hinduism is to dilute one's identification with the motherland.

As a Hindu, I reject that notion utterly. To suggest that an Indian Hindu becoming Christian is an anti-national act not only insults the millions of patriotic Indians who trace their Christianity to more distant forebears, including the Kerala Christians whose families converted to the faith of Saint Thomas centuries before the ancestors of many of today's Hindu chauvinists even learned to think of themselves as Hindu. It is an insult, too, to the national leaders, freedom fighters, educationists, scientists, military men, journalists and sportsmen of the Christian faith who have brought so much glory to the country through their actions and sacrifices. It is, indeed, an insult to the very idea of India. Nothing could be more anti-national than that.

One reader, Raju Rajagopal, writing 'as a fellow Hindu', expressed himself trenchantly in describing 'terrorism' and 'communal riots' as 'two sides of the same coin, which systematically feed on each other.' The only difference, he added, is 'that the first kind of terrorism is being unleashed by a fanatical few who swear no allegiance to the idea of India, whereas the second kind of terror is being unleashed by those who claim to love India more dearly than you and I, who are part of the electoral politics of India, and who know the exact consequences of their actions: creating deep fissures between communities, whose horrific consequences the world has witnessed once too often in recent decades.'

That is the real problem here. Nehru had warned that the communalism of the majority was especially dangerous because it could present itself as nationalist. Yet Hindu nationalism is not Indian nationalism. And it has nothing to do with genuine Hinduism either. A reader bearing a Christian name wrote to tell me that when his brother was getting married to a Hindu girl, the Hindu priest made a point of saying to him before the ceremony words to the effect of: 'When I say god, I don't mean a particular god.' As this reader commented: 'it's at moments like that that I can't help but feel proud to be Indian and to be moved by its religiosity—even though I'm an atheist.'

The real alternatives in our country are between those who believe in an India where differences arising from your birth, language, social status, mode of worship or dietary preferences shouldn't determine your Indianness, and those who define Indianness along one or more of these divisions. In other words the really important debate is not about conversions, but between the unifiers and the dividers—between those who think all Indians are 'us', whichever God they choose to worship, and those who think that Indians can be divided into 'us' and 'them'.

It is time for all Hindus to say: stop the politics of division.

We are *all* Indians.

PART THREE

TAKING BACK HINDUISM

7

TAKING BACK HINDUISM

If Hindutva is resisted by the vast majority of liberal Hindus, it is hardly paradoxical to suggest that Hinduism, India's ancient homegrown faith, can help strengthen Indianness in ways that the proponents of Hindutva have not understood. In one sense Hinduism is almost the ideal faith for the twenty-first century: a faith without apostasy, where there are no heretics to cast out because there has never been any such thing as a Hindu heresy. A faith that is eclectic and non-doctrinaire responds ideally to the incertitudes of a post-modern world.

So it was hard for a Hindu, proud of his faith's and his country's liberal traditions, not to be mortified, in 2015, when the visiting US President, Barack Obama, felt obliged to deliver a speech in New Delhi urging the government to live up to India's own values—and did it again in a post-Presidential visit in 2017.

'India will succeed so long as it is not split along the lines of religious faith,' Mr Obama said in 2015 in an implicit rebuke to the Hindutva brigades. The president was, of course, polite, couching his praise of religious diversity as a mutual strength of both India and the US, and speaking of his own challenges as a politician with the middle name of Hussein in a country increasingly hostile to Muslims. Many Obama critics in the US had alleged that he is a Muslim, not a Christian, the President acknowledged. 'There have been times when my faith has been questioned by people who don't know me…they said that I adhered to a different religion, as if that were somehow a bad thing,' he said.[1]

The president could hardly have been unaware, of course, that India's Hindutva-leaning prime minister had had a long track record of implying that belonging to a different religion than his own is indeed a bad thing—and that he depends for his political success on the support of people who have variously wanted all non-Hindus to convert 'back' to the mother faith or be driven out of the country. And he did it again on a visit to New Delhi in December 2017: 'A country shouldn't be divided into sectarian lines and that is something I have told Prime Minister Modi in person as well as to people in America,' Obama declared. 'For a country like India where there is a Muslim population that is successful, integrated and considers itself as Indian, which is not the case in some other countries, this should be nourished and cultivated.'

Obama's message on both occasions was pointed: if India did not resolve the problems of bigotry that are dividing the country, Mr Modi's proclaimed ambitious development plans would be thwarted. It was a message many of us in the political Opposition had also been giving Mr Modi and his colleagues. But coming from a US president, whose visit was being hailed by the government as a diplomatic triumph and whose 'bromance' with the Indian PM had seen first names being used and much friendly banter, it was a pointed reminder of the fundamental contradiction at the heart of Modi's regime.

As I had spelt out in my 2014 book *India Shastra*, Mr Modi's speeches and rhetoric appeared to recognise, and harness, a vital shift in our national politics from a politics of identity to a politics of performance; yet he had risen to power at the helm of a party, the BJP, which is ill-suited to the challenge of delinking India's polity from the incendiary issue of religious identity on which it had built its base.

Of course, Indians don't need an American visitor to tell them to uphold the ideal of freedom of religion, when our history is one of coexistence, the acceptance of religious diversity is deeply embedded in our culture and our Constitution reflects our pluralism. It's a great pity that a foreign leader is obliged to recognise that some Indians do not share the values on which India is built and which are reified in our

Constitution. As I have long argued, Indian democracy is all about the management of diversity, and if we don't respect our diversity we will no longer be the India that Mahatma Gandhi fought to free.

But for the first time, India has elected a prime minister who was himself named for 'severe violations of religious freedom' in reports by the US State Department from 2002 onwards, refused an American visa and was banned from entering the United States before he became prime minister. Mr Modi wasn't elected PM for condoning violence against minorities, but to fulfil an aspirational development vision he effectively articulated. Mr Obama's speech was a way of telling him he can't do that without abandoning his old religious intolerance that earned him those American strictures.

The problem is that the dominant strand in the ruling party cares far more about asserting Hindu chauvinism than it does about the economic reforms and investments that Mr Modi trumpeted—and which won him the support of voters who did not share his 'Hindutva' agenda. A party dependent on people who urge Hindu women to have four children—'no, ten!', as the Shankaracharya of Badrikashram said—not only shows profound disrespect to Hindu women[2] (who have to endure the labour to fulfil the Hindutva brigade's political fantasies) but proves itself out of touch with the real values and priorities of the Hindu masses in whose name it claims to speak.

The fact remains that the Modi regime has given free rein to the most retrograde elements in Indian society, who are busy rewriting textbooks to glorify Hindu leaders, extolling the virtues of ancient science over modern technology, beating the drums over 'love jihad', extolling *ghar wapsi*, and asserting that India's identity must be purely Hindu. Majoritarian communalism, as Nehru had long recognised, is a fundamental threat to our pluralist democracy. But throughout his life as an RSS *pracharak*, Modi has devoted himself to the very worldview that is undermining India's harmony.

TOLERANCE AND ACCEPTANCE

As a believing Hindu, I cannot agree with the followers of Hindutva. Indeed, I am ashamed of what they are doing while claiming to be acting in the name of my faith. The violence is particularly sickening: it has led hundreds of thousands of Hindus across India to protest with placards screaming, 'Not In My Name'. As I have explained throughout this book, and would like to reiterate, I have always prided myself on belonging to a religion of astonishing breadth and range of belief; a religion that acknowledges all ways of worshipping God as equally valid—indeed, the only major religion in the world that does not claim to be the only true religion. As I have often asked: How dare a bunch of thugs shrink the soaring majesty of the Vedas and the *Upanishads* to the petty bigotry of their brand of identity politics? Why should any Hindu allow them to diminish Hinduism to the raucous self-glorification of the football hooligan, to take a religion of awe-inspiring tolerance and reduce it to a chauvinist rampage?

Hinduism, with its openness, its respect for variety, its acceptance of all other faiths, is one religion which has always been able to assert itself without threatening others. But this is not the Hindutva that destroyed the Babri Masjid, nor that is spewed in hate-filled diatribes by communal politicians. It is, instead, the Hinduism of Swami Vivekananda, whom I have quoted at such length in this book. It is important to parse some of Swami Vivekananda's most significant assertions. The first is his assertion that Hinduism stands for 'both tolerance and universal acceptance. We believe not only in universal toleration, but we accept all religions as true.' He had quoted a hymn I have already cited, to the effect that as different streams originating in different places all flow into the same sea, so do all paths lead to the same divinity. He repeatedly asserted the wisdom of the Advaita belief that Truth is One even if the sages call It by different names. Vivekananda's vision—summarised in the credo '*sarva dharma sambhava*'—is, in fact, the kind of Hinduism practised by the vast majority of Hindus, whose instinctive acceptance of other faiths and forms of worship has long been the vital hallmark of our culture.

Of course it is true that, while Hinduism as a faith might privilege tolerance, this does not necessarily mean that all Hindus behave tolerantly. Nor should we assume that, even when religion is used as a mobilising identity, all those so mobilised act in accordance with the tenets of their religion. Nonetheless it is ironic that even the Maratha warrior-king Shivaji, after whom the bigoted Shiv Sena is named, exemplified the Hindu respect for other faiths. In the account of a critic, the Mughal historian Khafi Khan, Shivaji made it a rule that his followers should do no harm to mosques, the Quran or to women. 'Whenever a copy of the sacred Quran came into his hands,' Khafi Khan wrote, Shivaji 'treated it with respect, and gave it to some of his Mussalman followers'.[3] Other sources confirm Shivaji's standing orders to his troops that if they came across a Quran or a Bible they should preserve it safely until it could be passed on to a Muslim or Christian.

It is this doctrine of universal acceptance that has been increasingly called into question by the acolytes of Hindutva. Vivekananda had given his fellow Hindus a character certificate many of them no longer deserve. 'The Hindus have their faults,' Vivekananda added, but '...they are always for punishing their own bodies, and never for cutting the throats of their neighbours. If the Hindu fanatic burns himself on the pyre, he never lights the fire of Inquisition.'[4] These words have a tragic echo 125 years later in an India in which Hindu fanaticism is rising, and adopting a form that Vivekananda would not have recognised as Hindu.

The economist Amartya Sen made a related point in regretting the neglect by the votaries of Hindutva of the great achievements of Hindu civilisation in favour of its more dubious features. As Sen wrote about Hindu militants: 'Not for them the sophistication of the *Upanishads* or Gita, or of Brahmagupta or Sankara, or of Kalidasa or Sudraka; they prefer the adoration of Rama's idol and Hanuman's image. Their nationalism also ignores the rationalist traditions of India, a country in which some of the earliest steps in algebra, geometry, and astronomy were taken, where the decimal system emerged, where early philosophy—secular as well as religious—achieved exceptional sophistication, where people invented games like chess, pioneered sex education, and began the first systematic study of political economy. The Hindu militant chooses instead to present India—explicitly or implicitly—as a country of unquestioning idolaters, delirious fanatics, belligerent devotees, and religious murderers.'[5]

To discriminate against another, to attack another, to kill another, to destroy another's place of worship, is not part of the Hindu *dharma* so magnificently preached by Vivekananda, nor the Hinduism propagated in twenty-first-century India by popular spiritual leaders like Sri Sri Ravi Shankar (founder of the Art of Living) and Sadhguru Jaggi Vasudev (founder of the Isha Ashram), who preach a humane, practical faith using techniques of meditation and yoga as well as spiritual advice anchored in the ancient texts. Why, then, are the voices of Hindu religious leaders not being raised in defence of these fundamentals of Hinduism against those who would violently pervert it?

I reject the presumption that the purveyors of hatred speak for all or even most Hindus. The Hindutva ideology is in fact a malign distortion of Hinduism. It is striking that leaders of now-defunct twentieth-century political parties like the Liberal Party and the pro-free enterprise Swatantra Party were unabashed in their avowal of their Hinduism; the Liberal leader Srinivasa Sastry wrote learned disquisitions on the *Ramayana*, and the founder of Swatantra, C. Rajagopalachari ('Rajaji'), was a Sanskrit scholar whose translations of the Itihasas and lectures on aspects of Hinduism are still widely read, decades after his death. Neither would have recognised the intolerance and bigotry of Hindutva as in any way representative of the faith they held dear. Many leaders in the Congress Party are similarly comfortable in their Hindu beliefs while rejecting the political construct of Hindutva. It suits the purveyors of Hindutva to imply that the choice is between their belligerent interpretation of Hinduism and the godless Westernisation of the 'pseudo-seculars'. Rajaji and Sastry proved that you could wear your Hinduism on your sleeve and still be a political liberal. But that choice is elided by the identification of Hindutva with political Hinduism, as if such a conflation is the only possible approach open to practising Hindus.

I reject that idea. I not only consider myself both a Hindu and a liberal, but find that liberalism is the political ideology that most corresponds to the wide-ranging and open-minded nature of my faith.

A REFLECTION OF INSECURITY

The irony is that Hindutva reassertion is a reflection of insecurity rather than self-confidence. It is built on constant reminders of humiliation and defeat, sustained by tales of Muslim conquest and rule, stoked by stories of destroyed temples and looted treasures, all of which have imprisoned susceptible Hindus in a narrative of victimhood. Hindutva is an answer to a perception of failure and defeat, rather than a broad-minded story of a confident faith finding its place in the world. Looking back towards the failures of the past, it offers no hopes for the successes of the future.

This seems to be conceded even by one of the foremost voices of contemporary Hindutva, the American David Frawley. Hindus, he writes in his foundational screed *Arise Arjuna!* (1995), 'are generally suffering from a lack of self-esteem and an inferiority complex by which they are afraid to really express themselves or their religion. They have been beaten down by centuries of foreign rule and ongoing attempts to convert them'. Frawley's answer is for Indians to reassert Hindu pride, but his diagnosis calls that prescription into question.

As a Hindu and an Indian, I would argue that the whole point about India is the rejection of the idea that religion should be a determinant of nationhood. Our nationalist leaders did not jump to the conclusion that a Partition-formed Muslim state dictated an equivalent one for Hindus. To accept the idea of India you have to spurn the logic that divided the country in 1947. Your Indianness has nothing to do with which god you choose to worship, or not. We are not going to reduce ourselves to a Hindu Pakistan.

That is the real problem here. As I have mentioned earlier, Nehru had warned that the communalism of the majority was especially dangerous because it could present itself as nationalist. Yet, Hindu nationalism is not Indian nationalism. And it has nothing to do with genuine Hinduism either.

I too am proud of my Hinduism; I do not want to cede its verities to fanatics. I consider myself a Hindu and a nationalist, but I am not a Hindu nationalist. To discriminate against another, to attack another, to kill another, to destroy another's place of worship, on the basis of his faith is not part of Hindu *dharma*, as it was not part of Swami Vivekananda's. It is time to go back to these fundamentals of Hinduism. It is time to rescue Hindu *dharma* from the fundamentalists.

* * *

The misuse of Hinduism for sectarian minority-bashing is especially sad since Hinduism provides the basis for a shared sense of common culture within India that has little to do with religion. Bestselling authors like Amish Tripathi have achieved spectacular success by reinventing characters from Hindu mythology and the epics in stories accessible to modern readers, without surrendering to the prevalent chauvinism and bigotry of the Hindutva reassertion. Hindu festivals, from Holi to Diwali and of course Kerala's Onam, have already gone beyond their religious origins to unite Indians of all faiths as a shared experience (the revelry of Holi, the celebratory gift-giving of Onam, and the lights, firecrackers, mithais and social gambling of Diwali, have made all three into 'secular' occasions). Festivals—utsavas, melas, leelas—all 'Hindu' in origin, have become occasions for the mingling of ordinary Indians of all backgrounds. Religion lies at the heart of Indian culture, but not necessarily as a source of division; religious myths like the *Ramayana* and the *Mahabharata* provide a common idiom, a shared matrix of reference, to all Indians, and it was not surprising that when Doordarshan broadcast a fifty-two-episode serialisation of the *Mahabharata*, the script was written by a Muslim, Dr Rahi Masoom Raza. Hinduism and Islam are intertwined in India; both religions, after all, have shared the same history in the same space, and theirs is a cohabitation of necessity as well as fact.

To some degree, India's other minorities have found it comfortable to take on elements of Hindu culture as proof of their own integration into the national mainstream. The tennis-playing brothers Anand, Vijay and Ashok Amritraj all bear Hindu names, but they are Christian, the sons of Robert and Maggie Amritraj, and they played with prominent crosses dangling from their necks, which they were fond of kissing in supplication or gratitude at tense moments on court. But giving their children Hindu names must have seemed, to Robert and Maggie, more nationalist in these post-colonial times, and quite unrelated to which god they were brought up to worship. I would not wish to make too much of this, because Muslim Indians still feel obliged to adopt Arab names in deference to the roots of their faith, but the Amritraj case (repeated in many other Christian families I know) is merely an example of Hinduism serving as a framework for the voluntary cultural assimilation of minority groups, without either compulsion or conversion becoming an issue. Keralites almost unanimously consider the Christian singer Yesudas (whose very name is derived from Jesus!) to be the greatest-ever singer of Malayalam devotional songs and bhajans; for decades his songs were played at and around the Guruvayur temple while, as a Christian, the singer himself was not allowed in. (In September 2017 it was, however, announced that were he to make a formal request, he would be permitted entry as a confirmed *bhakt* of Lord Krishna).

HINDUISM AS CULTURE

It is to a great degree possible to speak of Hinduism as culture rather than as religion (a distinction the votaries of Hindutva distort in extolling Savarkar's enunciation of a similar view). The inauguration of a public project, the laying of a foundation stone or the launching of a ship usually start with the ritual smashing of a coconut, an auspicious practice in Hinduism but one which most Indians of other faiths cheerfully accept in much the same spirit as teetotallers acknowledge the role of champagne in a Western celebration. Interestingly, similar Hindu customs have survived in now-Muslim Java and now-Buddhist Thailand. Islamic Indonesians still cherish the *Ramayana* legend, now shorn (for them) of its religious associations. Javanese Muslims bear Sanskrit names. Hindu culture can easily be embraced by non-Hindus if it is separated from religious faith and treated as a heritage to which all may lay claim. I have often argued that the *Mahabharata* and the *Ramayana* should be taught in our schools just as the *Odyssey* and the *Iliad* are in Western ones, not as religious texts but as towering accomplishments of our culture and the source of so many legends and cultural references.

Amartya Sen is right to stress that Hinduism is not simply the Hindutva of Ayodhya or Gujarat; it has left all Indians a religious, philosophical, spiritual and historical legacy that gives meaning to the civilisational content of secular Indian nationalism. In building an Indian nation that takes account of the country's true Hindu heritage, we have to return to the pluralism of the national movement. This must involve turning away from the strident calls for Hindutva that would privilege a doctrinaire view of Hinduism at the expense of the minorities, because such calls are a denial of the essence of the Hinduism of Vivekananda. I say this not as a godless secularist, but as a proud Hindu who is mortified at what his own faith is being reduced to in the hands of bigots—petty men who know little about the beliefs, the traditions and the history of the faith in whose 'defence' they claim to act. They have distorted a pluralist religious philosophy in the process of instrumentalising it as a political ideology.

The way in which history and cultural memory informs contemporary attitudes varies from family to family. My mother's prosperous Nair family in Palakkad, for instance, lived in mortal terror of imminent attack by Tipu Sultan and lost most of its wealth in a foolish attempt to protect it from him by burying their treasures in an unknown location—they never found them again! But despite the stories that have been wryly and ruefully told and retold and passed down the generations over the two centuries since, my family and I never extended our dislike of Tipu and his marauders to a rejection of 'Muslims' as a whole, and certainly not to any Muslims of today. While we have no illusions about past attacks on temples by Muslim raiders, we did not bring up our children to use the past to justify bigotry in the present. One can appreciate history and leave it where it belongs.

Indians today have to find real answers to the dilemmas of running a plural nation. Nationalists often define their nation in terms of a cohesive group of people, held together by a common enemy. The common enemy of Indians is an internal one, but not the one identified by the Hindutva fanatics and their ilk. The common enemy lies in the forces of sectarian division that would, if unchecked, tear the country apart—or transform it into something that most self-respecting Hindus would refuse to recognise.

In many ways, the fundamental conflict of our times is the clash between, no, not civilisations, but doctrines—religious and ethnic fundamentalism on the one hand, secular consumerist capitalism on the other. The clash is taking place amidst a paradox. Thanks to globalisation, the world has been coming together into a single international market, just as it is simultaneously being torn apart by civil war, terrorism and the breakup of nations. Today there is a backlash, or more accurately two kinds of backlash: one a widely-noted current of economic anti-globalisation, as the 'losers' rebel against the elites who have been exporting their jobs to faraway lands; and the other what one can call cultural anti-globalisation, whose proponents seek the comforts of traditional identity. In many places in the West the two backlashes overlap, but in a country like India they do not; India's government seeks to be part of globalisation while rejecting the cultural diversity it implies. The Hindutva movement in India is part of this latter backlash against cosmopolitanism, multiculturalism and secularism in the name of cultural rootedness, religious or ethnic identity and nationalist authenticity.

In India this claim to authenticity and rootedness has taken on a majoritarian Hindu colouring under the BJP. It has sought to reduce Indians to a singular identity framed around their religious affiliation. Each individual, as I pointed out in my 1997 book *India: From Midnight to the Millennium*, has many identities. Sometimes religion obliges us to deny the truth about our own complexity by obliterating the multiplicity inherent in our identities. Religious fundamentalism, in particular, does so because it embodies a passion for pure belonging, a yearning intensified by the threatening tidal wave of globalisation as well as by the specificities of the devotees' politics. And it feeds on the inevitable sense among its adherents of being wounded, whether real or imagined. In this way, Hindutva reassertion draws from the same wellsprings as Islamist fanaticism and white-nationalist Christian fundamentalism.

What is to be done? We cannot delegitimise religion, and indeed there is something precious and valuable in a faith that allows a human being to see himself at one with others stretching their hands out towards God around the world. But can we separate religion from identity? Can we dream of a world in which religion has an honoured place but where the need for spirituality will no longer be associated with the need to belong? If we want religion to stop feeding fanaticism, terror and ethnic wars, we must find other ways of satisfying the need for identity. If identity can relate principally to citizenship rather than faith, to a land rather than a doctrine, and if that identity is one that can live in harmony with other identities, then we might still escape the worst horrors that the doomsayers (like Samuel Huntington, who two decades ago foretold a 'clash of civilisations') can conceive. A domestic 'clash of civilisations' would destroy India, which has survived and thrived as a civilisational medley.

Thanks, in many ways, to the eclectic inclusiveness of Hinduism, everything in India exists in countless variants. There was no single standard, no fixed stereotype, no 'one way'. This pluralism emerged from the very nature of the country; it was made inevitable by India's geography and reaffirmed by its history. There was simply too much of both to permit a single, exclusionist nationalism. When Hindutva's cadres demanded that all Indians declare 'Bharat Mata ki Jai (Victory to Holy Mother India)' as a litmus test of their nationalism, many of us insisted that no Indian should be obliged to mouth a slogan he did not believe in his heart. If some Muslims, for instance, felt that their religion did not allow them to hail their motherland as a goddess, the Constitution of India gave them the right not to. Hindutva wrongly seeks to deny them this right.

We were brought up to take this for granted, and to reject the sectarianism that had partitioned the nation when the British left. I was raised unaware of my own caste and unconscious of the religious loyalties of my schoolmates and friends. Of course, knowledge of these details came in time, but too late for any of it to matter, even less to influence my attitude or conduct. We were Indians: we were brought up (and constantly exhorted) to believe in an idea of nationhood transcending communal divisions. This may sound like the lofty obliviousness of the privileged, but such beliefs were held not only by elites: they were a reflection of how most Indians lived, even in the villages. Independent India was born out of a nationalist struggle in which acceptance of each other which we, perhaps unwisely, called secularism was fundamental to the nationalist consensus.

It is true that Hindu zealotry—which ought to be a contradiction in terms—is partly a reaction to other chauvinisms. As I have pointed out, the unreflective avowal by many Hindus of their own secularism has provoked the scorn of some Hindus, who despise the secularists as deracinated 'Macaulayputras' (sons of Macaulay) or 'Babur ke aulad' (sons of Babur). They see such Hindus as cut off from their own culture and heritage, and challenge them to rediscover their authentic roots, as defined by the proponents of Hindutva.

HINDUISM IS NOT A MONOLITH

But Hinduism is no monolith; its strength is found within each Hindu, not in the collectivity. Defining a 'Hindu' cause may well be a political reaction to the definition of non-Hindu causes: the Hindutva idea originated around the same time as the rise of a separate Muslim consciousness in the polity in the early twentieth century, and the resentments that spilled over into the destruction of the Babri Masjid in the century's last decade were largely articulated in opposition to the imagined 'appeasement' of India's minorities. The rage of the Hindu mobs is that of those who feel themselves supplanted in this competition of identities, who think that they are taking their country back from usurpers of long ago. They want revenge against history, but they do not realise that history is its own revenge.

The Hindutva fanatics seek to reinvent Hindu identity with a new belief structure and a new vocabulary. They seek to make Hinduism more like the Semitic religions they resent but wish to emulate: to pick fewer sacred books, notably the Gita, and exalt them would produce a less 'baggy', tighter version of the faith; to focus on fewer gods, notably Shiva, Rama and Krishna, with Ganesh and various forms of Devi thrown in, would sharpen Hindu divinity; to standardise religious practices around specific familiar festivals, rituals and gatherings, would provide a greater sense of community. Their associated efforts include a desire to control and restrict what Hindus eat, so their rejection of beef (even though several castes did eat it in the past) would itself become a marker of identity; to promote Hindi as a national language (though it is quite foreign to nearly half the country) so as to ensure that the vocabulary of Hindudom can be more easily transmitted; to mouth the same slogans ('Bharat Mata ki Jai!') and chant the same songs ('Vande Mataram' is a must), even though some Muslims are uncomfortable with both, in order to promote conformity. This invented Hinduism has much more to do with an era of political and cultural insecurity and a faltering new sense of aspiration than with the Vedas, the *Puranas* or the Bhakti movement: it denies the lived history of Hinduism even while claiming to speak in its name.

The central challenge of India is the challenge of accommodating the aspirations of different groups in the national dream. The ethos of Hinduism—inclusionist, flexible, agglomerative—helped the nation meet this challenge. The doctrine of Hindutva prefers uniformity to accommodation. The struggle for India's soul will be between two Hinduisms: the 'secularist' Indianism of the nationalist movement and the particularist fanaticism of the Ayodhya mob. It is a battle that rages still.

* * *

The inevitable backlash to my writings about Hindutva excesses, from the Babri Masjid demolition to the Gujarat horrors, has largely taken the form of belligerent emails and assorted social media fulminations from the less reflective of the Hindutva brigade. I have been excoriated as 'anti-Hindu' and described by several as a 'well-known leftist', which will no doubt amuse those of my friends who knew me in college thirty years ago as one of the very few supporters of Rajaji's conservative Swatantra Party—in those consensually socialist times. And from time to time a Hindutvavadi, reminding me of the religion that has been mine from birth, succumbed to the temptation to urge me predictably to heed that well-worn slogan: '*Garv se kaho ki hum Hindu hain*' (Say with pride that we are Hindus).

All right, let us take him up on that. I am indeed proud that I am a Hindu. But of what is it that I am, and am not, proud?

I am not proud of my co-religionists attacking and destroying Muslim homes and shops. I am not proud of Hindus raping Muslim girls, or slitting the wombs of Muslim mothers. I am not proud of Hindu vegetarians who have roasted human beings alive and rejoiced over the corpses. I am not proud of those who reduce the lofty metaphysical speculations of the

Upanishads to the petty bigotry of their own sense of identity, which they assert in order to exclude, not embrace, others.

I am proud that India's pluralism is paradoxically sustained by the fact that the overwhelming majority of Indians are Hindu, because Hinduism has taught them to live amidst a variety of other identities.

I am proud of those Hindus, like the Shankaracharya of Kanchi, who say that Hindus and Muslims must live like Ram and Lakshman in India. I am not proud of those Hindus, like 'Sadhvi' Rithambhara, who say that Muslims are like sour lemons curdling the milk of Hindu India.

I am not proud of those who suggest that only a Hindu, and only a certain kind of Hindu, can be an authentic Indian. I am not proud of those Hindus who say that people of other religions live in India only on their sufferance, and not because they belong on our soil. I am proud of those Hindus who realise that an India that denies itself to some of us could end up being denied to all of us.

I am proud of those Hindus who utterly reject Hindu communalism, conscious that the communalism of the majority is especially dangerous because it can present itself as nationalist. I am proud of those Hindus who respect the distinction between Hindu nationalism and Indian nationalism. Obviously, majorities are never seen as 'separatist', since separatism is by definition pursued by a minority. But majority communalism is in fact an extreme form of separatism, because it seeks to separate other Indians, integral parts of our country, from India itself. I am proud of those Hindus who recognise that the saffron and the green both belong equally on the Indian flag.

The reduction of non-Hindus to second-class status in their own homeland is unthinkable. As I have pointed out here, and elsewhere, it would be a second partition: and a partition in the Indian soul would be as bad as a partition in the Indian soil. For Hindus like myself, the only possible idea of India is that of a nation greater than the sum of its parts. That is the only India that will allow us to call ourselves not Brahmins, not Bengalis, not Hindus, not Hindi-speakers, but simply Indians.

How about another slogan for Hindus like me? *Garv se kaho ki hum Indian hain* (Say with pride that we are Indian).

* * *

There is an old Puranic story about Truth. It seems a brash young warrior sought the hand of a beautiful princess. Her father, the king, thought he was a bit too cocksure and callow. He decreed that the warrior could only marry the princess after he had found Truth.

So the warrior set out into the world on a quest for Truth. He went to temples and monasteries, to mountain tops where sages meditated, to remote forests where ascetics scourged themselves, but nowhere could he find Truth.

Despairing one day and seeking shelter from a thunderstorm, he took refuge in a musty cave. There was an old crone there, a hag with matted hair and warts on her face, the skin hanging loose from her bony limbs, her teeth yellow and rotting, her breath malodorous. But as he spoke to her, with each question she answered, he realised he had come to the end of his journey: she was Truth.

They spoke all night, and when the storm cleared, the warrior told her he had fulfilled his quest. Armed with his knowledge of Truth, he could go back to the palace and claim his bride.

'Now that I have found Truth,' he said, 'what shall I tell them at the palace about you?'

The wizened old creature smiled. 'Tell them,' she said, 'tell them that I am young and beautiful.'

So Truth exists, but is not always true. That subtle insight is typical of the wisdom of the ancient Hindus. It gives the lie to the petty bigotries, the glib certitudes, the righteous fanaticism of those who advocate Hindutva.

The tragedy for many Hindus is that the Hindu nationalists, often ironically referred to by their critics as *bhakts* (the 'devout'), are betraying daily the values of the very faith to which they claim to be committed. Since the original Bhakti movement began in Tamil Nadu in the sixth century, Hindu thought has stressed the personal nature of religion and emphasised the inclusive philosophy and all-embracing syncretism of the faith that Adi Shankara and Vivekananda taught to the world as Hinduism. The traditional Hindu texts, starting with the Vedas, were imbued with a sense of philosophical wonder, raising questions about creation, the nature of being and the meaning of life, and treating nothing as too sacred to interrogate. It is an act of treason to Hinduism to take this faith of mystery and doubt and reduce it to brazen certitudes, to shun diversity and extol dogma and to claim that it is the only authentic Hinduism.

The political project of Hindutva is nothing less than an assault on the religion; but where Hinduism has for millennia proved its resilience to external attacks, it is now revealing its vulnerability to attack from within. That is why Hindutva politics must be resisted; in presenting a view of Hinduism that is at odds with everything Hinduism has sought to stand for, it seeks to refashion Hinduism as something it has never been. Indeed, as the economist Kaushik Basu has argued, it reveals the insecurity of Hindutva's cheerleaders that they want to remake their country and religion in the very image of the countries and religions they claim to detest.

Hinduism attaches importance to *pramana* (instruments of warranted inference) in the pursuit of *jnana*, or knowledge. As long as you can demonstrate the validity or rigour of your *pramana*, you are entitled to the specific belief structure you wish to adhere to. It is this feature, unlike other traditions that rely on revelation as claims to truth, that ensures Hinduism is more open to diversity of belief. My friend Keerthik Sasidharan suggested to me, in twenty-first-century terms, that Hinduism is analogous to an open-source operating system on top of which others can build applications to be deployed in the receptive hardware of human brains. All Hinduism demands before the formation of any belief is analytical and logical consistency. Even the existence of God is subject to this test. The Nietzschean formulation that God created Man and Man returned the compliment is anticipated more than a millennium ago in this verse by Udayanacharya, the tenth-century logician, addressed to the deity Jagannatha of Puri:

> You're so drunk on wealth and power
> that you ignore my presence.
> Just wait: when the Buddhists come,
> your whole existence
> depends on me.[6]

(Yet it should be said that Udayanacharya is the very sage credited with so roundly trouncing Buddhists in debate that Buddhism never dared to challenge Hinduism in India thereafter.)

A RELIGION WITHOUT FUNDAMENTALS

When I stood for the post of UN Secretary General in 2006, journalists quizzed me about the role my Hindu faith played in my worldview. I conceded that it was true that faith can influence one's conduct in one's career and life. For some, it is merely a question of faith in themselves; for others, including me, that sense of faith emerges from a faith in something larger than ourselves. Faith is, at some level, what gives you the courage to take the risks you must take, and enables you to make peace with yourself when you suffer the inevitable setbacks and calumnies that are the lot of those who try to make a difference in the world. So I had no difficulty in saying openly that I am a believing Hindu. But I was also quick to explain what that phrase means to me. I'm not a 'Hindu fundamentalist'. As I have explained in this book, and said often in the past, the fundamental thing about Hinduism is that it is a religion without fundamentals. My faith in global diversity emerges from my Hindu beliefs as well, since we have an extraordinary diversity of religious practices within Hinduism, a faith with no single sacred book but many. Mine is a faith that allows each believer to reach out his or her hands to his or her notion of the godhead. I was brought up in the belief that all ways of worship are equally valid. I relished pointing out that my father prayed devoutly every day, but never used to oblige me to join him. In the Hindu way, he wanted me to find my own truth. And that was precisely the manner in which I brought up my own sons.

Finding my own truth gave me a truth that admits of the possibility that there might be other truths. I therefore bring to the world an attitude that is open, accommodating and tolerant of others' beliefs. Mine is not a faith for those who seek unquestioning dogmas, but there is no better belief-system for an era of doubt and uncertainty than a religion that cheerfully accommodates both.

The misuse of religion for political purposes is of course a sad, sometimes tragic, aspect of our contemporary reality. As UN

Secretary General Kofi Annan once said, the problem is never with the faith, but with the faithful. All faiths strive sincerely to animate the divine spark in each of us, but some of their followers, alas, use their faith as a club to beat others with, rather than a platform to raise themselves to the heavens. Since Hinduism believes that there are various ways of reaching the ultimate truth, as a Hindu I fully accepted the belief systems of others as equal to my own. That is why I cannot and do not accept the Hindutva fanatics' interpretation of the values and principles of my faith.

But what does it mean to me to be a practising Hindu? As I mentioned above, I have never been a frequent visitor to temples, though I do believe in praying every day, even if only for a couple of minutes. Many Hindus who can afford the space have a place for puja within their homes; at minimum, a picture, a little statue, or several. I too have maintained a little puja alcove at my homes where I try to reach out to the divine spirit. Yet, I believe in the Upanishadic doctrine that the Divine is essentially unknowable and unattainable by ordinary mortals. All prayer is an attempt to reach out to that which we cannot touch. While I do occasionally visit temples, and I appreciate how important they are to my mother and most other devout Hindus, I believe that one does not need any intermediaries between oneself and one's notion of the Divine. If God is in your heart, it matters little where else He resides.

So I take pride in the openness, the diversity, the range, the sublime philosophical aspirations of the Vedanta. I cherish the diversity, the lack of compulsion, and the richness of the various ways in which Hinduism is practised eclectically. And I admire the civilisational heritage of tolerance that makes Hindu societies open their arms to people of every other faith, to come and practise their beliefs in peace amidst Hindus. It is remarkable, for instance, that the only country on earth where the Jewish people have lived for centuries and never experienced a single episode of anti-Semitism is India. That is the Hinduism in which I gladly take pride.

Hinduism's suitability for the modern world lies in many ways in its recognition of uncertainty and its pragmatic non-dogmatism. The religion of 'maybe He does not know' is a faith for the non-dogmatic, one which looks beyond the blacks and whites, the grim certitudes of lesser mortals, to the acknowledgement of the scope for doubt, for different points of view on the great questions of life and death. Vivekananda's immortal 'We believe not only in universal toleration but we accept all religions as true' is a prescription for peace and coexistence among competing dogmatisms in a world full of too many dogmas. This is why it was perhaps the ideal faith for a candidate for United Nations Secretary General to profess. (And when I lost the race, my faith offered me consolation too, in the Bhagavad Gita's dictum that one did what was one's *dharma* to do, regardless of the consequences.)

Hinduism does not see the world in terms of absolutes. Blacks and whites are largely absent from its ethos. It sees competing notions of good and evil, duty and betrayal, everywhere, and seeks wisdom in finding the right approach suited for each specific circumstance. Vivekananda used to tell a parable of the frog in the well: 'I am a Hindu. I am sitting in my own little well and thinking that the whole world is my little well. The Christians sit in their little well and think the whole world is their well. The Muslims sit in their little well and think that is the whole world.' To Vivekananda, the world was one where each frog had much to learn from the others, if he would only look beyond his well.

Hinduism is not a totalising belief system; it offers a way of coping with the complexity of the world. It acknowledges that the truth is plural, that there is no one correct answer to the big questions of creation, or of the meaning of life. In its reverence for sages and rishis, it admits that knowledge may come from an exchange between two or more views, neither of which necessarily possesses a monopoly on the truth. The greatest truth, to the Hindu, is that which accepts the existence of other truths.

Hinduism sees life as an evolving dynamic, not a contest that can ever be settled once and for all. It is open to negotiation on ways of being and believing; it permits negotiation even with God. It offers rites and rituals, but leaves it up to each individual to choose which ones he wishes to adhere to. Each Hindu must find his own truth. Each individual achieves his own salvation and self-fulfilment.

At the same time Hinduism is also anchored in the real world. A superficial view of Hinduism sees its other-worldly 'timelessness'. But in fact the religion is anchored not in a world-denying spirituality, as Raimon Panikkar points out; in his words, it is not the timeless, but the 'time-full', which wins Vedic approbation. Time is depicted in hymns in the *Atharva Veda* as perpetually replenishing itself from a full vessel which, in spite of all efforts, can never be emptied. Since time transcends time, it is without beginning or end, without limit; and in that sense it is like God. 'Time am I, world-destroying,' says Krishna in the Bhagavad Gita, stressing 'I am imperishable Time'. As a verse in the *Maitreya Upanishad* puts it:

> *From time all beings emerge*
> *From time they advance and grow*
> *In time, too, they come to rest.*
> *Time is embodied and also bodiless.*

The harm religion does when it is passionately self-righteous—wars, crusades, communal violence, jihad—is arguably greater than the benefits religion produces when it does well (teaching morality, answering prayers, providing balm to troubled souls). In its long history, Hinduism has never launched an apocalyptic war of religion or tried to impose one correct answer on all of life. Hindus like to speak of theirs as a religion of peace, but then so do other faiths. Still, the Hindu scriptures are replete with hymns to peace, and are infused with the idea that human beings must seek peace within themselves and peace with all other human beings. Many Vedic mantras set out to achieve these ends; of these the Shanti Mantra is the most famous, and prays for peace in heaven, on earth and in the human heart. The words 'Om Shantih! Shantih! Shantihi!' are uttered three times at the end of every sacred action or after the recitation of a sacred text—three times because the Hindu seeks peace in all three realms. Humans cannot enjoy personal peace in the absence of peace on earth, but equally there cannot be peace in the world if there is no peace in the inner hearts of the human beings in the world. A verse of the *Yajur Veda* (xxxvi, 17) chants:

To the heavens be peace, to the sky and the earth,
To the waters be peace, to plants and all trees,
To the Gods be peace, to Brahman be peace,
To all men be peace, again and again—peace also to me![7]

The speaker of the Sixteenth Lok Sabha, the Lower House of the Indian parliament, the first in that office from the BJP, introduced the practice of uttering 'Om Shantih! Shantih! Shantihi!' after the otherwise ritualistic reading of obituary notices during each session. Though this implied the introduction of religious language into a secular Parliament, her words were echoed by many MPs, and not only those of her party. While as a liberal I was initially dismayed by her doing this, I soon came around to the view that as long as no one was obliged to follow her, calling for peace was hardly objectionable. A Hindu could be overtly Hindu, I felt, if in the process she was being all-embracing in her expression of her faith, while not imposing it on others.

Hinduism is a life-affirming religion of joy and play (*leela*). It sees the world as suffused with radiance rather than darkness; as the Bhagavad Gita says, 'That splendour which is from the sun, which illumines this whole world, which is in the moon and in fire—know that splendour is also mine.' In turn this refulgence is Man's, since he is enjoined by the *Upanishads* to see all beings in himself and himself in all things; he therefore radiates in his person the splendour of the Universe. Yes, the Hindu scriptures acknowledge the existence of human sorrow and suffering, but see them as part of an awakening to the transcendent. The Vedas do not ask why we suffer; they take human sorrow as a given, an affliction to be dealt with and overcome. The *Upanishads* are more questioning of suffering; they use a word, *dukha*, sadness and existential distress, a word not found in the Vedas. Ideally one must be detached from such suffering, as the Gita teaches, and by eliminating sorrow in oneself through self-realisation, help remove it from others. This seems impossible for most ordinary people, and so the easier solution is to take refuge in the Lord.

Similarly, the Hindu scriptures speculate about the mystery of what lies beyond human life, but they are not obsessed with death; as Panikkar brilliantly put it, 'they seem to describe an existential attitude that takes cognisance of the phenomenon of death but denies to it any character of ultimacy... It is by integrating the fact of death into life, by reabsorbing, as it were, death into life...by finding a ground that is common to both death and life, that we can find the proper Vedic perspective.' This notion of the continuity between life and death is a particularly Hindu idea, with death, as it were, inbuilt into life. Panikkar again: 'The beyond is the unfathomable ocean which makes the beaches on this side worth walking and playing on.'

Hindus believe that, at most, religion can create a platform upon which the beautiful things in life can be attained. Destiny, knowledge, reflection and prayer may equip you to achieve fulfilment. The Hindu is a seeker, but the holy grail he seeks is within himself. Hinduism urges you to explore your own mind and heart to discover the truths about life. The model of the ideal questing Hindu may be found in a description of the sage Narada in the Valmiki *Ramayana*: 'Dedicated to self-learning, fully in control of the senses, seeker of the truth'. Yoga, meditation, prayer, social service are all means to that end, but not the only ones. You have to work hard yourself to achieve those things that are worth achieving. The doctrine of *karma yoga* preached by both Vivekananda and Mahatma Gandhi is a doctrine of action, not of passivity or fatalism. There is no lassitude in the pursuit of the Purusharthas.

The wise Hindu can hold two or more opposing ideas together in her mind at the same time. That is the way the world is. For the Hindu texts uniquely operate from a platform of scepticism, not a springboard of certitude. The *Rig Veda* verse that says 'maybe He does not know' about the Creator is not an invention of post-modernism, but the wisdom of a timeless text that has lasted for three and a half millennia and will always be valid.

Most faiths prioritise one identity, one narrative and one holy book. Hinduism recognises that everyone has multiple identities, accepts diverse narratives and respects several sacred books. Indeed, the folk Hinduism of multiple beliefs cannot be forced into the Abrahamic framework of One Book, One Deity and one way of doing things. The more the Hindu grapples with the great questions, the more she understands how much is beyond our understanding.

Yet the Hindu lives in reality, in the here and now, conscious that on the way to renunciation and liberation from the world, there are worldly duties and responsibilities to family, community and nation that must be performed without regard to their rewards. Hindus do not shelter from the besieging forces of life behind the safety of their doctrinal battlements, the omniscience of their dogmas, the fatwas or encyclicals of their priests. They are unafraid to face the cross currents, acknowledging how little they know. Indeed Hindus are not awed by the complexity of the world, because they accept the world is complex, and much passes their understanding.

A RELIGION FOR THE 21ST CENTURY

In the twenty-first century, Hinduism has many of the attributes of a universal religion—a religion that is personal and individualistic, privileges the individual and does not subordinate one to a collectivity; a religion that grants and respects complete freedom to the believer to find his or her own answers to the true meaning of life; a religion that offers a wide range of choice in religious practice, even in regard to the nature and form of the formless God; a religion that places great emphasis on one's mind, and values one's capacity for reflection, intellectual enquiry, and self-study; a religion that distances itself from dogma and holy writ, that is minimally prescriptive and yet offers an abundance of options, spiritual and philosophical texts and social and cultural practices to choose from. In a world where resistance to authority is growing, Hinduism imposes no authorities; in a world of networked individuals, Hinduism proposes no institutional hierarchies; in a world of open-source information-sharing, Hinduism accepts all paths as equally valid; in a world of rapid transformations and accelerating change, Hinduism is adaptable and flexible, which is why it has survived for nearly 4,000 years.

In 1926, Professor Clement Webb suggested that Hinduism, with its tradition of openness, tolerance and acceptance of the Divine in the most diverse forms imaginable, 'could perhaps more easily than any other faith develop, without loss of continuity with its past, into a universal religion...' This remains true almost a century later. Universalism comes easily to Hinduism. Hindus respect the environment because it embodies the unity of all creation, and in this, too, theirs is a faith for the twenty-first century.

Dr Karan Singh, the former maharaja of Kashmir and Indian politician who is also a superbly readable scholar of Hindu philosophy, identifies five major principles in Hinduism that lend relevance and validity to the faith in today's world. At the risk of inadequate paraphrase, these are, according to him: the recognition of the unity of all mankind, epitomised in the Rig Vedic phrase '*vasudhaiva kutumbakam*', the world is one family; the harmony of all religions, epitomised in that Rig Vedic statement that was Swami Vivekananda's favourite, '*ekam sat vipra bahudha vadanti*'; the divinity inherent in each individual, transcending the social stratifications and hierarchies that have all too often distorted this principle in Hindu society; the creative synthesis of practical action and contemplative knowledge, science and religion, meditation and social service, in the faith; and finally, the cosmic vision of Hindu philosophy, incorporating the infinite galaxies of which the Earth is just a tiny speck. In Dr Singh's own words: 'such is the grandeur and mystery of the Atman that it can move towards a comprehension of the unutterable mystery of existence. We, who are children of the past and the future, of earth and heaven, of light and darkness, of the human and the divine, at once evanescent and eternal, of the world and beyond it, within time and in eternity, yet have the capacity to comprehend our condition, to rise above our terrestrial limitations, and finally, to transcend the throbbing abyss of space and time itself.' This, Dr Singh says, is the message of Hinduism, and it is a message that can and should resonate throughout the world.

Yet such a universal creed can only be the Hinduism described in this book, rather than the petty intolerant Hindutva being propagated by bigots in a travesty of the majesty of their faith. Swami Vivekananda had, as usual, put it best:

> 'if there is ever to be a universal religion, it must be one which will
> have no location in place or time; which will be infinite like the God
> it will preach, and whose sun will shine upon the followers of

Krishna and of Christ, on saints and sinners alike; which will not be Brahminic or Buddhistic, Christian or Mohammedan, but the sum total of all these...and still have infinite space for development; which in its catholicity will embrace in infinite arms, and find a place for every human being from the lowest grovelling savage, not far removed from the brute, to the highest man towering by the virtues of his head and heart almost above humanity, making society stand in awe of him and doubt his human nature. It will be a religion which will have no place for persecution or intolerance in its polity, which will recognise divinity in every man and woman, and whose whole scope, whose whole force, will be centered in aiding humanity to realise its own true, divine nature. Offer such a religion and all the nations will follow you.'

I am a Hindu who is proud to offer such a religion to the world. I do so conscious that Hinduism does not seek to proselytise, only to offer itself as an example that others may or may not choose to follow. Unlike the Abrahamic faiths it manifests no desire to universalise itself; yet its tenets and values are universally applicable. But first it must be revived and reasserted, in its glorious liberalism, its openness and acceptance, its eclecticism and universalism, in the land of its own birth. As the Hindu hymn (from the *Brihadaranyaka Upanishad*) says, in words that resonate with meaning for every human being on the planet:

> *Asato ma sad gamaya!*
> *Tamaso ma jyotir gamaya!*
> *Mrityor ma amritam gamaya!*

> Lead me from Untruth to Truth,
> Lead me from darkness to light,
> Lead me from death to immortality.

NOTES

PREFACE AND ACKNOWLEDGEMENTS

1. Right down to spellings, I have throughout eschewed the scholarly Romanised spellings of Sanskrit words favoured by the classic texts for simple versions that approximate the way the words are pronounced. This has led me to invent one spelling, 'mutth', for the Hindu monastery more frequently spelt '*mutt*' or '*math*', both of which might confuse or mislead the average English-speaker.

1. MY HINDUISM

1. Derived from Nanditha Krishna, *Hinduism and Nature*, New Delhi: Penguin Books, 2017, p. 5–6.
2. Debiprasad Chattopadhyaya and M. K. Gangopadhyaya (eds), *Carvaka/Lokayata: An Anthology of Source Materials and Some Recent Studies*, Indian Council of Philosophical Research, 1990, p. 352.
3. Mahatma Gandhi, *Hindu Dharma*, Ahmedabad: Navajivan Publishing House, 1950, p. 6.
4. Quoted in Sri Swami Sivananda, *All About Hinduism*, The Divine Life Society, 1947.
5. '[A] man can be as truly a Hindu as any without believing in the Vedas as an independent religious authority', V. D. Savarkar, *Hindutva: Who is a Hindu?* (originally published under the title *Essentials of Hindutva*), Bombay: Veer Savarkar Prakashan, 1923, p. 81.
6. Quoted in Jawaharlal Nehru, *The Discovery of India*, 1946.

7. Sarvepalli Radhakrishnan, *The Hindu Way of Life*, London: Geo. Allen & Unwin Ltd., 1927.

8. Swami Vivekananda, *The Complete Works of Swami Vivekananda*, Chennai: Manonmani Publishers, 2015.

9. Ibid.

10. Ibid.

11. Adapted from Friedrich Max Müller, *The Upanishads: Part II*, Oxford: Clarendon Press, 1884.

12. Raimon Panikkar, *The Vedic Experience: Mantramañjarı: An Anthology Of The Vedas For Modern Man*, Berkeley: University of California Press, 1977.

13. I am indebted to Dr Nanditha Krishna for this insight.

14. Robert L. Brown, *Ganesh: Studies of an Indian God*, New York: SUNY Press, 1991, p. 21.

15. 'Milk-drinking deities unleash mass hysteria', quoted in *Great Mysteries of the 20th Century*, Reader's Digest, 1999.

2. THE HINDU WAY

1. Shakunthala Jagannathan's translation.

2. François Bernier, *Travels in the Mogul Empire*, Manchester: Archibald Constable & Company, 1670.

3. S. Radhakrishnan, *The Hindu View of Life*, London: Geo. Allen & Unwin, 1926.

4. Diana L. Eck, *Encountering God: A Spiritual Journey from Bozeman to Banares*, Boston: Beacon Press, 1993, p. 76.

5. Herbert Risley, *The People of India*, Simla: Thacker, Spink & Co, 1915, p. 244.

6. Juan Mascaro, *The Upanishads*, London: Penguin Books, 1965.

7. The temple's riches are truly staggering. Donations from the public, the value of the thousands of kilos of hair they donate to the Lord through tonsuring their heads at the temple, the price of entry tickets, the specific fees paid for particular rituals and offerings, the sale of prasadam (usually in the form of the famous and patented Tirupati laddoo (milk sweets) and the cash deposited in the donation-urns or hundis within the temple itself. Tirupati's budget for 2015–2016 was c $392 million, compared to the Vatican's budget of c $274 million in the same year.

Since Lord Balaji is a particular favourite of those who pray for wealth, their gratitude for answered prayers is also munificent.

8. The ancient Indian science of Ayurveda groups foods into three categories, satvik, rajasik and tamasik, each category producing effects on the body of the consumer. Foods that grow under the ground, like onion and garlic, fall into the unhealthy tamasik category, along with meat, alcohol, coffee and tobacco.

9. In Tvastar's dwelling Indra drank the Soma, a hundredworth of juice pressed from the mortar, translated by Ralph T. H. Griffith.

10. Rutvij Merchant, 'Answering the ultimate question: who is a Hindu?', Firstpost.com, 24 September 2014.

11. See page 253.

12. K. Balasubramania Iyer, *Yaksha Prasna*, Bombay: Bhavan's Book Company, 1989.

13. I am indebted to Dr Nanditha Krishna for this insight.

14. Since the precise dates are impossible to establish, some authorities prefer a later date for the commencement of their composition.

15. Upinder Singh, *Political Violence in Ancient India*, Cambridge, MA: Harvard University Press, 2017, p. 236.

16. 'Having taken the bow furnished by the *Upanishads*, the great weapon and fixed in it the arrow rendered pointed by constant meditation and having drawn it with the mind fixed on the *Brahman*, hit, good looking youth! at that mark the immortal *Brahman*'. www.wisdomlib.org

17. Raimon Panikkar, *The Vedic Experience*, p. 66.

3. QUESTIONING HINDU CUSTOMS

1. Radhakrishnan, *The Hindu Way of Life*, London: Geo. Allen & Unwin, 1927.

2. Manu S. Pillai, 'Women, Lingayats and "the Hindus"', *LiveMint*, 25 September 2017.

3. Manu S. Pillai, 'The Kerala of the past and present', *LiveMint*, 2 September 2017.

4. Seema Chishti, 'Biggest caste survey: One in four Indians admit to practising untouchability', *Indian Express*, 29 November 2014.

5. A scholar friend finds the figure for Christians surprisingly low. In Tamil Nadu, she tells me, many churches have separate pews and burial

grounds for different castes, and some even make Dalits sit outside the church.

6. Amit Thorat, 'Mapping Exclusion', *Indian Express*, 3 December 2014.
7. Tejaswini Tabhane, 'No Mr Tharoor, I Don't Want to Enter Your Kitchen', www.roundtableindia.co.in, 16 September 2017.

4. GREAT SOULS OF HINDUISM

1. Michael Comans, *The Method of Early Advaita Vedanta: A Study of Gaud. apada, S'ankara, Sures'vara, and Padmapada*, Delhi: Motilal Banarsidass, 2000.
2. Raimon Panikkar, *The Vedic Experience: Mantramañjarı: An Anthology Of The Vedas For Modern Man*, Berkeley: University of California Press, 1977.
3. Adapted from Swami Vivekananda, *The Complete Works of Swami Vivekananda*, Chennai: Manonmani Publishers, 2015.
4. Friedrich Max Müller, *The Upanishads*, Oxford: Clarendon Press, 1884.
5. Dr Karan Singh, *Essays on Hinduism*, New Delhi: Ratna Sagar, 1987, p. 25.
6. Karigoudar Ishwara, *Speaking of Basava: Lingayat Religion and Culture in South Asia*, Boulder, Colarado: Westview Press, 1992, p. 212.
7. Manu S. Pillai, 'Basava and the Emergence of Lingayat identity', *LiveMint*, 28 July 2017.
8. Ibid.
9. In turn Sufism shows the influence of Hindu mysticism on Islam, but that is another story.
10. The period of Muslim conversions in the north saw the migration of several communities of Hindus southwards, bringing their religion and skills to other parts of India.
11. Gauri Shankar Bhatt, 'Brahmo Samaj, Arya Samaj, and the Church-Sect Typology', *Review of Religious Research*, 10, 1968, p. 24.
12. See page 253.
13. Christophe Jaffrelot, 'Hindu Nationalism: Strategic Syncretism in Ideology Building', *Economic and Political Weekly*, Vol. 28 No. 12/13, 20–27 March 1993.
14. Raimon Panikkar, *The Vedic Experience: Mantramañjarı: An Anthology Of The Vedas For Modern Man*, Berkeley: University of California Press, 1977.

15. S. Radhakrishnan, *The Hindu View of Life*, London: Geo. Allen & Unwin, 1926.

16. Ibid.

17. Ibid.

18. K. P. Shankaran, 'In Good Faith: Gandhi's radical Hinduism', *Indian Express*, 4 December 2017.

19. Ibid.

5. HINDUISM AND THE POLITICS OF HINDUTVA

1. T. N. Madan, 'Secularism in its place', *The Journal of Asian Studies*, vol. 46, No. 4, November 1987, pp. 747–759.

2. V. D. Savarkar, *Hindutva*, p. 3.

3. Ibid.

4. Ibid., pp. 3–4.

5. Quoted in M. J. Akbar, *India: The Siege Within: Challenges to a Nation's Unity*, New Delhi: UBSPD, 1996.

6. V. D. Savarkar, *Hindutva*, p. 3.

7. www.savitridevi.org/hindus-foreword.html

8. www.savitridevi.org/hindus-06.html

9. 3rd edition, Nagpur: Bharat Prakashan, 1945.

10. 4th impression, Bangalore: Vikrama Prakashan, 1968.

11. Golwalkar, *We, or Our Nationhood Defined*, pp. 52–53.

12. Ibid., p. 42.

13. Golwalkar, *Bunch of Thoughts*, p. 123.

14. Ibid., pp. 142–143.

15. Ibid., p. 22. ('Our concept of Hindu Nation is not a mere bundle of political and economic rights. It is essentially a cultural one.')

16. Ibid., p. 156.

17. Nietzsche in a letter to his friend Peter Gast, cited by Koenraad Elst in 'Manu as a weapon against egalitarianism: Nietzsche and Hindu political philosophy', paper presented at the annual conference of the Friedrich Nietzsche Society, Leiden, 2006.

18. Manu S. Pillai, 'Decoding RSS ideologue MS Golwalkar's nationalism', *Livemint*, 15 July 2017.

19. Ibid.

20. Ibid.

21. Golwalkar, *We, or Our Nationhood Defined*, p. 22.
22. Ibid.
23. Savarkar, *Hindutva*, p. 20.
24. Golwalkar, *We, or Our Nationhood Defined*, pp. 15, 16.
25. V. S. Naipaul, *Among the Believers: An Islamic Journey*, London: Penguin Books, 1982.
26. *Organiser*, 3 June 1979.
27. Golwalkar, *Bunch of Thoughts*, p. 142.
28. Golwalkar, *We, or Our Nationhood Defined*, pp. 104–105.
29. Golwalkar, *Bunch of Thoughts*, p. 102.
30. Ibid., p. 179.
31. Ibid., p. 186.
32. Golwalkar, *Bunch of Thoughts*, pp. 156.
33. Ramachandra Guha, 'They Too Wrote Our History', *Outlook*, 22 August 2005.
34. Golwalkar, *Bunch of Thoughts*, p. 131.
35. Manu S. Pillai, 'Decoding RSS ideologue MS Golwalkar's nationalism', *Livemint*, 15 July 2017.
36. Murad Ali Beg, 'Hindutva', *Frontier*, 6 June 2017.
37. Debapriya Mondal, 'Budget 2017: FM Jaitley announces Rs 4, 814 crore for Deen Dayal Upadhyaya Gram Jyoti Yojana, *Economic Times*, 1 February 2017. 'Budget 2016: Rs 200 cr for events on Deendayal Upadhyaya', *Times of India*, 29 February 2016. Deeptiman Tiwary, 'BJP going all out to resurrect Deen Dayal Upadhyaya's legacy', *Times of India*, 3 October 2014.
38. Jyoti Malhotra, 'New pedestal for a saffron pioneer', *India Today*, 14 October 2015.
39. Bhavdeep Kang, 'Who is this man who features in every Modi speech?', Grist Media, 6 October 2014.
40. K. S. Bharathi, *The Political Thought of Pandit Deendayal Upadhyaya*, New Delhi: Concept Publishing Company, 1998, p. 86.
41. Bhishkar, C. P., *Pt. Deendayal Upadhyay Ideology & Perception—Part 5: Concept of The Rashtra*, New Delhi: Suruchi Prakashan, 2014, p. 4.
42. The Direction of National Life, Lucknow: Lohit Prakashan, 1971.
43. Golwalkar, *Bunch of Thoughts*, p. 227.
44. Quoted in V. V. Nene, *Pandit Deendayal Upadhyaya: Ideology and Perception*, trans. by M. K. Paranjape and D. R. Kulkarni, New Delhi: Suruchi Prakashan, 1988, pp. 10–11.

45. C. P. Bhishkar, *Pt. Deendayal Upadhyay Ideology & Perception—Part 5: Concept of The Rashtra*, New Delhi: Suruchi Prakashan, 2014, p. 156.

46. Ibid., p. 17.

47. Ibid., p. 18.

48. Ibid., p. 155.

49. Ibid., pp. 109–110.

50. Ibid., p. 157.

51. Ibid., p. 87.

52. Ibid., p. 179.

53. Dattopant Bapurao Thengadi, *Pandit Deendayal Upadhyaya: Ideology and Perception*, Vol. 2, New Delhi: Suruchi Prakashan, 1988, p. 50.

54. V. V. Nene, *Pt. Deendayal Upadhyay Ideology & Perception—Part-2: Integral Humanism*, New Delhi: Suruchi Prakashan, 2014, p. 77.

55. 'Ramzada vs haramzada: Outrage over Union Minister Sadhvi's remark', *Indian Express*, 2 December 2014.

56. Bhishkar, C. P., *Pt. Deendayal Upadhyay Ideology & Perception—Part 5: Concept of The Rashtra*, New Delhi: Suruchi Prakashan, 2014, p. 93. ('[Bharat] has always given a warm welcome and shelter to social groups... like the Parsis and Jews.')

57. Suchitra Mohanty, 'Rohingya refugees "threat to national security", Centre tells Supreme Court', *LiveMint*, 14 September 2017.

58. Dilip Awasthi, 'Ayodhya, December 6, 1992: A nation's shame', *India Today*, 31 December 1992.

59. The militant violence in Kashmir, and the terror attacks of 26/11 in Mumbai, which have been planned and directed from across the border by Pakistan, are beyond the scope of this book.

60. Akshaya Mukul, 'Savarkar had begged the British for mercy', *Times of India*, 3 May 2002.

61. 'Vajpayee wanted Modi to quit over Gujarat riots, but party said no: Venkaiah Naidu', *India Today*, 9 March 2014.

62. Prabhat Patnaik, 'The Fascism of Our Times', *Social Scientist*, Vol. 21 No. 3/4, 1993.

63. Ashis Nandy, 'Obituary of a Culture', *Seminar*, 2002.

64. *Dr. Ramesh Yeshwant Prabhoo vs Shri Prabhakar Kashinath Kunte & Others*, 1996 SCC (1) 130.

65. Manu S. Pillai, 'Why the BJP wouldn't have risen the way it did with Vajpayee', *Livemint*, 28 January 2017.

66. Vishwadeepak, 'We should remove secularism, socialism from the Constitution: Govindacharya', *National Herald*, updated on www.nationalheraldindia.com, 2 October 2017.

67. Ibid.

6. BEYOND HOLY COWS: THE USES AND ABUSES OF HINDU CULTURE AND HISTORY

1. Vamadev Shastri, 'Sarva Dharma Sambhava: Unity or Confusion of Religions?', www.hinduhumanrights.info, 18 August 2013.

2. David Frawley, *Awaken Bharata: A Call for India's Rebirth*, New Delhi: Voice of India, 1998, p. xxv.

3. David Frawley, *Arise Arjuna: Hinduism and the Modern World*, New Delhi: Voice of India, 1995, p. 15.

4. David Frawley, *Awaken Bharata: A Call for India's Rebirth*, New Delhi: Voice of India, 1998, p. xxv.

5. K. N. Panikkar, 'In the Name of Nationalism', *Frontline*, 13 March 2004.

6. K. Thangaraj and G. Chaubey, 'Too early to settle the Aryan migration debate', *The Hindu*, 13 July 2017.

7. Ibid. Also see Michael Danino, 'Aryans and the Indus Valley Civilization: Archaeological, Skeletal and Molecular Evidence' in *A Companion to South Asia in the Past* edited by Gwen Robbins Schug and Subhash R. Walimbe, Oxford: John Wiley & Sons, 2016; and Danino's response ('The problematics of genetics and the Aryan issue', *The Hindu*, 29 June 2017) to Tony Joseph, 'How genetics is settling the Aryan migration debate', *The Hindu*, 16 June 2017.

8. P. L. Kessler, 'South East Asia–Cambodia, www.historyfiles.co.uk.

9. This is not to imply that all the recent appointees to such bodies are Hindutvavadis, merely that some with Hindutva credentials have been placed in key positions.

10. Dick Teresi, *Lost Discoveries: The Ancient Roots of Modern Science from the Babylonians to the Maya*, New York: Simon & Schuster, 2002.

11. Audrey Truschke, *Aurangzeb: The Man and the Myth*, New Delhi: Penguin Books, 2017.

12. Girish Shahane, 'Aurangzeb was a bigot not just by our standards but also by those of his predecessors and peers', *Scroll.in*, 1 November 2017.

13. Audrey Truschke, '"Some of the hate mail is chilling": Historian Audrey Truschke on the backlash to her Aurangzeb book', *Scroll.in*, 25 May 2017.

14. Ross Colvin and Sruthi Gottipati, 'Interview with BJP leader Narendra Modi', Reuters, 12 Juy 2013.

15. '"All Indians Originally Hindus", RSS Chief Mohan Bhagwat Says Hinduism's Door Open To All', *Outlook*, 12 September 2017.

16. 'Giriraj Singh wanted to send PM critics to Pakistan. Now, he is a minister', www.NDTV.com, 10 November 2014.

17. 'Shiv Sena MP Force-Feeds Man Who Was Fasting for Ramzan', www. NDTV.com, 23 July 2014.

18. Pheroze L. Vincent, 'Bengali slum dwellers caught in crossfire' *The Hindu*, 10 December 2014.

19. Full text of the judgment at: Sanjay Kishan Kaul, 'There should be freedom for the thought we hate', *Outlook*, 8 May 2008.

20. D. N. Jha, 'What the Gods Drank', *Indian Express*, 29 July 2017.

21. 'UP CM Yogi Adityanath's anti-Romeo squads: "Moral policing", "Taliban-like", international media has its say,' *Indian Express*, 3 April 2017.

22. Annie Gowen, 'Is India neglecting the Taj because it was built by Muslims?', *Washington Post*, 3 October 2016.

23. 'Adityanath: Foreign dignitaries are now being gifted the Gita and not 'un-Indian' Taj Mahal replicas', *Scroll.in*, 16 June 2017.

24. 'Taj Mahal is a "blot on Indian culture", was built by traitors, says BJP leader Sangeet Som', *Scroll.in*, 16 October 2017.

25. 'Yogi Adityanath slams SRK, compares him with Hafiz Saeed', *The Hindu*, 4 November, 2015.

26. Sowmiya Ashok, 'Don't get into why Taj Mahal was built, when or how… Taj a gem, will protect it: Yogi Adityanath', *Indian Express*, 27 October 2017.

27. Nayantara Sahgal, 'A Hindu Speaks', www.indiancultureforum.in, 11 October 2017.

28. Jawaharlal Nehru, *The Discovery of India*, Calcutta: The Signet Press, 1946.

29. Alison Saldanha, 'Cow-Related Hate Crimes Peaked in 2017, 86% of Those Killed Muslim', *thewire.in*, 8 December 2017.

30. '4 Dalits stripped, beaten up for skinning dead cow', *Times of India*, 13 July 2016.

31. Siddharth Ranjan Das, 'Muslim Women Beaten Over Beef Rumour, Spectators Film Attack, Cops Watch', www.NDTV.com, 27 July 2016.

32. Amulya Gopalakrishnan, 'We Are All Gau Rakshaks: Whether or not we care about cows, we certainly don't mind vigilantism', *Times of India*, 1 August 2016.

33. Venkitesh Ramakrishnan, 'The Cow Menace', *Frontline*, 10 November 2017.

34. 'It was not that the cow was not sacred in Vedic times, it was because of her sacredness that it is ordained in the *Vajasaneyi Samhita* that beef should be eaten.' From *Dharma Shastra Vichar* (Marathi) by Panduranga Vaman Kane, quoted in B. R. Ambedkar, *The Untouchables: Who Were They and Why They Became Untouchables?*, 1948. Accessed via www.ambedkarintellectuals.in on 15 December 2017.

35. Jha, D. N., *The Myth of the Holy Cow*, London: Verso Books, 2004, pg 139. ('The Vedas mention about 250 animals out of which at least 50 were deemed fit for sacrifice, by implication for divine as well as human consumption. The *Taittiriya Brahmana* categorically tells us, "Verily the cow is food" (atho annam vai gauh) and Yajnavalkya's insistence on eating the tender (amsala) flesh of the cow is well known.')

36. 'Nevertheless Yagnavalkya said, "I, for one, eat it, provided that it is tender."' In *The Satapatha Brahmana According to the Text of the Madhyandina School* translated by Julius Eggeling, Oxford: Clarendon Press, 1885, p. 11.

37. Nandagopal Rajan, '#PoMoneModi: Angry Kerala responds to PM Modi's Somalia comparision', *Indian Express*, 13 May 2016.

7. TAKING BACK HINDUISM

1. Suhasini Haider, 'India will succeed if it is not splintered along religious lines: Barack Obama', *The Hindu*, 28 January 2015.

2. Sandeep Joshi, 'Hindu women should have 10 children: Shankaracharya', *The Hindu*, 19 January 2015.

3. Percival Spear, Vincent Smith (trans.), *The Oxford History of India*, 4th edn, London: Oxford University Press, p. 412.

4. Makarand R. Paranjape (ed.), *Swami Vivekananda: A Contemporary Reader*, New Delhi: Routledge, 2015.

5. Amartya Sen, 'Threats to Secular India', *Social Scientist*, Volume 21, 1993.

6. http://prekshaa.in/story-verse-udayanacharya-nyaya-tarka-vaisheshika-shastra-buddhism-puri-jagannath/
7. Raimon Panikkar, *The Vedic Experience*.

BIBLIOGRAPHY

Agrawala, Vasudev Sharan, *Padmavat: Malik Muhammad Jayasi krit Mahakavya (Mool Aur Sanjeevani Vyakhya)*, Jhansi: Sahitya Sadan, 1955.

Ananthamurthy, U. R., *Hindutva or Hind Swaraj*, New Delhi: HarperCollins, 2016.

Andersen, Walter K. and Damle, Shridhar D., *The Brotherhood in Saffron: The Rashtriya Swayamsevak Sangh and Hindu Revivalism*, New Delhi: Vistaar Publications, 1987.

Basham, A. L., *The Wonder That Was India*, London: Picador, 2004.

Chinmayananda, Swami, *The Holy Geeta*, Mumbai: Chinmaya Mission Trust, 1992.

Coomaraswamy, Ananda, *A New Approach to the Vedas: An Essay in Translation and Exegesis*, New Delhi: South Asia Books, 1994.

Deshpande, C. R., *Transmission of the Mahabharata Tradition*, Simla: Indian Institute of Advanced Study, 1978.

Doniger, Wendy, *On Hinduism*, New Delhi: Aleph Book Company, 2013.

———, *The Hindus: An Alternative History*, New Delhi: Penguin Books, 2009.

Eck, Diana, *India: A Sacred Geography*, New York: Harmony Books, 2013.

Elst, Koenraad, *Bharatiya Janata Party Vis-a-vis Hindu Resurgence*, New Delhi: Voice of India, 1997.

Embree, Ainslie T., *Sources of Indian Tradition, Vol. 1: From the Beginning to 1800*, New York: Columbia University Press, 1958.

Gambhirananda, Swami, trans., *Eight Upanishads with the Commentary of Sankaracarya*, Second Revised Edition, vols I and II, Kolkata: Advaita Ashrama, 1989 and reprinted 2006.

Ganeri, Jonardon, *Artha: Meaning (Foundations of Philosophy in India)*, New Delhi: Oxford University Press, 2011.

Golwalkar, M. S., *Bunch of Thoughts*, Fourth imp, Bangalore: Vikram Prakashan, 1968.

————, *We, or Our Nation Defined*, Third edn, Nagpur: Bharat Publications, 1945.

Guru, Nataraja, *The Word of the Guru: The Life and Teaching of Guru Narayana*, New Delhi: DK Printworld, 2003.

Jaffrelot, Christophe, *Hindu Nationalism: A Reader*, Princeton: Princeton University Press, 2007.

————, *The Hindu Nationalist Movement and Indian Politics: 1925 to the 1990s*, London: Hurst, 1996.

Jagannathan, Shakunthala, *Hinduism*, Bombay: Vakil, Feffer and Simons, 1984.

Jha, D. N., *The Myth of the Holy Cow*, New Delhi: Navnayana Books, 2009.

————, 'What the gods drank', *Indian Express*, 29 July 2017.

Khan, Ansar Hussain, *The Rediscovery of India: A New Subcontinent*, Hyderabad: Orient Longman, 1995.

Krishna, Nanditha and Jagannathan, Shakunthala, *Ganesha: The Auspicious... The Beginning*, Bombay: Vakil, Feffer And Simons, 1992.

Kumaran, Murkkoth, *The Biography of Sree Narayana Guru*, Sivagiri: Sivagiri Madom, 2011.

Lannoy, Richard, *The Speaking Tree: A Study of Indian Culture and Society*, New York & London: Oxford University Press, 1971.

Mandeville, John, *The Travels of Sir John Mandeville*, Moseley, C. (trans.), London: Penguin Books, 2005.

Mascaro, Juan, *The Upanishads*, London: Penguin Books, 1965.

Menon, Ramesh, *Bhagavata Purana*, New Delhi: Rupa Publications, 2007.

Nehru, Jawaharlal, *The Discovery of India*, Calcutta: The Signet Press, 1946

Pandey, Gyanendra, 'Which of Us are Hindus?' in *Hindus and Others: The Question of Identity in India Today*, New Delhi: Viking, 1993.

Panikkar, Raimon, *The Vedic Experience: Mantramañjari: An Anthology of the Vedas for Modern Man*, Berkeley: University of California Press, 1977.

Parthasarathy, Swami A., *Vedanta Treatise: The Eternities*, Bombay: Vakil & Sons, 1978.

Prakashan, Bharat, *Shri Guruji: The Man and His Mission, On the Occasion of His 51st Birthday*, Delhi: Bharat Prakashan, 1955.

Prasad, Swami Muni Narayana, *The Philosophy of Narayana Guru*, New Delhi: DK Printworld, 2003.

Radhakrishnan, S., *The Hindu View of Life*, London: Geo. Allen & Unwin Ltd., 1927.

Ramachandran, R., *A History of Hinduism: From the Origins to the Present* (unpublished manuscript), 2017.

Saraswati, Swami Satyananda, *Four Chapters on Freedom: Commentary on the Yoga Sutras of Patanjali*, Munger: Yoga Publications Trust, 1976.

Savarkar, V. D., *Essentials of Hindutva* (available only on PDF) & *Hindutva: Who Is a Hindu?*, 1928, reprint Gorakhpur: Gita Press, 1993.

————, *Hindutva: Who is a Hindu?*, Bombay: Veer Savarkar Prakashan, 1923.

Sen, K. M., *Hinduism*, London: Penguin Books, 1978.

Singh, Dr Karan, *Essays on Hinduism*, Delhi: Ratna Sagar, 1989.

Singh, Upinder, *The Idea of Ancient India: Essays on Religion, Politics, and Archaeology*, New Delhi: Sage Publications, 2016.

Swami, Shri Purohit, *The Geeta: The Gospel of Lord Shri Krishna*, London: Faber and Faber, 1935.

Thapar, Romila: *The Penguin History of Early India from the Origins to AD 1300*, New Delhi: Penguin Books, 2003.

Tharoor, Shashi, *India: From Midnight to the Millenium and Beyond*, New Delhi: Penguin Books, 2012.

————, *Inglorious Empire: What the British Did in India*, London: Hurst, 2017.

————, *India Shastra: Reflections on the Nation in our Time*, New Delhi: Aleph Book Company, 2015.

————, *The Great Indian Novel*, New Delhi: Penguin Books, 1989.

The Life of Swami Vivekananda by his Eastern and Western Disciples, 2 vols, Kolkata: Advaita Ashrama Trust, 1999.

Upadhyaya, Deendayal, *Rashtra Jeevan Ki Disha*, Lucknow: Lokhit Prakashan, 1976, 2010.

Viswanathan, Ed, *Am I a Hindu?*, New Delhi: Rupa Publications, 1993.

Vivekananda, Swami, *The Complete Works of Swami Vivekananda*, Chennai: Manonmani Publishers, 2015.

Zaehner, R. C., *Hinduism*, London: Oxford University Press, 196.

INDEX